Director® 8.5
Shockwave® Studio
Interface
Design

New
Riders

epic software group, inc.™

DIRECTOR 8.5 SHOCKWAVE STUDIO INTERFACE DESIGN

International Standard Book Number: 0-7357-1218-2

Library of Congress Catalog Card Number: 2001096470

Printed in the United States of America

First Printing: March 2002

06 05 04 03 02   7 6 5 4 3 2 1

Interpretation of the printing code: The rightmost double-digit number is the year of the book's printing; the rightmost single-digit number is the number of the book's printing. For example, the printing code 02-1 shows that the first printing of the book occurred in 2002.

TRADEMARKS

WARNING AND DISCLAIMER

PUBLISHER
David Dwyer

ASSOCIATE PUBLISHER
Stephanie Wall

EXECUTIVE EDITOR
Steve Weiss

PRODUCTION MANAGER
Gina Kanouse

MANAGING EDITOR
Sarah Kearns

ACQUISITIONS EDITOR
Theresa Gheen

DEVELOPMENT EDITOR
Grant Munroe

PROJECT EDITOR
Stacia Mellinger

COPY EDITOR
Keith Cline

PRODUCT MARKETING MANAGER
Kathy Malmloff

PUBLICITY MANAGER
Susan Nixon

MANUFACTURING COORDINATOR
Jim Conway

COVER DESIGNER
Rick Rodriguez of epic software group, inc.™

INTERIOR DESIGNER
Wil Cruz

COMPOSITOR
Amy Parker

PROOFREADER
Debbie Williams

INDEXER
Lisa Stumpf

MEDIA DEVELOPERS
epic software group inc.™ and
Jay Payne of New Riders

CONTENTS AT A GLANCE

TABLE OF CONTENTS

ABOUT THE AUTHORS

For the past twelve years, the artists, animators, and programmers at **epic software group, inc.**™ have been help-ing their clients use the power of the computer to tell their stories in ways that are not possible with traditional media. epic creates applications such as multimedia presentations, electronic catalogs, computer-based training, interactive brochures, and touch-screen kiosks. Their work is distributed on CD-ROM, DVD, and the Internet.

In 1997, epic entered the world of publishing when the company was chosen to create over 100 3D illustrations for the Happy and Max series of children's books. In 2000, epic authored *Macromedia Flash 5—From Concept to Creation*, followed by *Macromedia Director Game Development—from Concept to Creation*. In 2001, epic produced *LightWave 6.5 & 7 Applied* and *Excel 2002 Plain & Simple*. Book projects currently in the works by epic include two titles for Flash and *The World's Greatest 3D Graphics*, scheduled for release at Siggraph 2002.

ABOUT THE TECH EDITOR

Jerome Givens is an Interactive Designer from Indianapolis, Indiana. He studied multimedia at Indiana University and developed a proficiency in programming through his work with Macromedia Director over the past five years. He has been involved with several interactive media projects ranging from business applications to 3D gaming applications to DVD-ROM titles.

DEDICATION

Interface design and development requires the understanding of technology, aesthetics, and human behavior. This book is dedicated to those innovative artists and programmers who are on a never-ending quest to bring their creative ideas to life on the computer. Sometimes they might fail; but through hard work, tenacity, and a wonderful sense of humor, they ultimately succeed in finding a vastly superior way to communicate using this new media. This book is dedicated to everyone with the curiosity and courage to try something that has never been done, and to whom "great" just isn't good enough.

ACKNOWLEDGMENTS

It takes a great deal of time and effort to put together a book like this. Many people contributed to the content and design; others provided encouragement and support.

When I founded epic software group, inc. in 1990, I realized that the most successful projects would be team efforts, with each person contributing his or her best work. And that was indeed the case with *Director 8.5 Shockwave Studio Interface Design*. Without a doubt, it would have remained just another interesting idea had it not been for the combined efforts of this talented team. I would like to offer my heartfelt appreciation to the following people:

First and foremost, I thank our Author and Multimedia Programmer, Cliff Jones, whose knowledge of Director never ceases to amaze me. This is his second book on Director, and he continues to find ingenious ways to ring every ounce of power out of this incredible authoring tool. Not only is he able to explain complex subjects in terms we can all understand, he can do it while juggling a number of other equally challenging tasks! He is a joy to work with and puts 110% into everything he sets his mind on accomplishing.

Next, I thank Robert Bailey, our Sr. Multimedia Director Project Manager. Robert has "lived" in Director for more than five years. He does not simply write programs, he attacks them. The "impossible" might take the whole day to do; doing something in Director that "has never been done before" may stretch out to two days. Robert sticks with it until a program works flawlessly—never mind what time of day it is. I can think of no better manager for a multimedia assignment. No matter how complex the project, Robert will get it done on time and within budget.

Many of the 3D graphics in the book were created by Danny Duhon, our Creative Director and Lead 3D Artist. Danny's work has been showcased in a number of 3D books and periodicals. Derek Hughes is our 2D Artist. It is wonderful to watch concepts from a brainstorming session magically appear in pencil sketches, storyboards, illustrations, and vector animations. I am very proud of their work. Thanks guys, for all the wonderful eye candy.

One of the most important aspects of any software book is getting the details right. Our Proofreader, Sharon Howerton, kept us in line by checking and rechecking every line of copy in the book. Copy Editing was done by Keith Cline, one of the best.

Also on the homefront, I thank our support staff at epic who were instrumental in driving this book to completion. My gratitude goes to Victor M. Cherubini and Rod Afshar, two young and talented programmers whose experience in programming and design seems to far exceed their age.

Perhaps the folks we have to thank the most are our friends at New Riders. Steve Weiss is the Executive Editor at New Riders Publishing. We had been discussing the project for months and were about to come to an agreement on September 10, 2001. And then the world changed, and most of our clients halted all work. We felt sure this project would also be delayed, but Steve believed in this book and gave it the Green Light. Steve, we will always admire your courage and vision even in a time of chaos.

Acquisition Editor Theresa Gheen (who I am convinced is the Patron Saint of the Chronologically Challenged) really helped us understand New Riders style and format. The book has benefited enormously from the revisions that her suggestions prompted. Many thanks also to Development Editor Grant Munroe for fine-tuning the book's organization, making it as user-friendly as possible. More thanks to the Technical Editor, Jerome Givens, who went through everything with a fine-toothed comb. We also thank the support staff at New Riders—Stacia Mellinger, Jay Payne, Wil Cruz, Sarah Kearns, and Lisa Stumpf—all of whom did such a fine job producing and perfecting the book. Thank you, everyone.

Vic Cherubini
President
epic software group, inc.

A Message from New Riders

As the reader of this book, you are our most important critic and commentator. We value your opinion and want to know what we're doing right, what we could do better, in what areas you'd like to see us publish, and any other words of wisdom you're willing to pass our way.

As Executive Editor at New Riders, I welcome your comments. You can fax, email, or write me directly to let me know what you did or didn't like about this book—as well as what we can do to make our books better. When you write, please be sure to include this book's title, ISBN, and author, as well as your name and phone or fax number. I will carefully review your comments and share them with the authors and editors who worked on the book.

Please note that I cannot help you with technical problems related to the topic of this book, and that due to the high volume of email I receive, I might not be able to reply to every message. Thanks.

Fax: 317-581-4663

Email: steve.weiss@newriders.com

Mail: Steve Weiss
            Executive Editor
            New Riders Publishing
            201 West 103rd Street
            Indianapolis, IN 46290 USA

Visit Our Web Site: www.newriders.com

On our web site, you'll find information about our other books, the authors we partner with, book updates and file downloads, promotions, discussion boards for online interaction with other users and with technology experts, and a calendar of trade shows and other professional events with which we'll be involved. We hope to see you around.

Email Us from Our Web Site

Go to www.newriders.com and click on the Contact Us link if you

- ➤ Have comments or questions about this book.
- ➤ Want to report errors that you have found in this book.
- ➤ Have a book proposal or are interested in writing for New Riders.
- ➤ Would like us to send you one of our author kits.
- ➤ Are an expert in a computer topic or technology and are interested in being a reviewer or technical editor.
- ➤ Want to find a distributor for our titles in your area.
- ➤ Are an educator/instructor who wants to preview New Riders books for classroom use. In the body/comments area, include your name, school, department, address, phone number, office days/hours, text currently in use, and enrollment in your department, along with your request for either desk/examination copies or additional information.

*"It is not enough to do your best; you must know
what to do and then do your best."*
—W. Edwards Deming

▼▼▼ introduction

A DIFFERENT APPROACH

In the past, interface design books followed a specific formula. They first discussed the basics of visual design and then led the reader through the finer points of user interaction. The major theories of design gradually became clear to the reader, but only after countless hours of study. When the reader was fully confident in his or her design skills, he would invest in a programming book to learn how to put the theories into practice. The problem with studying advanced design theory before learning even the basics of interface creation is that the reader has no time to develop his skills and see the trade-offs of style and convenience firsthand.

Director 8.5 Shockwave Studio Interface Design uses a slightly different teaching method. As you progress through the chapters in the *Background Information* section, you will learn about the principles of interface design and then move on to the basic elements of Director that you will learn to master in the remainder of the book. If you have any questions about programming in Lingo while you are walking through the book's interface chapters, refer to Appendix B, "Guide to Lingo Programming."

HISTORY OF MACROMEDIA DIRECTOR

In June 1985, a company called MacroMind created the major precursor to Director. It was an animation program called VideoWorks and was available only for Macintosh computers. A few years later, MacroMind combined an updated version of VideoWorks with a few other multimedia utilities, such as GraphicWorks and MusicWorks, to create Director 1.0. MacroMind often referred to early versions of Director as VideoWorks Interactive. Its major purpose was the creation of graphical presentations, guided tours, and kiosks.

Eventually, MacroMind changed its name to Macromedia and created a Windows version of Director. Originally, they were going to split Director into two separate tools. One version would handle interactive development and allow powerful programming, and the other would cover only animation. This change might have made simple animation easier for some, but overall, Director is much more convenient as a single package.

The growth of the Internet quickly prompted Macromedia to develop web browser plug-ins that allowed Director programs to be accessible all over the world. Director content for the Internet soon became known as Shockwave, and the rush began to find new compression methods. The ideas Macromedia came up with allowed Shockwave content to download more quickly than ever before. Today, Shockwave is one of the most common forms of interactive multimedia on the Internet (see Figure I.1).

Figure I.1 *The splash screen of Director 8.5 Shockwave Studio.*

ADVANTAGES OF USING DIRECTOR

Director enables programmers to create quality interactive multimedia quickly and easily for the Internet, Macintosh, and PC. Director's drag-and-drop interface and simplified programming language help to free programmers from wasting their time on common or repetitive tasks. The Shockwave player lets Internet users view online Director applications. Most computers with Internet access currently use the Shockwave player, and virtually all computer manufacturers preinstall the player on new computers. With such a wide audience available, you can be sure that they will notice your Director applications.

OVERVIEW OF THE CHAPTERS

Chapter 1, "Designing Interfaces," and Chapter 2, "Using Director," cover the basics of interface design and Macromedia Director. If you are already familiar with these elements, you may want to go straight to the interface chapters. You should, however, at least look over these chapters to make sure that you are comfortable with all the information they cover.

Chapter 3, "The Basics," walks you through the basic techniques involved in creating a simple interface application (see Figure I.2). This is the only interface chapter that does not use a template file to get you started. You build the entire The Basics interface from scratch just by following the chapter's numbered steps.

Figure I.2   *The Basics interface in action.*

Chapter 4, "Ten-Step Guide," illustrates the advantages of offering the user two navigation options. It also takes you through the creation and implementation of a simple vector shape. Unlike the The Basics interface, the Ten-Step Guide interface uses transition animations to enhance its aesthetic appeal (see Figure I.3). You will learn how to set up a multisection interface using tweening effects in the Score.

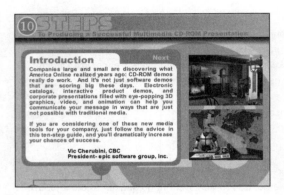

Figure I.3   *The Ten-Step Guide interface in action.*

Chapter 5, "Television," introduces global variables and frame behaviors. It also uses the Background Transparent ink to create a simple transparency mask. The contents of the television screen show through a transparent section of the television sprite's image (see Figure I.4). This gives the programmer the freedom to move items on and off the television screen without fear of items overlapping the television itself.

Figure I.4   *The Television interface in action.*

Chapter 6, "Classic Jukebox," walks you through the creation of a complex button behavior. It is generic enough to work on any button image with an Over and a Down state. The interface uses QuickTime movies to immerse the user in the otherwise two-dimensional environment. Just placing introduction and exit animations in an interface can change its feel completely (see Figure I.5).

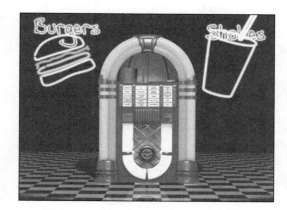

Figure I.5 *The Classic Jukebox interface in action.*

Chapter 7, "epic Model Library," illustrates the use of behavior parameters. Parameters enable the programmer to make a single behavior that can function in a variety of ways, depending on the values passed from its associated sprites. This chapter then goes on to explain the details of creating scrolling text fields through Lingo and interpreting user interaction with multiline text (see Figure I.6).

Figure I.6 *The epic Model Library interface in action.*

Chapter 8, "Cluttered Desktop," demonstrates the use of rollover status messages and dynamic background images. When the user's mouse enters the bounds of an item on the desk, the computer monitor displays a status message, and the background image becomes gray and blurry (see Figure I.7). The interface also introduces simple scrolling image fields. When the user uses the scrollbars, the portfolio image sprite's cast member changes to give the appearance of scrolling.

Figure I.7 *The Cluttered Desktop interface in action.*

Chapter 9, "Video Game," introduces the creation and implementation of film loops. In addition to animation, this chapter also covers the fundamentals of accepting user input through the keyboard. You can use the arrow keys to move the video game character around the Stage. When the user presses the Enter key (Return on Macintosh), the interface reacts based on the position of the playback head within the Score and the character sprite within the Stage (see Figure I.8).

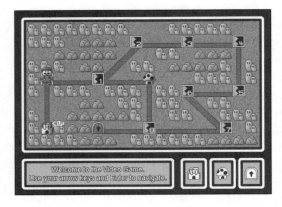

Figure I.8 *The Video Game interface in action.*

Chapter 10, "Media Browser," illustrates the basics of creating graphical, resizable windows for your Director interfaces. In addition, the interface also uses a method for scrolling images and text that is very similar to a web browser. You can add page items directly to the Score, and the Media Browser interface will display them based on their channel order. You can even specify item properties such as alignment and resizing based on the window dimensions (see Figure I.9).

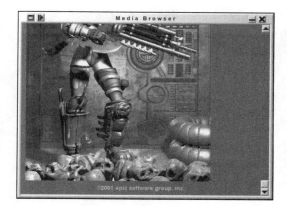

Figure I.9 *The Media Browser interface in action.*

Chapter 11, "Vector Sampler," discusses the use of complex vector graphics within Director interfaces. It walks you through creating vector shapes and compiling them into film loops. After you create the film loops, you can use the compiled vector graphics much as you would any other sprite. The chapter also covers a basic technique used for importing media files through Lingo (see Figure I.10).

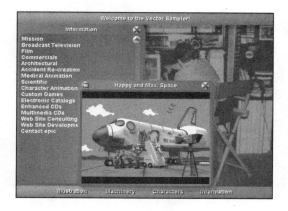

Figure I.10 *The Vector Sampler interface in action.*

Chapter 12, "epic Portfolio," explains how to create complex image overlays and dynamic menu buttons. Because the different sections of the portfolio do not contain the same number of items each, each menu button must repeatedly decide whether it should be visible. The chapter also explains how to create a spotlight effect that follows a specified sprite around the Stage (see Figure I.11).

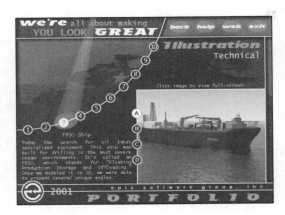

Figure I.11 *The epic Portfolio interface in action.*

Chapter 13, "Woodlands Waterway," walks you through the creation and implementation of rollover caption messages. When the user's mouse moves over an active building link in the interface's main menu, a short description appears directly below the user's cursor. In many situations, you can use rollover captions messages in place of status messages (see Figure I.12).

Figure I.12 *The Woodlands Waterway interface in action.*

Chapter 14, "Chopper-Bot," explains how to manipulate the volume of sound channels through Lingo. As the playback head moves through the Score, the volume of the looping helicopter noise must adjust to create smooth aural transitions. To create an immersive first-person view in the interface's main menu, the robot's hand moves in place of the mouse cursor to press the menu buttons. This gives the user the feeling that she actually is the robot (see Figure I.13).

Figure I.13 *The Chopper-Bot interface in action.*

Chapter 15, "Holiday House," discusses the creation of various interactive animations. Sometimes, animating through Lingo is just more convenient than using the Score. The chapter also discusses the use of multiple sound channels. Because the user may want several sounds to play simultaneously, the interface must decide when to interrupt busy sound channels and when to leave them alone (see Figure I.14).

Figure I.14 *The Holiday House interface in action.*

Chapter 16, "Company Headquarters," explains how to incorporate QuickTime VR movies into your Director interfaces. QuickTime VR is a tool that enables programmers to display immersive panoramic content on web sites or inside presentations. After defining hot spots inside a QuickTime VR movie, you can import the movie into a Director interface and determine the user interaction based on the hot spots being manipulated (see Figure I.15).

Figure I.15 *The Company Headquarters interface in action.*

Chapter 17, "3D Gallery," introduces Shockwave 3D and explains how to affect 3D sprites through Lingo. The chapter covers topics such as model rotation, camera movement, and working with texture overlays. For a detailed explanation of Shockwave 3D and how to use it, refer to Appendix C, "Guide to Shockwave 3D."

After you have finished rebuilding and customizing these interfaces, you can move on to the "Conclusion." Unlike many computer books, this book's "Conclusion" is more than just a simple restatement of what you have learned. The "Conclusion" contains descriptions of a wide variety of web resources on Director and interface design. It even provides access to several producers of Xtra extensions, which enable a programmer to expand Director's functionality. Just because you finish this book doesn't mean that your education in interface development must finish as well.

USING THE CD-ROM

You can access most elements of the accompanying CD-ROM through its multimedia interface. If you want to view one of the interfaces featured in this book, for instance, you just click its menu link. After you have finished browsing the interface, press the Escape key or use the interface's Exit button.

If you choose not to run the multimedia interface, however, you can access all files on the CD-ROM from your operating system's browsing utility (such as Windows Explorer). Within the browsing utility, you may want to copy the contents of the CD-ROM onto your hard drive for increased speed and convenience. You can run the CD-ROM's multimedia interface at any time by double-clicking `start.exe` (`macstart` on Macintosh). If you prefer, however, you can open source files through Director and then save them to your hard drive as specified in Appendix A, "Guide to Common Tasks."

Whether or not you decide to use the CD-ROM's multimedia interface, you should copy the contents of the CD-ROM's Fonts folder to you system's Fonts folder. For example, the Windows Fonts folder is generally named Fonts and located in the Windows directory. For more information on installing these fonts, view your operating system's Help system.

GETTING STARTED

The best place to start learning about designing multimedia interfaces is by reading Chapter 1 of this book. Then, if you are already familiar with Lingo and you just want to learn more about different aspects of Director interface development, you can jump to any chapter you want and complete its tutorial. If you have never used Director before, however, you should definitely complete Chapter 2 and look through Appendix B before proceeding to any interface chapters. Each interface chapter assumes that you have a basic understanding of Director and its programming language, Lingo.

>>> **part 1**
background information

"Never express yourself more clearly than you are able to think."
—Niels Bohr

▼▼▼

chapter 1
designing interfaces

BASIC PRINCIPLES OF DESIGN

When designing any visual interface, you must always try to see things from the user's point of view. Remember that your goal is to make the user as comfortable and involved as possible. The first basic principle that a designer must keep in mind is *simplicity*. Never squeeze so many items onto one screen that the user is forced to search for information. Major topics of interest should jump out at the user and lead smoothly to more information. Figure 1.1 shows an example of simplistic design. If you find yourself questioning whether an element of your interface is necessary, you should most likely get rid of it. Too much information can be as harmful as not enough.

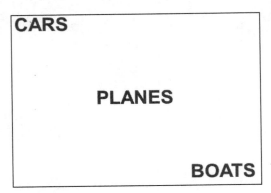

Figure 1.1 *Incorporating the concept of simplicity into design.*

Consider the idea of *proximity* as you position interface elements on the screen. Basically, this principle states that like items should be placed near each other, and unlike items should not. A photo's proximity to its caption in a newspaper makes their relationship obvious. If two unrelated items are positioned close to each other, the user's initial reaction is confusion. Don't be afraid to leave enough white space, or blank area, to separate groups of interface elements. White space is a necessary element of interface design. It gives the eyes a chance to rest when they are otherwise busy scanning the screen elements. Figure 1.2 shows an example of a design that accounts for proximity.

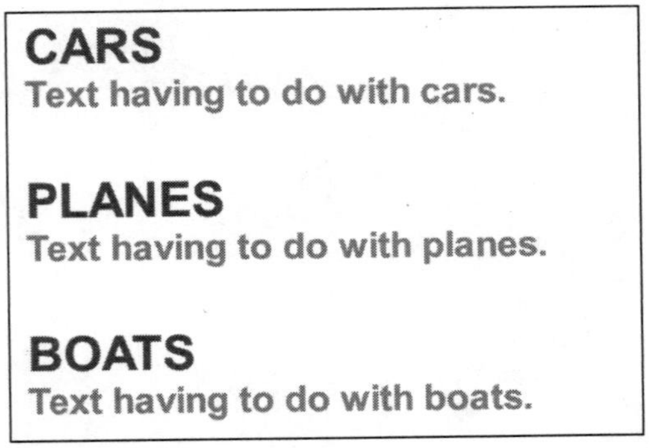

CARS
Text having to do with cars.

PLANES
Text having to do with planes.

BOATS
Text having to do with boats.

Figure 1.2 *Using proximity in design.*

Another way to indicate a relationship between interface elements is through *alignment*. Items should never be placed randomly on the screen. Be conscious of each item's alignment as you position it on the screen (see Figure 1.3). Always maintain a sense of balance. In other words, if you position an interface element on the left side of your screen, you should probably have another element on the right side of your screen to keep the user's attention more or less centered. Your white space should be evenly distributed across the screen.

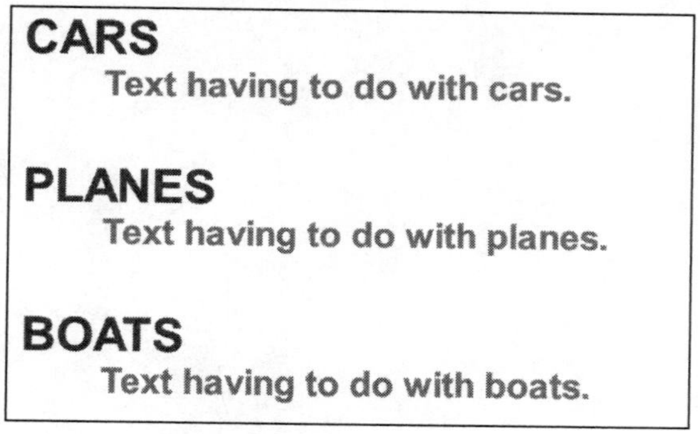

CARS
Text having to do with cars.

PLANES
Text having to do with planes.

BOATS
Text having to do with boats.

Figure 1.3   *Using alignment in design.*

To give your interfaces a smooth, consistent feel, apply the principle of *repetition*. If you use a certain font, color, or graphic at one point in your interface, be sure to use it again. Elements with a similar function should always appear similar to give the user a sense of predictability and continuity (see Figure 1.4). Never just abandon a font style after using it only once. Repeat the use of it so that it doesn't seem out of place or different from the rest of your interface.

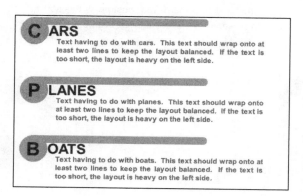

Figure 1.4   *Using repetition in design.*

Another principle to remember is *contrast*. If two colors or font styles do not appear exactly alike, they should appear very different. Choose no more than a few styles per interface and stick with them (see Figure 1.5). Similar but not identical styles can sometimes come across as sloppiness or even mistakes that were never caught. Basically, always keep the user from having to figure out what the style he is looking at is meant to indicate. It should be obvious. Appropriately applying the idea of contrast to your interface can accentuate important items and clarify subtle differences between interface elements.

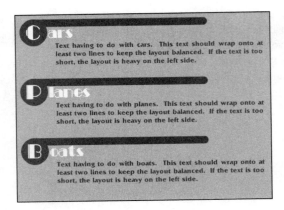

Figure 1.5 *Contrast draws attention to section headings.*

KNOWING YOUR AUDIENCE

When designing interfaces, always keep the best interest of your audience in mind. If you have a specifically defined audience (such as children, musicians, or programmers), you might be able to make certain assumptions about what the user knows. Musicians, for example, generally know how to read music or at least can identify certain instruments by name. Programmers are generally familiar with basic terms such as *variables*, *functions*, and *loops*. However, you might not always be so fortunate as to have a clear definition of your audience. Most interfaces are meant to reach a very wide audience and must therefore be designed with people's diversity in mind.

Some users might already be familiar with the sort of interface you have built. For these users, you must be sure that all the elements of your interface are easily accessible with no delays. Experienced users will not want to sit through endless instructions on operating an interface that is already familiar to them. You must allow this sort of user to do as she wants and not be distracted with gratuitous help screens, as a user might be with the interface shown in Figure 1.6.

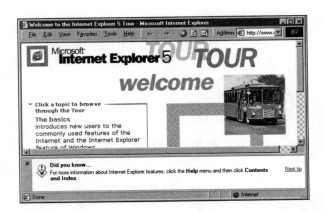

Figure 1.6 *Users already familiar with this interface might not appreciate the help directives.*

On the other hand, never dump the user right into an interface and assume that he knows how to use it. Give the user clues to point him in the right direction. Unless your interface is unusually complicated, most users will be able to navigate without a problem. However, you must not forget the user who prefers explicit instruction to random exploration. This user would much rather spend time reading an extensive help file than risk making a mistake. It is for this user that you must always provide a help screen that is easily accessible from any point within your interface. Figure 1.7 shows a help system for Internet Explorer.

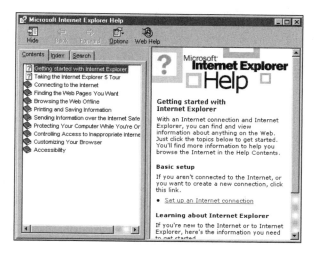

Figure 1.7 *A fully functional help system.*

Every user wants a few simple things from an interface. The user wants to be in control at all times, to never have to stop for instructions, and to never have to wait unnecessarily. In some situations, these goals cannot be met completely, but you must always do your best. Remember that the purpose of an interface is to bring information to the user. Nothing should get in the way of this basic idea. Only if you keep the user's priorities in mind will your interface be truly intuitive and convenient to use.

GIVING THE USER CONTROL

In any situation, the user wants to think that she is in charge of the computer's activities. For every action the user takes, the interface should have an obvious and immediate reaction. The user should never feel like the interface is in control and that she is just watching and waiting. Such an environment can result in the user losing interest and abandoning the interface altogether.

Be *explicit*. Any clickable element of an interface should be set apart from the rest of the interface by a drop shadow, a highlight, or some other method. The bottom line is that all controls should be obvious. This means not only accentuating active items but also diminishing items that could be confused for buttons, links, or other control elements. If an item looks like a button, it should function as one (see Figure 1.8). The user should never be surprised.

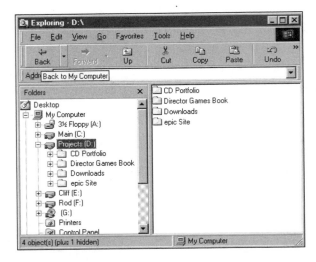

Figure 1.8   *Be explicit by accentuating an active button.*

Be *flexible*. Every user is different. If a user is disinterested with a section of an interface, he should be able to skip to a more entertaining section without having to wait for a video or animation sequence to complete. A good way to be flexible is to provide the user with more than one way to accomplish a task. Of course, this idea does not necessarily apply to simple interfaces with only a few tasks available to the user. Figure 1.9 shows an example of a flexible interface.

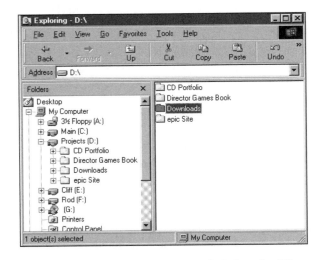

Figure 1.9   *Be flexible by offering two methods of accessing folders.*

Be *forgiving*. The user should not have to be afraid of making a mistake while she is exploring an interface. Create an environment that enables users to do whatever they want with no annoying error messages to discourage them. Any action the user can take should be easily reversible because people make mistakes, change their minds, and sometimes push buttons just to discover their functions. If an action is not reversible (such as exiting the interface), be sure to give the user advance warning (see Figure 1.10).

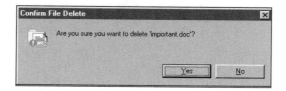

Figure 1.10 *Forgiving user mistakes through a warning message.*

PROVIDING FEEDBACK

The purpose of feedback is to inform the user about his interaction with the interface. It tells the user something about what he can do, is doing, or has done. Without explicit feedback, the user has no indication that the computer has received his input and will assume it has not. Feedback is a vital element of interface design and must never be overlooked. Problems can arise if the designer does not plan all aspects of an interface's feedback carefully. A user given ambiguous feedback might misinterpret that information. This can lead to user error.

Possibly the most helpful type of feedback is commonly referred to as *future feedback*. Future feedback is given to the user before an interaction occurs. Figure 1.11 shows the user selecting a command. The status bar explains that this command copies items to the Clipboard. The feedback in the status bar tells the user what will happen if a certain action is carried out. A good example of future feedback is the rollover, or mouse-over, state of buttons and hyperlinks. When the mouse moves over a button in some applications, a helpful description of the command appears in the status bar at the bottom of the screen, as shown in Figure 1.11.

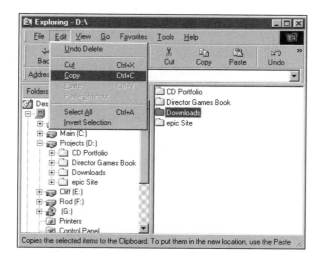

Figure 1.11 *The status bar displaying feedback to the user.*

Present feedback is supplied to the user as an interaction is taking place. It lets the user know that something is happening and often gives an indication of when the task will be completed. Many programs display an empty bar that gradually fills with color as a task progresses or a file downloads. Present feedback is generally most useful for tasks that take more than a few seconds. Figure 1.12 shows an example of feedback taking place while a user is performing a task.

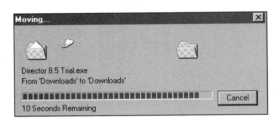

Figure 1.12 *Feedback happening in the present tense while the user is moving files.*

The last type of feedback is of course *past* feedback (see Figure 1.13). Past feedback occurs after an interaction has occurred and gives the user information about what has just happened. Its purpose is to tell the user how his action has affected the system or the interface. After a long download has finished, your Internet browser might alert you with a message that says `Download complete`. This message tells you that it is time to move on to a new task such as opening or virus-checking the downloaded file.

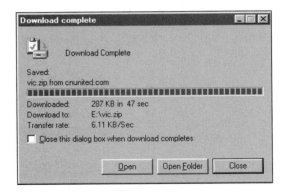

Figure 1.13 *An example of past feedback after downloading a file.*

USING METAPHORS EFFECTIVELY

A *metaphor*, in the context of interface design, is a representation of a physical object that is meant to give the user an idea of how an interface operates. For example, a media player whose interface resembles a television requires little or no instruction to use. Everyone knows how to use a television. Therefore, by translating physical activities into mouse clicks, the user can figure out how to operate the media player. All media can be displayed in the television's screen, and all buttons can function much like they would on an actual television, as shown in Figure 1.14.

Figure 1.14 *The television's knobs and buttons control the media.*

The designer might run into problems, however, when deciding where to place additional elements, such as user preferences, music play lists, and external plug-ins. One possible solution is to make all additional elements accessible by clicking the television's screen. This method works just fine, but now the television behaves more like a touch-screen kiosk. The metaphor has been overextended and the interface has no room for additional features. This disconnection between the way you would expect to control a real TV and the way the interface works is referred to as *interface magic*. Figure 1.15 shows the television interface with controls directly on its screen.

Figure 1.15 *An example of a television metaphor using magic to extend its functionality.*

A little bit of interface magic is okay. Computer software should be able to do more than its physical predecessors. The problem is that some interfaces stray from their chosen metaphor too far and wind up with confusing results. A classic example of a metaphor gone wrong is the Trash icon on the desktop of Macintosh computers. The Trash icon functions much like a trash can would in the real world. When users drag and drop files into Trash, the files are deleted. The designers apparently were stumped when it came time to figure out how users should eject disks from their computers. They settled on the slightly upsetting method of dragging a disk icon into Trash. Users might initially think that they are deleting the contents of the disk when in actuality they are merely removing the disk from the computer. It is a tough metaphor to follow.

Some designers try to cut down on interface magic by constantly adjusting their interface to fit the chosen metaphor. They become so attached to the metaphor that, instead of abandoning it altogether, they end up damaging the usability of the interface. Such a sacrifice is never a good idea. A good metaphor should help the user understand how to operate an interface. It should never confuse or annoy the user.

REPRESENTING IDEAS WITH IMAGES

In general, people process information better visually than they do textually. Of course, people can learn by reading, but seeing something done is generally more effective than reading how to do it. The brain simply processes images faster than text because text is a human invention. For example, your brain's initial reaction to a picture of a dog would be "dog." Then, your brain would move on to ask, "Which dog?" Your brain's initial reaction to the word *dog* written on a piece of paper is "text." Then, your brain would ask, "What does it say?" The conclusion is simple: Use images rather than text whenever possible.

An image or symbol used to represent an action or idea is commonly called an *icon*. Icons are used in a wide variety of situations both inside and outside of computers. For example, almost every road sign is made up of some sort of icon. The reasoning behind this is that icons have the potential to be recognized more quickly and accurately than ordinary text. When people are driving down the road at 60 miles per hour, they have very little time to read road signs, and missing one could mean getting into a collision.

Another reason to use icons is that they generally take up much less room onscreen than their equivalent text commands. Most applications offer access to their major commands through both text options (in drop-down menus) and icon buttons (in toolbars or floating palettes). When presented with the option, most users prefer using icon buttons. A good illustration of this is the System menu in Windows (see Figure 1.16). Each application in Windows contains a System menu accessible by clicking the program icon in the upper-left corner of its window. Users generally ignore this menu, however, because its commands are available as icon buttons as well in the upper-right corner of the window.

Figure 1.16 *Accessing the System menu in Windows via the icon.*

When designing an icon, you must consider several different aspects of your situation. No formula applies to icon design. Before you start thinking about picture ideas, stop and think whether an icon already in existence could fit the idea you want to represent. For example, a folder icon means "open," and a disk icon means "save." You have no reason to design a new icon if a perfectly good one already exists. Borrowing icons from existing software is not a form of giving up on designing an original icon. It just means that some users will be familiar with the icons before even viewing your interface. Remember that the convenience of the user is always your first priority.

If you conclude that your situation requires a completely original icon, you must begin the design process by thinking about the idea you are trying to represent. Try to simplify the idea down to its core components. Concentrate on the images that come into your head and put them on paper. Now try to look at your drawings objectively. Which images would bring the idea to mind if you weren't already thinking about it? Compose a few icon designs and have people try to guess what each design represents. Don't be discouraged if no one guesses correctly at first. Just try to make your icon as simple and obvious as possible.

If, after all your efforts, you still cannot seem to create an intuitive icon with an obvious meaning, you might have to settle for a slightly ambiguous icon design. If this is the case, however, be sure to inform the user of your icon's meaning. Never leave the user to guess the function of any control in your interface. Depending on your situation, of course, explicit instructions could defeat the purpose of using an icon altogether.

The downside of using icons in place of text is that they are inherently vaguer and more open to interpretation. Different cultures could interpret the same icon in very different ways. One user might see a picture of a cow and think "beef." Another might interpret the image as "milk." Still another might think "rodeo." When a precise message must be delivered, nothing works better than old-fashioned text.

BELLS AND WHISTLES

As you enter the world of multimedia interface design, you might be tempted to fill your interfaces with as many eye-catching effects and animations as possible. Just remember that a solid design plus lots of bells and whistles does not necessarily equal a good interface. When it comes to special effects, it's possible to go too far. Always ask yourself whether the effect you are adding will contribute to the interface as a whole or just add clutter and disrupt its aesthetic continuity. Never add special effects just because you can.

*"The artist is nothing without the gift, but the
gift is nothing without work."*

—Emile Zola

▼▼▼ chapter 2
using director

INSTALLING AND RUNNING DIRECTOR

Director is a powerful multimedia-authoring tool designed to create interactive content for the Internet, CD-ROM, and DVD-ROM. Most multimedia development utilities are designed for either noninteractive presentations such as Microsoft PowerPoint, or powerful but complicated applications such as Borland C++. Director is a hybrid that enables developers to produce powerful multimedia applications with considerably less effort than its predecessors required. With enough practice, anyone can create impressive interfaces in no time. To install the trial version of Director 8.5 Shockwave Studio on your computer, follow the steps outlined in Procedure 2.1.

Procedure 2.1 Installing the Trial Version of Director 8.5 Shockwave Studio

1. Insert the CD that accompanies this book into your CD-ROM drive. If an application does not run automatically, as shown in Figure 2.1, browse your CD-ROM drive and run start.exe (macstart on Macintosh).

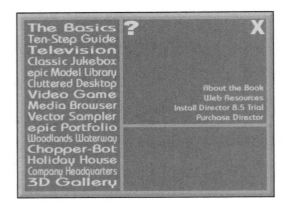

Figure 2.1 *The book's CD-ROM interface, as it should appear.*

2. Follow the onscreen instructions to install Director 8.5 Shockwave Studio on your computer.
3. When the Director installation program finishes, run director.exe from your Director 8.5 folder.

With so many unusual-looking windows, Director's interface may seem overwhelming at first. If you learn Director one piece at a time, however, everything will fall into place. Each window in Director serves a specific and unique purpose. You will not need every window open all the time; but to keep confusion to a minimum right now, do not close any windows unless instructed to do so.

USING THE STAGE WINDOW

The Stage is like a canvas that contains all the visible elements of a Director movie, or application. Much like its theatrical counterpart, Director's Stage is the only area of a movie visible to the audience. The Stage itself is just a solid rectangle that appears behind everything else. In fact, most Director movies cover the Stage up completely with a background image. Nevertheless, the Stage is the most important part of any Director movie. To view the Stage window within Director, follow the steps outlined in Procedure 2.2.

Procedure 2.2   Viewing the Stage Window

1. If you do not see the Stage window, click the Stage button within the toolbar (see Figure 2.2). Director will display the Stage window.

Figure 2.2   *The Stage button within the toolbar.*

2. If you want to reposition the Stage window within Director, drag its title bar to the position you want.
3. If you want to resize the Stage window within Director, drag its lower-right corner to the size you want.
4. If you want to zoom the Stage window in or out, click the Zoom Menu drop-down list and select an option (see Figure 2.3). Director will update the Stage window.

Note:
Resizing the Stage window does not actually change the size of your Stage, just the amount visible in Authoring mode. Use the Stage window's scroll bars if the entire Stage is not visible.

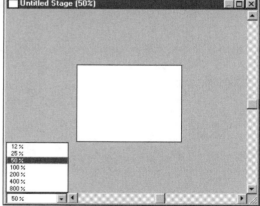

Figure 2.3   *The Stage at 50 percent zoom within the Stage window.*

To play a Director movie, you must create at least one *sprite*. A sprite is a visible item, such as a text field or an image that exists on the Stage. One simple way to create sprites is to use the Tool Palette window. To add a customized text sprite to the Stage using the Tool Palette window, follow the steps outlined in Procedure 2.3.

Figure 2.4 *The Text button within the Tool Palette window.*

Procedure 2.3 Adding Customized Text Sprite to the Stage

1. If you do not see the Tool Palette window within Director, click the Window menu and select the Tool Palette option. Director will display the Tool Palette window.

2. Within the Tool Palette window, click the Text button (see Figure 2.4). Director will select the Text tool.

3. In the Stage window, click near the middle of the Stage. Director will display a new text field within the Stage.

4. In the text field you created, type your desired text.

5. Next, in the text field you created, select all your text. Click the Modify menu and select the Font option. The Font dialog box appears (see Figure 2.5).

6. Using the Font dialog box, click and hold your mouse on the Color button and select a color swatch. Director will set the color of your text to whichever color you select.

7. In the Font Selection box, click the font option of your choice. Director will set the font of your text to whichever font you select.

8. Click the Size drop-down list and select the size option of your choice. Director will set the size of your text to whichever size you select.

9. Click the OK button. Director will apply your font selections to your text in the text field you created.

10. Within the Stage window, drag one of the text field's corners to the size you want.

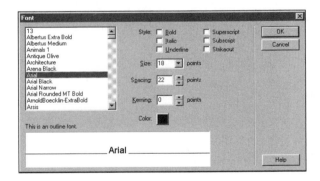

Figure 2.5 *Modifying your font within the Font dialog box.*

Note:
A text field with a framing of Adjust to Fit (the default framing) cannot have a height that exceeds the height of the text within that field.

So far, you have learned how to create customized text within a Director movie. Surprisingly, Director doesn't get all that much more complicated. You are on your way to developing fully interactive graphical user interfaces. Now that you know how to use the Stage window, you are ready to move on to the Property Inspector, one of the most important tools in Director.

USING THE PROPERTY INSPECTOR WINDOW

The Property Inspector window is the easiest way to customize the properties of anything and everything within Director. You will use the Property Inspector at least as much as any of Director's other windows. Before you begin creating your movie, change a few of its properties such as the size and the color of its Stage. To modify your movie's properties, follow the steps outlined in Procedure 2.4.

Procedure 2.4   Using the Property Inspector Window

1. If you do not see the Property Inspector window, click the Property Inspector button within the toolbar, as shown in Figure 2.6. Director will display the Property Inspector window.

Figure 2.6   *The Property Inspector button within the toolbar.*

2. Click the Movie tab. Director will display the Movie sheet.

3. Next click the Stage Size button and select the 640 × 480 option. Director will resize the Stage to 640 pixels wide and 480 pixels high.

4. Finally, click and hold your mouse on the button to the right of the Stage Fill Color icon and select a color swatch (see Figure 2.7). Director will change the color of the Stage to whichever color you select.

Note:
You can choose any Stage size you want, but keep in mind that the resolution of some monitors is often as low as 640 × 480 pixels.

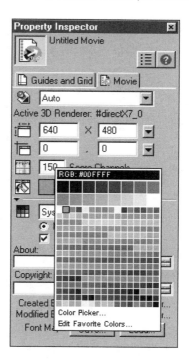

Figure 2.7   *Changing the Stage fill color within the Property Inspector window.*

The Property Inspector window can do more than just modify your movie's properties. You can also use the Property Inspector window to modify the properties of sprites. To modify the properties of the text you created earlier, follow the steps outlined in Procedure 2.5.

Note:

You are not required to name things such as text and graphics in Director, but as your movies become increasingly complicated, you will certainly be glad you did. It is difficult to keep track of unnamed media.

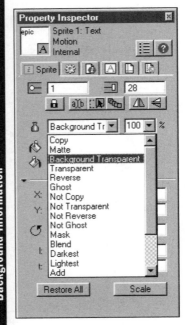

Figure 2.8 *The Ink drop-down list within the Property Inspector window.*

Procedure 2.5 Modifying Text Properties

1. Click the text you created. Director will update the Property Inspector window.

2. In the Property Inspector window, click the Member tab. Director will display the Member sheet.

3. Next, in the Name field, type **Motion** and press the Enter key (Return on Macintosh). Director will name the text that you created *Motion*.

4. Click the Sprite tab. Director will display the Sprite sheet.

5. Click the Ink drop-down list and select the Background Transparent option, as shown in Figure 2.8. Director will remove the background from the Motion sprite.

6. In the Rotation Angle field, type a number to be used as the rotation angle of the Motion sprite and press the Enter key (Return on Macintosh). Director will rotate the Motion sprite to whatever angle you type.

7. Click the Moveable button. Director will allow the user to drag the Motion text around the Stage while the movie is playing.

8. Within the toolbar, click the Play button. Director will preview your movie within the Stage window. Drag the Motion text around the Stage to make sure that your movie is working properly.

9. Click the Rewind button. Director will stop previewing your movie within the Stage window and return it to frame 1.

By now, you have a fully functioning, interactive Director movie. However, dragging text around an empty screen really isn't very high in entertainment value. Although your Director skills are improving, you are a long way from creating a truly impressive interface. Keep your chin up. You are about to get to the fun stuff.

USING THE SCORE WINDOW

The Score is the element that sets Director apart from many other development tools. The Score window consists mainly of a grid with columns called frames and rows called sprite channels. You can position all the graphical elements of your interface in different frames to create animation. Using the Score, you can create an entire multimedia presentation without any programming knowledge. Interactive interfaces can sometimes require a great deal of programming, however, and sometimes do not use the Score for animation at all. Still, the Score is an important tool for layering and organizing your movie's sprites. To view the Score window within Director, follow the steps outlined in Procedure 2.6.

Procedure 2.6 Using the Score Window

1. If you do not see the Score window, click the Score Window button within the toolbar, as shown in Figure 2.9. Director will display the Score window.

2. If you want to reposition the Score window within Director, drag its title bar to the position you want.

3. If you want to resize the Score window within Director, drag its lower-right corner to the size you want.

Figure 2.9 *The Score Window button within the toolbar.*

To animate a sprite using the Score, it must be under Score control. By default, all sprites are under the control of the Score. The Motion sprite, however, is draggable. If a sprite is supposed to follow the user's mouse, Director will ignore any attempt to move it using the Score. To remove the dragability of the Motion sprite, and create movement for it using the Score, follow the steps outlined in Procedure 2.7.

Procedure 2.7 Animating a Sprite Using the Score

1. In the Stage window, click the Motion sprite. Director will update the Property Inspector window.

2. In the Property Inspector window, click the Moveable button. Director will no longer enable the user to drag the Motion text around the Stage while the movie is playing.

3. Within the Score window, drag cell 28 of channel 1 to frame 50. Director will extend the Motion sprite to frame 50 (see Figure 2.10).

Note:
When you created the Motion sprite, Director put it in the first sprite channel. Director creates sprites with a default length of 28 frames. Therefore, the Motion sprite begins in frame 1 and ends in frame 28. Individual spots in the Score's grid of frames and channels are called cells.

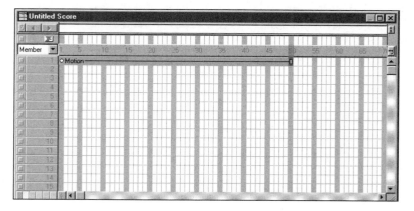

Figure 2.10 *Extending the Motion sprite within the Score window.*

4. Click cell 50 of channel 1. Director will display frame 50 of your movie within the Stage window.

5. Click the Insert menu and select the Keyframe option. Director will mark cell 50 of channel 1 as a keyframe.

6. Within the Score window, click cell 10 of channel 1. Director will display frame 10 of your movie within the Stage window.

7. Click the Insert menu and select the Keyframe option. Director will mark cell 10 of channel 1 as a keyframe.

>>>

8. Within the Stage window, drag the Motion sprite to a new location on the Stage. Director will display a path outline between the old and new positions of the Motion sprite within the Stage (see Figure 2.11).

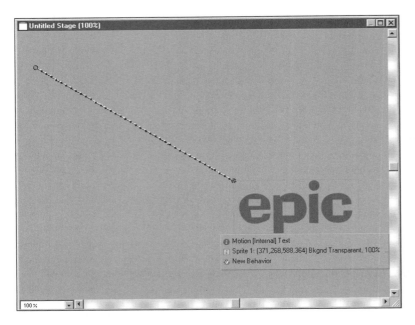

Figure 2.11 *The path outline of the Motion sprite.*

9. Within the Score window, click cell 40 of channel 1. Director will display frame 40 of your movie within the Stage window.

10. Click the Insert menu and select the Keyframe option. Director will mark cell 40 of channel 1 as a keyframe.

11. Within the Stage window, drag the Motion sprite to a new location on the Stage. Director will display a path outline between the old and new positions of the Motion sprite within the Stage window.

12. Click the Modify menu, select the Sprite submenu, and then select the Tweening option. Director will display the Sprite Tweening dialog box.

13. Within the Sprite Tweening dialog box, drag the Ease-In slider to around 25%. Director will update the path outline preview to show acceleration at the beginning of the path.

14. Drag the Ease-Out slider to around 25%. Director will update the path outline preview to show deceleration at the end of the path.

15. Click the Continue at Endpoints check box. Director will update the path outline preview to show a smooth, connected path (see Figure 2.12).

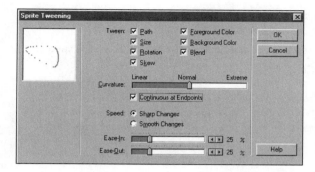

Figure 2.12 *The path outline preview within the Sprite Tweening dialog box.*

16. Now click the OK button. Director will update the path outline of the Motion sprite within the Stage window.

17. Within the toolbar, click the Play button. Director will preview your movie within the Stage window. Notice how the text accelerates at the beginning of the game and decelerates at the end.

18. Click the Rewind button. Director will stop previewing your movie within the Stage window and return it to frame 1.

Note:
Try clicking different cells within the Score window and changing the rotation and skew angles of the Motion sprite. Director will apply tweening, or transitioning, to more than just a sprite's location. If you add more sprites in channels with higher numbers, they will overlap the Motion sprite.

Perhaps you're wondering by now exactly which window stores media such as text and graphics. You know that the Stage window does not store media, because its contents can vary from frame to frame. The Score window cannot store media either, because programming code can cause media elements to change while a movie is playing. The window that actually stores media such as text and graphics is called the *Cast window*.

USING THE CAST WINDOW

Director stores all media elements and programming scripts in groups called *casts*. In every new movie, Director creates a cast named *Internal*. Until you get a bit more practice with Director, you will store all your text, graphics, and other cast members in the Internal cast. To view and work in the Cast window, follow the steps outlined in Procedure 2.8.

Procedure 2.8 Using the Cast Window

1. Click the Cast Window button, as shown in Figure 2.13. Director will display the Cast window.

Figure 2.13 *The Cast Window button within the toolbar.*

2. If you want to reposition the Cast window, drag its title bar to the position you want.

3. If you want to resize the Cast window, drag its lower-right corner to the size you want.

>>>

Note:
The Thumbnail View style arranges thumbnail previews of the cast members in numeric order. The List View style sorts cast members by name with no thumbnail images. The List View style is more useful for finding cast members by name than by the order chosen by the programmer.

4. Within the Cast window, click the Cast View Style button. Director will change the way it displays cast members within the Cast window.

5. If the Cast window is currently in List View style, click the Cast View Style button. Director will return the Cast window's view style to Thumbnail mode.

By now, you may be wondering how to incorporate graphics into your Director movie. Creating graphical cast members is a simpler process than you might think. To create a new bitmap graphic in the Internal cast and add it to the Stage, follow the steps outlined in Procedure 2.9.

Procedure 2.9   Creating a New Bitmap Image

1. Within the toolbar, click the Paint Window button, as shown in Figure 2.14. Director will display the Paint window and add a new bitmap member to the Internal cast.

Figure 2.14   *The Paint Window button within the toolbar.*

Note:
Generally, when you create graphics for your interfaces, you will build them in external programs rather than inside Director. For information on importing media into Director, refer to Appendix A, "Guide to Common Tasks."

2. In the Paint window, use Director's built-in paint tools to create an image or paste an image from an external graphics program.

3. In the Cast Member Name field, type **Graphic** and press the Enter key (Return on Macintosh). Director will name the bitmap you created *Graphic*.

4. Click the Paint Window button. Director will close the Paint window.

5. Drag the Graphic member from the Cast window into cell 1 of channel 2 of the Score window. Director will display the Graphic bitmap within the Stage window.

6. Within the Score window, drag cell 28 of channel 2 to frame 50. Director will extend the Graphic bitmap to frame 50.

Now that you have created a graphic, you can use it as many times as you want within your Director movie. A sprite is just an instance of a cast member. If you delete a cast member, all sprites associated with it in the Score and on the Stage will appear blank. Although the differences between sprites and cast members may seem confusing at first, you'll get the hang of it in no time.

USING THE SCRIPT WINDOW

The programming language associated with Director is named *Lingo*. Lingo was designed to make graphical programming easy. If you want to learn how to write Lingo programming code, refer to Appendix B, "Guide to Lingo Programming." To write a Lingo behavior script and apply it to the Graphic bitmap, follow the steps outlined in Procedure 2.10.

Procedure 2.10 Applying a Lingo Behavior Script to a Bitmap

1. Click the Script Window button within the toolbar, as shown in Figure 2.15. Director will display the Script window.

Script Window [Ctrl+0]

Figure 2.15 *The Script Window button within the toolbar.*

2. In the Script window, in the Cast Member Name text field, type **Graphic Behavior** and press the Enter key (Return on Macintosh). Director will name the new script *Graphic Behavior*.

Note:
For more information about programming in Lingo, refer to Appendix B.

3. Within the Property Inspector window, click the Script tab. Director will display the Script sheet.

4. Next click the Script Type drop-down list and select the Behavior option. Director will mark the Graphic Behavior script as a behavior script.

5. Within the Script window, type Lingo code to be stored within the Graphic Behavior script.

6. Click the Script Window button on the toolbar. Director will close the Script window.

7. In the Stage window, click the Graphic sprite. Director will update the Property Inspector window.

8. Now in Property Inspector window, click the Behavior Popup button and select the Graphic Behavior option. Director will apply the Graphic Behavior to the Graphic sprite, as shown in Figure 2.16.

9. Click the Play button. Director will preview your movie within the Stage window. The Graphic Behavior should affect the Graphic sprite.

10. Click the Rewind button. Director will stop previewing your movie within the Stage window and return it to frame 1.

By now, you should possess the basic skills required to create an interface in Director. The main difference between the Director movie you just created and the interfaces of the following chapters is complex Lingo programming code and a little hard work. As you read this book, you will gain the skill and experience you need to create as complex an interface as you desire.

Figure 2.16 *Applying the Graphic Behavior script to the Graphic bitmap.*

PUTTING IT ALL TOGETHER

Now that you have mastered the individual elements of Director, you should start thinking about the best way to arrange Director's windows to suit your needs. If possible, keep the Stage window, the Score window, the Cast window, and the Property Inspector window fully visible at all times. Such a goal may be difficult to meet at a resolution as low as 800 × 600 pixels (see Figure 2.17).

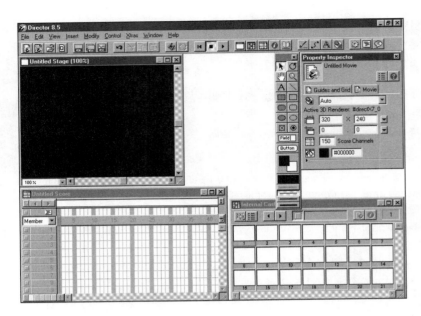

Figure 2.17 *Arranging Director's windows to suit your needs.*

If you find yourself having trouble fitting Director's windows on your screen, you might consider adjusting your computer's resolution, or screen area. You can accomplish this task by finding and opening the Display or Monitor section of your operating system's control panel. Your goal is to give yourself as much room to work as possible without shrinking everything down so far that small text is blurry and illegible. Choose a resolution that is convenient for you.

>>> **part 2**
simple interfaces

"What we call results are beginnings."
—Ralph Waldo Emerson

>>> chapter 3
the basics

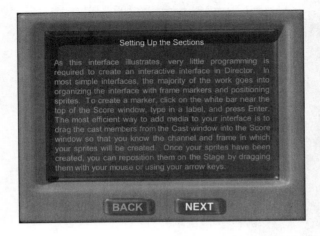
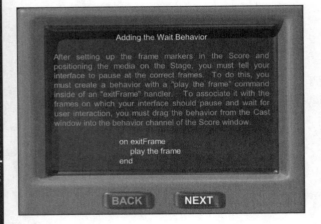
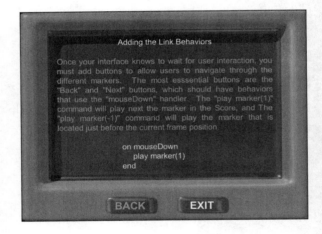

Figures 3.1-3.4   *The Basics interface in action.*

APPROACHING "THE BASICS" INTERFACE

Before you attempt to create any sort of complex interface within Director, you should first build a very simple interface from start to finish. You might be surprised at the amount of work that goes into the creation of a simple interface such as The Basics. Every interactive interface contains at least some media cast members to appear within the Stage as sprites, Lingo scripts to be applied to the interactive elements of the interface, and organization of information within the Score.

UNDERSTANDING THE BASICS INTERFACE

The Basics interface contains four sections, each with its own frame marker and Wait behavior on its first frame. When Director's playback head enters one of the interface sections, the Wait behavior of the first frame of the section makes it stay on the current frame and go no farther. Every frame of the interface contains two buttons that, when clicked, moves Director's playback head to the frame marker directly to the left or to the right of the current frame. When the playback head reaches the new marker, the frame's Wait behavior pauses the interface again to wait for more user interaction. To view the various Lingo scripts of the Internal cast, follow the steps outlined in Procedure 3.1.

Procedure 3.1   Viewing Lingo Scripts of the Internal Cast

1. Open the `tb.dir` file from the 03 - The Basics folder as specified in Appendix A, "Guide to Common Tasks." The Internal cast contains the four Lingo scripts shown in Table 3.1.

Table 3.1   Internal Cast Lingo Scripts

Script Name	Description
Wait	Makes the movie repeat the current frame over and over until otherwise specified.
Back Link	Changes the color of its associated sprite based on mouse interaction and plays the marker just before the playback head when the user clicks its associated sprite.
Next Link	Changes the color of its associated sprite based on mouse interaction and plays the marker just after the playback head when the user clicks its associated sprite.
Exit Link	Changes the color of its associated sprite based on mouse interaction and exits the interface when the user clicks its associated sprite.

2. Click the Wait member. Director will update the Cast window.
3. Click the Cast Member Script button. Director will display the Wait script within the Script window.
4. Use the Previous Cast Member and Next Cast Member buttons to view each of the Lingo scripts in the Internal cast.

After browsing through The Basics interface scripts and taking a look at its organization in the Score, you should have a good understanding of the logic behind this interface. If some of its aspects are still not clear, you may want to refer to Appendix B, "Guide to Lingo Programming." Although understanding the innerworkings of The Basics interface at this time is not completely necessary, it should make things easier for you as you re-create the interface throughout the rest of this chapter.

SETTING UP THE MOVIE

The first step in the creation of an interface is, of course, the creation of a new Director movie. After you have saved a new movie to your hard drive, make sure that the Stage has the correct color and dimensions for your interface. You can change these properties at any time, but you should set them up first to make arranging sprites on the Stage easier for yourself. If you change the size of the Stage after you have set up your interface sprites, the sprites might be misaligned or even off the screen entirely. To create a new movie and set its Stage properties, follow the steps outlined in Procedure 3.2.

Procedure 3.2   Creating a New Movie

1. Click the New Movie button (see Figure 3.5). Director will close the `tb.dir` file and create a new Director movie.

Figure 3.5   *The New Movie button.*

Figure 3.6   *Changing the Stage fill color.*

2. Save the new file to your hard drive as specified in Appendix A.

3. Within the Property Inspector window, click the Movie tab. Director will display the Movie sheet.

4. Click the Stage Size button and select the 640 × 480 option. Director will resize the Stage to 640 pixels wide and 480 pixels tall.

5. Click and hold the button to the right of the Stage Fill Color icon and select the black swatch (see Figure 3.6). Director will change the color of the Stage to black.

Now that you know how to set up a Director movie from scratch, you won't have to wade through such basic instructions throughout the rest of this book. The other interface chapters instruct you to open a template file that contains a partially complete version of the respective chapter's interface. Simple or repetitive tasks are completed for you so that you can spend your time learning what makes each interface unique.

CREATING THE MEDIA CAST MEMBERS

Multimedia interfaces consist of a variety of images, text, and other media elements organized on the screen. Nevertheless, before you can even begin to set up an interface on the Stage, you must either create or import its media elements in a cast. Both of The Basics interface graphic elements are available as external files for you to import, but because you must format text within Director, you need to create the text cast members from scratch. You can shorten the time it takes to create the text cast members by copying, pasting, and then modifying some of the cast members. To create the bitmap and text cast members needed for The Basics interface, follow the steps outlined in Procedure 3.3.

Procedure 3.3   Creating a Bitmap and Text Cast Members

1. Import the `background.bmp` file from The Basics folder and name its cast member **Background** as specified in Appendix A.

2. Import the `title.bmp` file from The Basics folder and name its cast member **Title** as specified in this book's Appendix A.

3. On the toolbar, click the Text Window (see Figure 3.7). Director will display the Text window.

Figure 3.7 *The Text Window button.*

4. In the Text window, click the Size drop-down list and select 18 (see Figure 3.8). Director will set the font size to 18 within the Text window.

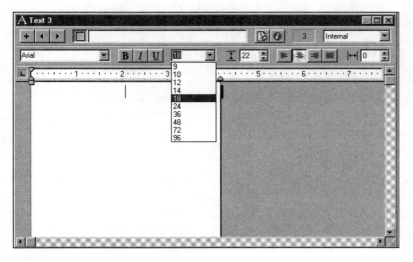

Figure 3.8 *Changing the font size.*

5. Click on the Align Center button. Director will center-align the text cursor within the Text window.

6. In the Tool Palette window, click and hold the Foreground Color button and select the white swatch (see Figure 3.9). Director will set the foreground color to white within the Text window.

7. Click and hold the Background Color button and select the black swatch. Director will set the background color to black within the Text window.

8. In the Text window, type **Click on the Next button to continue**. Director will update the Text window.

9. In the Cast Member Name field, type **Introduction Text** and press the Enter key (Return on Macintosh), as shown in Figure 3.10. Director will name your new text cast member Introduction Text.

10. Click the Introduction Text member. Director will highlight the Introduction Text member.

11. Click the Edit menu and select the Copy Cast Members option. Director will hold a copy of the Introduction Text member in memory.

12. Click an empty section of the Internal cast. Director will deselect the Introduction Text member.

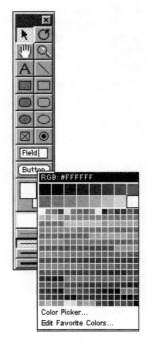

Figure 3.9 *Changing the foreground color.*

>>>

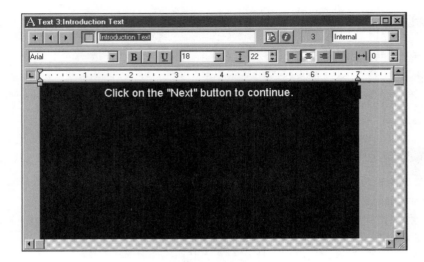

Figure 3.10 *Naming the new cast member.*

13. Click the Edit menu and select the Paste option. Director will paste a copy of the Introduction Text member into the Internal cast from memory.

14. In the Cast Member Name field, type **Instructions 1 Text** and press the Enter key (Return on Macintosh), as shown in Figure 3.11. Director will rename the new Introduction Text member to Instructions 1 Text.

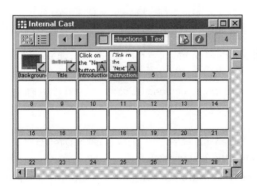

Figure 3.11 *Naming the new cast member.*

15. Click an empty section of the Internal cast. Director will deselect the Instructions 1 Text member.

16. Click the Edit menu and select the Paste option. Director will paste a copy of the Introduction Text member into the Internal cast from memory.

17. In the Cast Member Name field, type **Instructions 2 Text** and press the Enter key (Return on Macintosh). Director will rename the new Introduction Text member to Instructions 2 Text.

18. Click an empty section of the Internal cast. Director will deselect the Instructions 2 Text member.

19. Click the Edit menu and select the Paste option. Director will paste a copy of the Introduction Text member into the Internal cast from memory.

20. In the Cast Member Name field, type **Instructions 3 Text** and press the Enter key (Return on Macintosh). Director will rename the new Introduction Text member to Instructions 3 Text.

21. Click an empty section of the Internal cast. Director will deselect the Instructions 3 Text member.

22. Click the Edit menu and select the Paste option. Director will paste a copy of the Introduction Text member into the Internal cast from memory.

23. In the Cast Member Name field, type **Back Link Text** and press the Enter key (Return on Macintosh). Director will rename the new Introduction Text member to Back Link Text (see Figure 3.12).

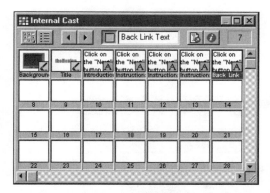

Figure 3.12 *The new text cast members.*

24. Double-click the Instructions 1 Text member. Director will display the text of Instructions 1 Text within the Text window.

25. Select the Instructions 1 Text member's existing text and replace it with the text that you want to appear in the first section of your interface (see Figure 3.13).

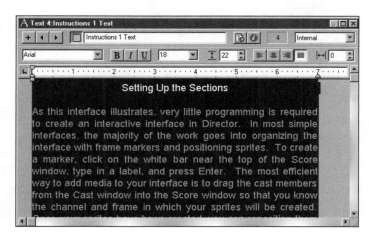

Figure 3.13 *Editing the Instructions 1 Text member.*

>>>

26. Double-click the Instructions 2 Text member. Director will display the text of Instructions 2 Text within the Text window.

27. Select the Instructions 2 Text member's existing text and replace it with the text that you want to appear in the second section of your interface.

28. Double-click the Instructions 3 Text member. Director will display the text of Instructions 3 Text within the Text window.

29. Select the Instructions 3 Text member's existing text and replace it with the text that you want to appear in the third section of your interface.

30. Double-click the Back Link Text member. Director will display the text of Back Link Text within the Text window.

31. Select the Back Link Text member's existing text and replace it with **BACK**.

32. Select the Back Link Text member's text and click the Bold button. Director will make the selected text boldface.

33. Click the Size drop-down list and select 24. Director will set the font size of the selected text to 24 (see Figure 3.14).

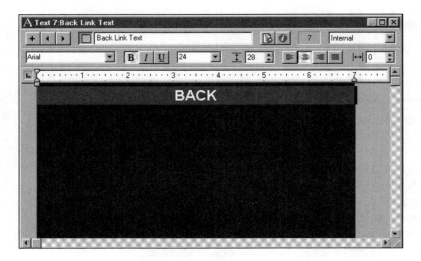

Figure 3.14 *Editing the Back Link Text member.*

34. In the Tool Palette window, click and hold the Foreground Color button and select the black swatch. Director will set the foreground color of the selected text to black.

35. Click and hold the Background Color button and select the white swatch. Director will set the background color to white within the Text window.

36. Click the Back Link Text member. Director will highlight the Back Link Text member.

37. Click the Edit menu and select the Copy Cast Members option. Director will hold a copy of the Back Link Text member in memory.

38. Click an empty section of the Internal cast. Director will deselect the Back Link Text member.

39. Click the Edit menu and select the Paste option. Director will paste a copy of the Back Link Text member into the Internal cast from memory.

40. In the Cast Member Name field, type **Next Link Text** and press the Enter key (Return on Macintosh). Director will rename the new Back Link Text member to Next Link Text.

41. Click an empty section of the Internal cast. Director will deselect the Next Link Text member.

42. Click the Edit menu and select the Paste option. Director will paste a copy of the Back Link Text member into the Internal cast from memory.

43. In the Cast Member Name field, type **Exit Link Text** and press the Enter key (Return on Macintosh). Director will rename the new Back Link Text member to Exit Link Text (see Figure 3.15).

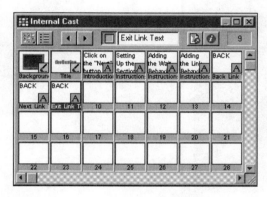

Figure 3.15 *The new text cast members.*

44. Double-click the Next Link Text member. Director will display the Next Link Text text within the Text window.

45. Select the Next Link Text member's existing text and replace it with **NEXT**.

46. Double-click the Exit Link Text member. Director will display the Exit Link Text text within the Text window.

47. Select the Exit Link Text member's existing text and replace it with **EXIT**.

48. Within the toolbar, click the Text Window button. Director will close the Text window.

At this point, your movie's Internal cast should contain all the media cast members necessary to build The Basics interface. If you were to preview your movie right now, however, you would see nothing but a blank screen. The user never sees any of the contents of the Cast window. Remember that casts are just a place to store media elements and programming code behind the scenes.

SETTING UP THE SCORE

Any time you drag a cast member onto the Stage it will show up in the Score. The reverse is also true. Dragging cast members into the Score window is the most efficient way to add sprites to your Director movie because only in the Score can you fully control the frames and channel in which a sprite is visible. Of course after you have positioned a sprite in the Score, you may want to reposition it or resize it within the Stage. Generally, however, the cleanest way to position a sprite on the Stage is to modify its properties in the Property Inspector window. To position the interface sprites within the Score, follow the steps outlined in Procedure 3.4.

Procedure 3.4 Positioning Interface Sprites Within the Score

1. Drag the Background member from the Cast window into cell 1 of channel 1 of the Score window. Director will display the Background sprite within the Stage window (see Figure 3.16).

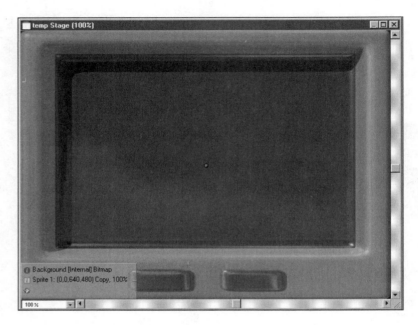

Figure 3.16 *The Background sprite.*

2. Drag cell 28 of channel 1 to frame 74. Director will extend the Background sprite to frame 74.

3. Drag the Exit Link Text member from the Cast window into cell 1 of channel 2 of the Score window. Director will display the Exit Link Text sprite within the Stage window.

4. Drag cell 28 of channel 2 to frame 29. Director will extend the Exit Link Text sprite to frame 29.

5. Drag the Back Link Text member from the Cast window into cell 30 of channel 2 of the Score window. Director will display the Back Link Text sprite within the Stage window.

6. Drag cell 57 of channel 2 to frame 74. Director will extend the Back Link Text sprite to frame 74.

7. Drag the Next Link Text member from the Cast window into cell 1 of channel 3 of the Score window. Director will display the Next Link Text sprite within the Stage window.

8. Drag cell 28 of channel 3 to frame 59. Director will extend the Next Link Text sprite to frame 59.

9. Drag the Exit Link Text member from the Cast window into cell 60 of channel 3 of the Score window. Director will display the Exit Link Text sprite within the Stage window.

10. Drag cell 87 of channel 3 to frame 74. Director will curtail the Exit Link Text sprite to frame 74 (see Figure 3.17).

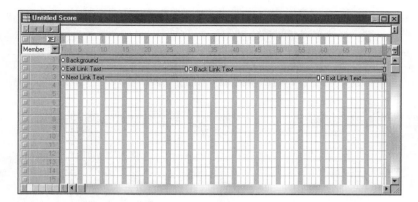

Figure 3.17 *The new sprites.*

11. Drag the Title member from the Cast window into cell 5 of channel 4 of the Score window. Director will display the Title sprite within the Stage window.

12. Drag cell 32 of channel 4 to frame 29. Director will curtail the Title sprite to frame 29.

13. Drag the Instructions 1 Text member from the Cast window into cell 30 of channel 4 of the Score window. Director will display the Instructions 1 Text sprite within the Stage window.

14. Drag cell 57 of channel 4 to frame 44. Director will curtail the Instructions 1 Text sprite to frame 44.

15. Drag the Instructions 2 Text member from the Cast window into cell 45 of channel 4 of the Score window. Director will display the Instructions 2 Text sprite within the Stage window.

16. Drag cell 72 of channel 4 to frame 59. Director will curtail the Instructions 2 Text sprite to frame 59.

17. Drag the Instructions 3 Text member from the Cast window into cell 60 of channel 4 of the Score window. Director will display the Instructions 3 Text sprite within the Stage window.

18. Drag cell 87 of channel 4 to frame 74. Director will curtail the Instructions 3 Text sprite to frame 74.

19. Drag the Introduction Text member from the Cast window into cell 15 of channel 5 of the Score window. Director will display the Introduction Text sprite within the Stage window.

20. Drag cell 42 of channel 4 to frame 29. Director will curtail the Introduction Text sprite to frame 29.

You may have noticed that although the Score looks perfectly in order, the Stage window is cluttered with overlapping sprites. Finally, the media elements are a visible part of your interface, but they are by no means organized and accessible. Stage organization is just as important as Score organization. To position the interface sprites within the Stage, follow the steps outlined in Procedure 3.5.

Procedure 3.5   Positioning Interface Sprites Within the Stage

1. Within the Score window, click cell 1 of channel 2, hold down the Shift key, and then click cell 74 of channel 2. Director will highlight the contents of channel 2.

2. In the Property Inspector window, type **190** into the X field, **434** into the Y field, **100** into the W field, and then press the Enter key (Return on Macintosh). Director will update the selected sprites within the Stage window.

>>>

The Basics

3. Click the Ink drop-down list and select the Background Transparent option (see Figure 3.18). Director will remove the background from the selected sprites.

4. Within the Property Inspector window, in the Foreground Color field, type **#C0C0FF** and press the Enter key (Return on Macintosh), as shown in Figure 3.19. Director will set the foreground color of the selected sprites to light blue.

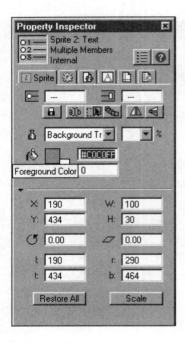

Figure 3.18 *Setting the ink of the sprites in channel 2 to Background Transparent.*

Figure 3.19 *The Foreground Color field.*

5. Within the Score window, click cell 1 of channel 3, hold down the Shift key, and then click cell 74 of channel 3. Director will highlight the contents of channel 3.

6. Within the Property Inspector window, type **350** into the X field, **434** into the Y field, **100** into the W field, and then press the Enter key (Return on Macintosh). Director will update the selected sprites within the Stage window.

7. Click the Ink drop-down list and select the Background Transparent option. Director will remove the background from the selected sprites.

8. In the Foreground Color field, type **#C0C0FF** and press the Enter key (Return on Macintosh). Director will set the foreground color of the selected sprites to light blue.

9. Within the Score window, click cell 6 of channel 4. Director will highlight the Title sprite.

10. Within the Property Inspector window, type **220** into the Y field and press the Enter key (Return on Macintosh). Director will update the Title sprite within the Stage window.

11. Click the Ink drop-down list and select the Background Transparent option. Director will remove the white background from the Title sprite.

12. Within the Score window, click cell 30 of channel 4, hold down the Shift key, and then click cell 74 of channel 4. Director will highlight the Instructions 1 Text, Instructions 2 Text, and Instructions 3 Text sprites in channel 4.

13. Within the Property Inspector window, type **80** into the X field, **60** into the Y field, **480** into the W field, and then press the Enter key (Return on Macintosh). Director will update the selected sprites within the Stage window.

14. Click the Ink drop-down list and select the Background Transparent option. Director will remove the background from the selected sprites.

15. Within the Score window, click cell 16 of channel 5. Director will highlight the Introduction Text sprite.

16. Within the Property Inspector window, type **80** into the X field, **350** into the Y field, **480** into the W field, and then press the Enter key (Return on Macintosh). Director will update the Introduction Text sprite within the Stage window.

17. Click the Ink drop-down list and select the Background Transparent option. Director will remove the background from the Introduction Text sprite (see Figure 3.20).

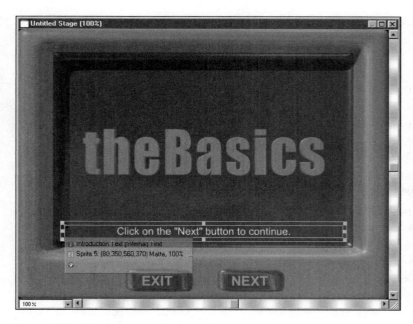

Figure 3.20 *The Introduction Text sprite within the Stage window.*

Now that your sprites are all in their proper positions, you can learn about a process called *tweening*. Tweening occurs when a sprite is told to be in one position in one frame and another position in a later frame. Frames that tell Director to make changes to a sprite are called *keyframes*. In the empty frames between two keyframes, Director attempts to create smooth motion. In addition to changing a sprite's position, keyframes also can affect a sprite's dimensions, color, rotation, or any of several other properties. Unless otherwise specified, Director will create smooth transitions between keyframes any time a sprite's appearance changes. To create an introduction animation for your interface, follow the steps outlined in Procedure 3.6.

Procedure 3.6 Creating an Introduction Animation

1. Within the Score window, click cell 14 of channel 1. Director will highlight the Background sprite.

2. Click the Insert menu and select the Keyframe option. Director will mark cell 14 of channel 1 as a keyframe.

3. Click cell 14 of channel 2. Director will highlight the Exit Link Text sprite.

4. Click the Insert menu and select the Keyframe option. Director will mark cell 14 of channel 2 as a keyframe.

5. Click cell 14 of channel 3. Director will highlight the Next Link Text sprite.

6. Click the Insert menu and select the Keyframe option. Director will mark cell 14 of channel 3 as a keyframe.

7. Click cell 14 of channel 4. Director will highlight the Title sprite.

8. Click the Insert menu and select the Keyframe option. Director will mark cell 14 of channel 4 as a keyframe.

9. Click cell 1 of channel 1. Director will highlight cell 1 of the Background sprite.

10. Within the Property Inspector window, in the Blend drop-down list, type **0**, and press the Enter key (Return on Macintosh). Director will set the opacity of cell 1 of the Background sprite to zero percent.

11. In the Score window, click cell 1 of channel 2. Director will highlight cell 1 of the Back Link Text sprite.

12. From the Property Inspector window, in the Blend drop-down list, type **0**, and press the Enter key (Return on Macintosh). Director will set the opacity of cell 1 of the Exit Link Text sprite to zero percent.

13. Within the Score window, click cell 1 of channel 3. Director will highlight cell 1 of the Next Link Text sprite.

14. In the Property Inspector window, from the Blend drop-down list, type **0**, and press the Enter key (Return on Macintosh). Director will set the opacity of cell 1 of the Next Link Text sprite to zero percent.

15. Within the Score window, click cell 5 of channel 4. Director will highlight cell 5 of the Title sprite.

16. In the Property Inspector window, type **503** into the W field, **100** into the H field, and then press the Enter key (Return on Macintosh). Director will update cell 5 of the Title sprite within the Stage window.

17. Within the Property Inspector window, in the Blend drop-down list, type **0** and press the Enter key (Return on Macintosh), as shown in Figure 3.21. Director will set the opacity of cell 5 of the Title sprite to zero percent.

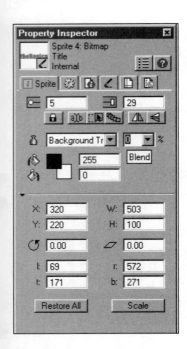

Figure 3.21   *The Blend drop-down list within the Property Inspector window.*

If you were to preview your movie at this point, you would see the interface load properly, display the first section, and then move on to display the other sections. Without any Lingo code to tell the interface to stop, it would play through in only a few seconds. To make the interface pause as soon as it enters a section, you must create a looping behavior and apply it to the first frame of each section. To add a frame marker and a looping behavior to each section of the interface, follow the steps outlined in Procedure 3.7.

Procedure 3.7   Adding a Frame Marker and a Looping Behavior

1. Add a marker named Introduction to frame 15 as specified in Appendix A.

2. Add a marker named Section 1 to frame 30 as specified in Appendix A.

3. Add a marker named Section 2 to frame 45 as specified in Appendix A.

4. Add a marker named Section 3 to frame 60 as specified in Appendix A.

5. Create a behavior script named Wait as specified in Appendix A.

6. In the Cast window, click the Wait member. Director will highlight the Wait member.

7. Click the Cast Member Script button. Director will display the Wait script within the Script window.

8. Within the Script window, type the following code:

```
on exitFrame
   play the frame
end
```

9. From the toolbar, click the Script Window button. Director will close the Script window.

10. Apply the Wait behavior to frames 15, 30, 45, and 60 as specified in Appendix A.

If you were to leave your interface in its current condition, its sections would be fully formed but inaccessible. The interface would pause as soon as it reached the Wait behavior in the frame that contains the Introduction marker. To complete this interface, you must activate its buttons by applying behavior scripts to them.

WRITING AND APPLYING THE LINK BEHAVIORS

Each of the behavior scripts for the link buttons contains three event handlers. For all three, the mouseEnter handler changes the color of its associated sprite to white, and the mouseLeave handler changes the color back to light blue. The mouseDown handler is unique for each behavior. It contains the Lingo code that will execute when the user actually clicks a button. The Back Link behavior's mouseDown handler plays the previous marker, the Next Link behavior's handler plays the next marker, and the Exit Link behavior's handler stops the movie entirely. To create the three link behaviors and apply them to their appropriate sprites, follow the steps outlined in Procedure 3.8.

Procedure 3.8   Creating Link Behaviors

1. Create a behavior script named Back Link as specified in Appendix A.

2. Within the Cast window, click the Back Link member. Director will highlight the Back Link member.

3. Click the Cast Member Script button (see Figure 3.22). Director will display the Back Link script within the Script window.

>>>

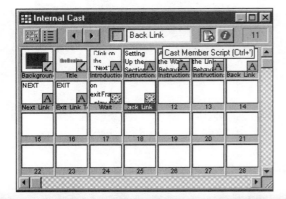

Figure 3.22   *The Cast Member Script button within the Cast window.*

4. Within the Script window, type the code that follows throughout this step:

```
on mouseDown
  play marker(-1)
end
```

The previous handler plays the marker directly to the left of the playback head when the user clicks the associated sprite.

The following handler changes the associated sprite's foreground color to white when the user's mouse enters the boundaries of the associated sprite:

```
on mouseEnter me
  sprite(me.spriteNum).color = rgb(255, 255, 255)
end
```

The following handler changes the associated sprite's foreground color to light blue when the user's mouse leaves the boundaries of the associated sprite:

```
on mouseLeave me
  sprite(me.spriteNum).color = rgb(192, 192, 255)
end
```

5. Create a behavior script named Next Link as specified in Appendix A.

6. From the Cast window, click the Next Link member. Director will highlight the Next Link member.

7. Click the Cast Member Script button. Director will display the Next Link script within the Script window.

8. Within the Script window, type the following code:

```
on mouseDown
  play marker(1)
end

on mouseEnter me
  sprite(me.spriteNum).color = rgb(255, 255, 255)
end

on mouseLeave me
  sprite(me.spriteNum).color = rgb(192, 192, 255)
end
```

Note that the handler plays the marker directly to the right of the playback head when the user clicks the associated sprite.

9. Create a behavior script named Exit Link as specified in Appendix A.

10. Within the Cast window, click the Exit Link member. Director will highlight the Exit Link member.

11. Click on the Cast Member Script button. Director will display the Exit Link script within the Script window.

12. From the Script window, type the following code:

```
on mouseDown
  halt
end

on mouseEnter me
  sprite(me.spriteNum).color = rgb(255, 255, 255)
end

on mouseLeave me
  sprite(me.spriteNum).color = rgb(192, 192, 255)
end
```

Note that the preceding handler stops the movie entirely when the user clicks the associated sprite.

13. On the toolbar, click the Script Window button. Director will close the Script window.

14. Apply the Back Link behavior to the Back Link Text sprite that begins in cell 30 of channel 2 as specified in Appendix A.

15. Apply the Next Link behavior to the Next Link Text sprite that begins in cell 1 of channel 3 as specified in Appendix A.

16. Apply the Exit Link behavior to the Exit Link Text sprite that begins in cell 1 of channel 2 and the Exit Link Text sprite that begins in cell 60 of channel 3 as specified in Appendix A.

Try previewing your movie now. Your interface should function exactly like The Basics interface on the companion CD-ROM. Of course your section text will differ from the original, but you shouldn't worry about that. The main concern of an interface designer is building a framework in which to store information. The information within a properly constructed interface should be able to be updated or reorganized at any given time.

MAKING ADJUSTMENTS

Now that your interface is fully constructed, you might be wondering what use it is to you. When you construct an interface, you want it to be original, not just a copy of someone else's design. Actually, with a few simple moves, you can convert The Basics interface into a totally new creation. You can replace the bitmaps of the Background and Title members, change the font style of the text members, and even rearrange the interface elements within the Stage. If necessary, you can even add more sections to the Score by creating new markers, complete with Wait behaviors, and extending the sprites accordingly. The sections themselves can contain any sort of media element, not just text. The basic two-button interface has a wide variety of applications.

"Great things are not done by impulse, but by a series of small things brought together."
—Vincent Van Gogh

▼▼▼ **chapter 4**
ten-step guide

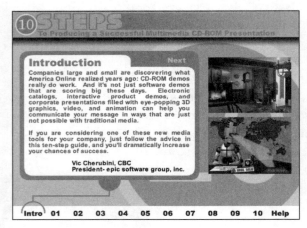
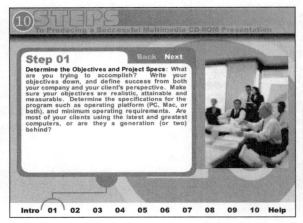

Figures 4.1-4.4   *The Ten-Step Guide interface in action.*

APPROACHING THE "TEN-STEP GUIDE" INTERFACE

The Ten-Step Guide interface is quite similar to The Basics interface in that they both contain sequential sections connected by Back and Next links. The Ten-Step Guide interface, however, also provides a second navigation option, which makes the interface much more flexible. At any point in the presentation, the user can click a link at the bottom of the screen and skip to a completely new section. Because of this second navigation method, the user can access the sections of the Ten-Step Guide interface in any order he or she chooses.

UNDERSTANDING THE TEN-STEP GUIDE INTERFACE

If you were to remove all the animation sequences and flashy graphics from the Ten-Step Guide interface, you would be left with an interface not very different from The Basics interface. The only important new elements are the section links at the bottom of the Stage. Each of these links uses the same behavior yet points to different sections of the presentation. This is possible because the names of the frame markers correspond to the text of the links. The Section Link behavior just plays the marker whose name matches the associated link's text. If the user were to click a link labeled Help, the interface would play the frame marker labeled Help. This technique prevents the programmer from having to create a new behavior for each section link. To view the various Lingo scripts of the Scripts cast, follow these steps:

1. Open the `ts.dir` file from the 04 - Ten-Step Guide folder as specified in Appendix A, "Guide to Common Tasks." The Scripts cast contains the four Lingo scripts shown in Table 4.1.

Table 4.1 The Scripts Cast Lingo Scripts

Script Name	Description
Wait	Makes the movie repeat the current frame over and over until otherwise specified.
Back Link	Changes the color of its associated sprite based on mouse interaction and plays the frame that is nine frames to the left of the playback head when the user clicks its associated sprite.
Next Link	Changes the color of its associated sprite based on mouse interaction and plays the frame directly to the right of the playback head when the user clicks its associated sprite.
Section Link	Changes the color of its associated sprite based on mouse interaction and plays the marker whose name matches its cast member's text when the user clicks its associated sprite.

2. In the Cast window, click the Wait member. Director will update the Cast window.

3. Click the Cast Member Script button. Director will display the Wait script within the Script window.

4. Use the Previous Cast Member and Next Cast Member buttons to view each of the Lingo scripts in the Scripts cast.

After browsing through the Ten-Step Guide interface scripts and taking a look at its organization in the Score, you should have a good understanding of the logic behind this interface. If some of its aspects are still not clear, you may want to refer to Appendix B, "Guide to Lingo Programming." Although understanding the innerworkings of the Ten-Step Guide interface at this time is not completely necessary, it should make things easier for you as you re-create the interface throughout the rest of this chapter.

DRAWING THE CIRCLE VECTOR SHAPE

Vector graphics differ from bitmap, or raster, graphics in that they are made up of curves and vertices rather than pixels. Basically, vector images contain shapes that the computer must convert into pixels to display on the screen. One good attribute of vector images is that they can be scaled and distorted without any loss of quality. In addition, they tend to have considerably smaller file sizes than ordinary raster images. Overly complex vector images, however, can bog down a computer with unnecessary calculations. When developing interfaces in Director, you will generally use vector graphics only for simple, geometric shapes. To draw a circle into the Circle member of the Shapes cast, follow the steps outlined in Procedure 4.1.

Procedure 4.1 Drawing a Circle Vector Shape

1. Open the `tbtemp.dir` file from the 04 - Ten-Step Guide folder and save it to your hard drive as specified in Appendix A.

2. In the Cast window, click the Choose Cast button and select the Shapes option. Director will display the Shapes cast within the Cast window.

3. Double-click the Circle member. Director will display the Circle shape within the Vector Shape window.

>>>

4. Within the Vector Shape window, click the Filled Ellipse button (see Figure 4.5). Director will select the Filled Ellipse tool.

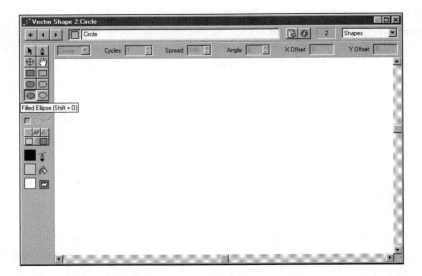

Figure 4.5   *The Filled Ellipse button.*

5. Next click and drag to create a circle.

6. Click and hold the button to the left of the Fill Color icon and select the Color Picker option (see Figure 4.6). Director will display the Color dialog box.

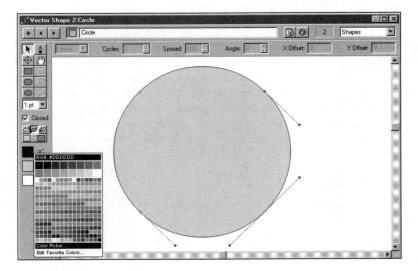

Figure 4.6   *Selecting the Color Picker option.*

7. In the Color dialog box, type **200** into the Red field, **100** into the Green field, **0** into the Blue field, and then click the OK button. Director will set the fill color to dark orange within the Vector Shape window.

8. In the Vector Shape window, click the Stroke Width drop-down list and select 0 pt (see Figure 4.7). Director will set the Circle shape's stroke width to zero.

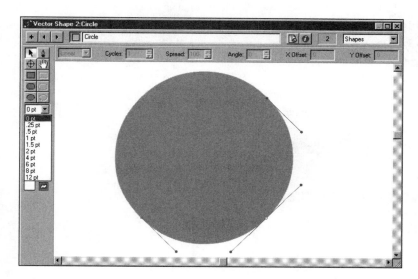

Figure 4.7 *Selecting the 0 pt option.*

9. From the toolbar, click the Vector Shape Window button (see Figure 4.8). Director will close the Vector Shape window.

Figure 4.8 *The Vector Shape Window button.*

As you may have noticed, the Shapes cast contains several other vector shapes, which are already built for you. Some of these shapes are relatively complex. Presently, Director's vector graphics capabilities are somewhat limited. There are no real shortcuts to creating complex vector graphics within Director. You must just start with a basic shape, such as a circle, and then move its vertices around to suit your needs. If you find yourself trying to create a very complex vector graphic within Director, you would probably be better off using an external paint program to create a raster image.

SETTING UP THE BACKGROUND ELEMENTS

After the opening animation brings the interface elements into place, several of the elements do not change throughout the remainder of the presentation. These items (such as the large 10 logo and the top title bar) appear behind the interface's changing graphics, text, and links. In general, most interfaces tend to have static, or constant, elements in the background and dynamic, or changing, elements in the foreground. This feels the most natural to the user because, in nature, objects in the distance are either still or very slow-moving, and he can only manipulate objects that are close by. To position the background elements of the interface within the Score and the Stage, follow the steps outlined in Procedure 4.2.

Procedure 4.2   Setting the Background Elements

1. In the Cast window, click the Choose Cast button and select the Bitmaps option. Director will display the Bitmaps cast within the Cast window.

2. Drag the Large 10 member from the Cast window into cell 60 of channel 1 of the Score window. Director will display the Large 10 sprite within the Stage window.

3. Using the Score window, drag cell 64 of channel 1 to frame 119. Director will extend the Large 10 sprite to frame 119.

4. Next click cell 61 of channel 1. Director will highlight the Large 10 sprite (see Figure 4.9).

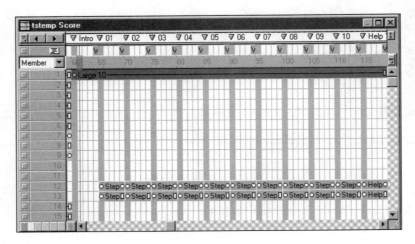

Figure 4.9   *The Large 10 sprite within the Score window.*

5. In the Property Inspector window, type **450** into the X field, **290** into the Y field, and then press the Enter key (Return on Macintosh). Director will update the Large 10 sprite within the Stage window.

6. Click the Ink drop-down list and select the Matte option. Director will remove the white border from the Large 10 sprite.

7. Click the Blend drop-down list and select the 50 option (see Figure 4.10). Director will set the opacity of the Large 10 sprite to 50 percent.

8. Drag the Shadow member from the Cast window into cell 60 of channel 2 of the Score window. Director will display the Shadow sprite within the Stage window.

9. In the Score window, drag cell 64 of channel 2 to frame 119. Director will extend the Shadow sprite to frame 119.

10. Click cell 61 of channel 2. Director will highlight the Shadow sprite.

11. From the Property Inspector window, type **70** into the Y field, **640** into the W field, and then press the Enter key (Return on Macintosh). Director will update the Shadow sprite within the Stage window.

12. Click the Ink drop-down list and select the Subtract Pin option. Director will make the Shadow sprite subtract the RGB values of its pixels from the portion of the Stage it covers.

13. Drag the Steps Fade member from the Cast window into cell 60 of channel 4 of the Score window. Director will display the Steps Fade sprite within the Stage window.

14. Using the Score window, drag cell 64 of channel 4 to frame 119. Director will extend the Steps Fade sprite to frame 119.

15. Click cell 61 of channel 4. Director will highlight the Steps Fade sprite.

16. In the Property Inspector window, type **350** into the X field, **23** into the Y field, and then press the Enter key (Return on Macintosh). Director will update the Steps Fade sprite within the Stage window.

17. Drag the Small 10 member from the Cast window into cell 60 of channel 6 of the Score window. Director will display the Small 10 sprite within the Stage window.

18. From the Score window, drag cell 64 of channel 6 to frame 119. Director will extend the Small 10 sprite to frame 119.

19. Click cell 61 of channel 6. Director will highlight the Small 10 sprite.

20. In the Property Inspector window, type **30** into the X field, **30** into the Y field, and then press the Enter key (Return on Macintosh). Director will update the Small 10 sprite within the Stage window.

21. Click the Ink drop-down list and select the Matte option. Director will remove the white border from the Small 10 sprite (see Figure 4.11).

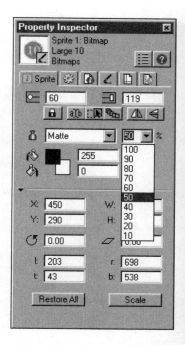

Figure 4.10 *Selecting the 50 option in the Property Inspector window.*

Figure 4.11 *The Small 10 sprite.*

22. In the Cast window, click the Choose Cast button and select the Shapes option. Director will display the Shapes cast within the Cast window.

23. Drag the Rectangle member from the Cast window into cell 60 of channel 3 of the Score window. Director will display the Rectangle shape within the Stage window.

24. Within the Score window, drag cell 64 of channel 3 to frame 119. Director will extend the Rectangle shape to frame 119.

25. Click cell 61 of channel 3. Director will highlight the Rectangle shape (see Figure 4.12).

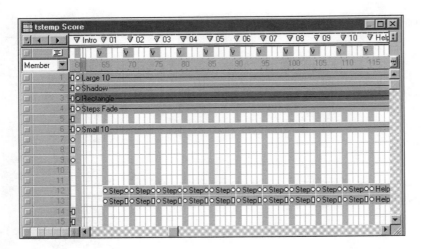

Figure 4.12   *The Rectangle shape within the Score window.*

26. Using the Property Inspector window, type **0** into the X field, **0** into the Y field, **640** into the W field, **60** into the H field, and then press the Enter key (Return on Macintosh). Director will update the Rectangle shape within the Stage window.

27. In the Foreground Color field, type **#FFA000** and press the Enter key (Return on Macintosh). Director will set the foreground color of the Rectangle shape to orange.

28. Drag the Circle member from the Cast window into cell 60 of channel 7 of the Score window. Director will display the Circle shape within the Stage window.

29. In the Score window, drag cell 64 of channel 7 to frame 119. Director will extend the Circle shape to frame 119.

30. Click cell 61 of channel 7. Director will highlight the Circle shape.

31. Using the Property Inspector window, type **215** into the X field, **390** into the Y field, **50** into the W field, **50** into the H field, and then press the Enter key (Return on Macintosh). Director will update the Circle shape within the Stage window.

32. Click the Ink drop-down list and select the Background Transparent option. Director will remove the background from the Circle shape.

33. Drag the Rounded Rectangle member from the Cast window into cell 60 of channel 8 of the Score window. Director will display the Rounded Rectangle shape within the Stage window.

34. Within the Score window, drag cell 64 of channel 8 to frame 119. Director will extend the Rounded Rectangle shape to frame 119.

35. Click cell 61 of channel 8. Director will highlight the Rounded Rectangle shape.

36. In the Property Inspector window, type **215** into the X field, **240** into the Y field, **400** into the W field, **300** into the H field, and then press the Enter key (Return on Macintosh). Director will update the Rounded Rectangle shape within the Stage window.

37. Next click the Ink drop-down list and select the Background Transparent option. Director will remove the background from the Rounded Rectangle shape.

38. Drag the Text Background member from the Cast window into cell 60 of channel 9 of the Score window. Director will display the Text Background shape within the Stage window.

39. Within the Score window, drag cell 64 of channel 9 to frame 119. Director will extend the Text Background shape to frame 119.

40. In the Score window, click cell 61 of channel 9. Director will highlight the Text Background shape.

41. Using the Property Inspector window, type **215** into the X field, **240** into the Y field, **380** into the W field, **280** into the H field, and then press the Enter key (Return on Macintosh). Director will update the Text Background shape within the Stage window.

42. Click the Ink drop-down list and select the Background Transparent option. Director will remove the background from the Text Background shape (see Figure 4.13).

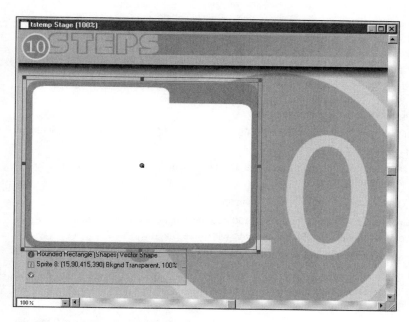

Figure 4.13 *The Text Background shape.*

43. In the Cast window, click the Choose Cast button and select the Text option. Director will display the Text cast within the Cast window.

44. Drag the To Producing Text member from the Cast window into cell 60 of channel 5 of the Score window. Director will display the To Producing Text sprite within the Stage window.

45. From the Score window, drag cell 64 of channel 5 to frame 119. Director will extend the To Producing Text sprite to frame 119.

46. Using the Score window, click cell 61 of channel 5. Director will highlight the To Producing Text sprite.

47. In the Property Inspector window, type **50** into the X field, **38** into the Y field, and then press the Enter key (Return on Macintosh). Director will update the To Producing Text sprite within the Stage window.

>>>

48. Click the Ink drop-down list and select the Background Transparent option. Director will remove the background from the To Producing Text sprite.

49. In the Foreground Color field, type **#C86400** and press the Enter key (Return on Macintosh). Director will set the foreground color of the To Producing Text sprite to dark orange.

Now that you have positioned all the static background elements on the Stage, your interface should be starting to take shape. Look at the interface so far and think about where you would expect to find the various foreground elements such as the section title, paragraph text, and navigation links. When positioning the elements of your interfaces, you should always try to imagine where the user would naturally look for a particular item. You should never surprise the user with illogical item placement. Always keep the basic principles of interface design in mind.

ADDING THE BACK AND NEXT LINKS

To make your interface functional, only two elements are technically required. The Back link and the Next link provide the user with minimal control over interface navigation. Unlike the background elements of this interface, the Back and Next links do not exist in every frame. You must remember that the first section needs no Back link, and the last section needs no Next link. Some interfaces choose to include both links in every section and have the navigation path lead in a circle. For the purposes of the Ten-Step Guide, however, this would only lead to confusion. To position the Next and Back links within the Score and the Stage, follow the steps outlined in Procedure 4.3.

Procedure 4.3   Positioning Links in the Score and Stage

1. Drag the Back Link member from the Cast window into cell 65 of channel 10 of the Score window. Director will display the Back Link sprite within the Stage window.

2. In the Score window, drag cell 69 of channel 10 to frame 119. Director will extend the Back Link sprite to frame 119.

3. Click cell 66 of channel 10. Director will highlight the Back Link sprite.

4. In the Property Inspector window, type **280** into the X field, **100** into the Y field, and then press the Enter key (Return on Macintosh). Director will update the Back Link sprite within the Stage window.

5. Click the Ink drop-down list and select the Background Transparent option. Director will remove the background from the Back Link sprite.

6. In the Foreground Color field, type **#FFC864** and press the Enter key (Return on Macintosh). Director will set the foreground color of the Back Link sprite to light orange.

7. Drag the Next Link member from the Cast window into cell 60 of channel 11 of the Score window. Director will display the Next Link sprite within the Stage window.

8. Using the Score window, drag cell 64 of channel 11 to frame 114. Director will extend the Next Link sprite to frame 114.

9. Click cell 61 of channel 11. Director will highlight the Next Link sprite (see Figure 4.14).

10. From the Property Inspector window, type **340** into the X field, **100** into the Y field, and then press the Enter key (Return on Macintosh). Director will update the Next Link sprite within the Stage window.

11. Click the Ink drop-down list and select the Background Transparent option. Director will remove the background from the Next Link sprite.

12. In the Foreground Color field, type **#FFC864** and press the Enter key (Return on Macintosh). Director will set the foreground color of the Next Link sprite to light orange.

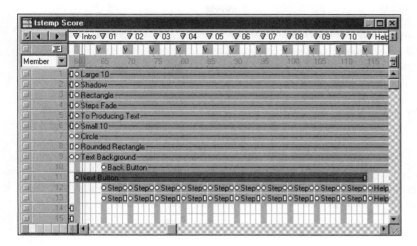

Figure 4.14 *The Next Link sprite within the Score window.*

Now that you have positioned the Back and Next links in both the Score and the Stage, activating them is all that remains. The simplest way to do this is by giving each link its own behavior script. Because both links should change color when the user's mouse moves over them, the two behavior scripts will have identical `mouseEnter` and `mouseLeave` handlers. The `mouseDown` handler, however, will be different because the two links must respond differently to mouse clicks. The two behaviors have been partially completed for your convenience. To complete and apply the Back Link and Next Link behavior scripts, follow the steps outlined in Procedure 4.4.

Procedure 4.4   Completing and Applying the Back Link and Next Link Behaviors

1. In the Cast window, click the Choose Cast button and select the Scripts option. Director will display the Scripts cast within the Cast window.

2. Click the Back Link member. Director will highlight the Back Link member.

3. Next click the Cast Member Script button. Director will display the Back Link script within the Script window.

4. In the Script window, in the `mouseDown` handler, type the following code. Note that the following line plays the marker directly to the left of the playback head:

   ```
   play marker(-1)
   ```

5. In the Cast window, click the Next Link member. Director will highlight the Next Link member.

6. Click the Cast Member Script button. Director will display the Next Link script within the Script window.

7. From the Script window, in the `mouseDown` handler, type the following code. Note that the following line plays the marker directly to the right of the playback head:

   ```
   play marker(1)
   ```

8. From the toolbar, click the Script Window button. Director will close the Script window.

9. Apply the Back Link behavior to the Back Link sprite that begins in cell 65 of channel 10 as specified in Appendix A.

10. Apply the Next Link behavior to the Next Link sprite that begins in cell 60 of channel 11 as specified in Appendix A.

>>>

If you were to preview your movie at this point, you would find that you could access every section of the interface by using only the Back and Next links. The first section has been left blank so that you can rebuild it and see what sort of work goes into setting up the foreground elements of a section. Because all the sections are set up in virtually the same manner, there is no reason for you to rebuild each of them.

SETTING UP THE FOREGROUND ELEMENTS

As you can see by looking in the Score window, the Introduction section does not contain all the same elements as the other sections. You will need to add the Introduction section's title text, body text, and screen shot images to complete the section's foreground. The title text and screen shot images both use keyframes to give the illusion that they are actually moving onto the screen as the section first loads. This sort of tweening effect has no real practical purpose but can add to the aesthetic appeal of your interface. To position the foreground elements of the Introduction section within the Score and the Stage, follow the steps outlined in Procedure 4.5.

Procedure 4.5   Positioning Foreground Elements

1. In the Cast window, click the Choose Cast button and select the Text option. Director will display the Text cast within the Cast window.

2. Drag the Introduction member from the Cast window into cell 60 of channel 12 of the Score window. Director will display the Introduction sprite within the Stage window.

3. In the Score window, click cell 61 of channel 12. Director will highlight the Introduction sprite.

4. From the Property Inspector window, type **35** into the X field, **100** into the Y field, and then press the Enter key (Return on Macintosh). Director will update the Introduction sprite within the Stage window.

5. Click the Ink drop-down list and select the Background Transparent option. Director will remove the background from the Introduction sprite.

6. Next, in the Foreground Color field, type **#C86400** and press the Enter key (Return on Macintosh). Director will set the foreground color of the Introduction sprite to dark orange.

7. In the Score window, click cell 64 of channel 12. Director will highlight cell 64 of the Introduction sprite.

8. Click the Insert menu and select the Keyframe option. Director will mark cell 64 of channel 12 as a keyframe (see Figure 4.15).

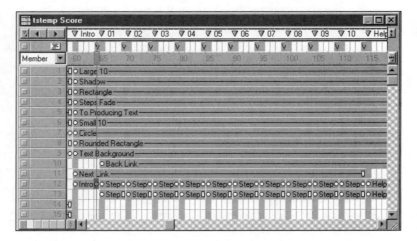

Figure 4.15   *Cell 64 of the Introduction sprite.*

9. Click cell 60 of channel 12. Director will highlight cell 60 of the Introduction sprite.

10. Using the Property Inspector window, in the Blend drop-down list, type **0** and press the Enter key (Return on Macintosh). Director will set the opacity of cell 60 of the Introduction sprite to zero percent.

11. Drag the Introduction Text member from the Cast window into cell 60 of channel 13 of the Score window. Director will display the Introduction Text sprite within the Stage window.

12. In the Score window, click cell 61 of channel 13. Director will highlight the Introduction Text sprite.

13. Using the Property Inspector window, type **35** into the X field, **135** into the Y field, and then press the Enter key (Return on Macintosh). Director will update the Introduction Text sprite within the Stage window.

14. Click the Ink drop-down list and select the Background Transparent option. Director will remove the background from the Introduction Text sprite.

15. In the Cast window, click the Choose Cast button and select the Bitmaps option. Director will display the Bitmaps cast within the Cast window.

16. Drag the Shot 1 member from the Cast window into cell 61 of channel 31 of the Score window. Director will display the Shot 1 sprite within the Stage window.

17. In the Score window, click cell 62 of channel 31. Director will highlight the Shot 1 sprite.

18. From the Property Inspector window, type **527** into the X field, **171** into the Y field, and then press the Enter key (Return on Macintosh). Director will update the Shot 1 sprite within the Stage window.

19. Using the Score window, click cell 63 of channel 31. Director will highlight the Shot 1 sprite.

20. Click the Insert menu and select the Keyframe option. Director will mark cell 63 of channel 31 as a keyframe (see Figure 4.16).

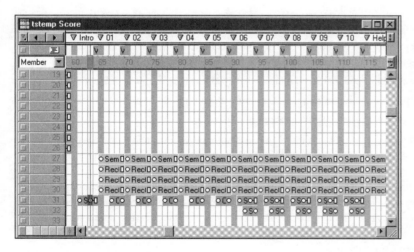

Figure 4.16 *Cell 63 of the Shot 1 sprite.*

21. Click cell 61 of channel 31. Director will highlight cell 61 of the Shot 1 sprite.

22. From the Property Inspector window, type **684** into the X field, **500** into the W field, and then press the Enter key (Return on Macintosh). Director will update cell 61 of the Shot 1 sprite within the Stage window (see Figure 4.17).

>>>

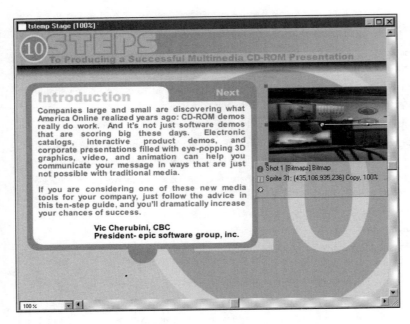

Figure 4.17 *Cell 61 of the Shot 1 sprite within the Stage window.*

23. Drag the Shot 2 member from the Cast window into cell 62 of channel 32 of the Score window. Director will display the Shot 2 sprite within the Stage window.

24. In the Score window, click cell 63 of channel 32. Director will highlight the Shot 2 sprite.

25. Within the Property Inspector window, type **527** into the X field, **311** into the Y field, and then press the Enter key (Return on Macintosh). Director will update the Shot 2 sprite within the Stage window.

26. In the Score window, click cell 64 of channel 32. Director will highlight cell 64 of the Shot 2 sprite.

27. Click the Insert menu and select the Keyframe option. Director will mark cell 64 of channel 32 as a keyframe.

28. Click cell 62 of channel 32. Director will highlight cell 62 of the Shot 2 sprite.

29. In the Property Inspector window, type **684** into the X field, **500** into the W field, and then press the Enter key (Return on Macintosh). Director will update cell 62 of the Shot 2 sprite within the Stage window.

By now, your interface should be looking fairly complete. It contains 12 fully functional sections, a Back link and a Next link to provide access to those sections, and an arrangement of background graphics to organize everything on the screen. Preview your movie and navigate through the different sections. The Back and Next links are actually inconvenient if you want to access a specific section such as Help. Therefore, you must add a second navigation option to make things more convenient for the user.

ADDING A SECOND NAVIGATION OPTION

The most obvious, and in this case most convenient, way to provide access to a number of sections is to create a link for each individual section. This way, if the user has a particular section in mind, she can move directly to that section without having to pass through any others. The Ten-Step Guide interface not only displays the section links but also includes a graphic to indicate which link would lead to the current section. This graphic gives the user a sense of her progress in the presentation. To position the section links' neighboring shapes within the Score and the Stage, follow the steps outlined in Procedure 4.6.

Procedure 4.6 Positioning Section Links

1. In the Cast window, click the Choose Cast button and select the Shapes option. Director will display the Shapes cast within the Cast window.

2. Drag the Rectangle member from the Cast window into cell 60 of channel 14 of the Score window. Director will display the Rectangle shape within the Stage window.

3. Using the Score window, drag cell 64 of channel 14 to frame 119. Director will extend the Rectangle shape to frame 119.

4. Click cell 61 of channel 14. Director will highlight the Rectangle shape.

5. From the Property Inspector window, type **0** into the X field, **450** into the Y field, **640** into the W field, **30** into the H field, and then press the Enter key (Return on Macintosh). Director will update the Rectangle shape within the Stage window.

6. Click and hold the button to the right of the Foreground Color icon and select a white swatch. Director will set the foreground color of the Rectangle shape to white (see Figure 4.18).

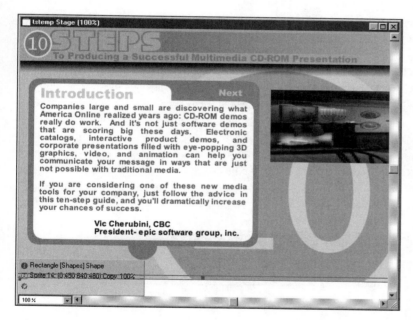

Figure 4.18 *The Rectangle sprite.*

7. Drag the Semicircle member from the Cast window into cell 60 of channel 27 of the Score window. Director will display the Semicircle shape within the Stage window.

8. In the Score window, click cell 61 of channel 27. Director will highlight the Semicircle shape.

9. Using the Property Inspector window, type **45** into the X field, **460** into the Y field, **50** into the W field, **50** into the H field, **45** into the Rotation Angle field, and then press the Enter key (Return on Macintosh), as shown in Figure 4.19. Director will update the Semicircle shape within the Stage window.

>>>

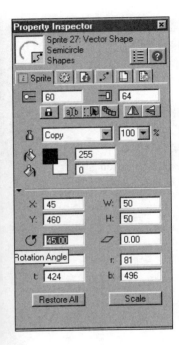

Figure 4.19 *The Rotation Angle field.*

10. Click the Ink drop-down list and select the Background Transparent option. Director will remove the background from the Semicircle shape.

11. Drag the Rectangle member from the Cast window into cell 60 of channel 28 of the Score window. Director will display the Rectangle shape within the Stage window.

12. In the Score window, click cell 61 of channel 28. Director will highlight the Rectangle shape.

13. From the Property Inspector window, type **45** into the X field, **425** into the Y field, **170** into the W field, **3** into the H field, and then press the Enter key (Return on Macintosh). Director will update the Rectangle shape within the Stage window.

14. In the Foreground Color field, type **#C86400** and press the Enter key (Return on Macintosh). Director will set the foreground color of the Rectangle shape to dark orange.

15. Drag the Rectangle member from the Cast window into cell 60 of channel 29 of the Score window. Director will display the Rectangle shape within the Stage window.

16. In the Score window, click cell 61 of channel 29. Director will highlight the Rectangle shape.

17. Using the Property Inspector window, type **213** into the X field, **413** into the Y field, **3** into the W field, **15** into the H field, and then press the Enter key (Return on Macintosh). Director will update the Rectangle shape within the Stage window.

18. In the Foreground Color field, type **#C86400** and press the Enter key (Return on Macintosh). Director will set the foreground color of the Rectangle shape to dark orange.

19. Drag the Rectangle member from the Cast window into cell 60 of channel 30 of the Score window. Director will display the Rectangle shape within the Stage window.

20. In the Score window, click cell 61 of channel 30. Director will highlight the Rectangle shape (see Figure 4.20).

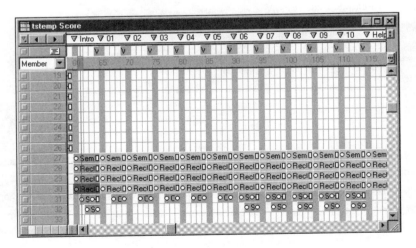

Figure 4.20 *The Rectangle shape.*

21. Using the Property Inspector window, type **43** into the X field, **425** into the Y field, **3** into the W field, **15** into the H field, and then press the Enter key (Return on Macintosh). Director will update the Rectangle shape within the Stage window.

22. In the Foreground Color field, type **#C86400** and press the Enter key (Return on Macintosh). Director will set the foreground color of the Rectangle shape to dark orange.

Now that you have set up the section indicator for the Introduction section and the links' background rectangle, you can see approximately where the different section links must be located. Each section contains a set of vector shapes that point from the bottom of the text rectangle to the location of that particular section's link. It is very important that the section links be placed in the same order that the sections occur in the Score so that the section indicator moves smoothly from left to right if the user chooses to use the Back and Next links. To position the section links within the Score and the Stage, follow the steps outlined in Procedure 4.7.

Procedure 4.7   Positioning the Links within the Score and Stage

1. In the Cast window, click the Choose Cast button and select the Text option. Director will display the Text cast within the Cast window.

2. Click the Intro Link member, press and hold the Shift key, and then click the Help Link member. Director will highlight members 27 through 38 of the Text cast (see Figure 4.21).

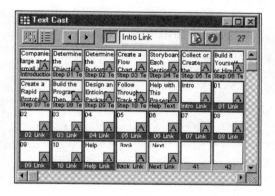

Figure 4.21 *The selected cast members.*

3. Drag the selected cast members from the Cast window into cell 60 of channel 15 of the Score window. Director will display the new sprites shape within the Stage window.

4. Using the Score window, click cell 60 of channel 15, press and hold the Shift key, and then click cell 64 of channel 26. Director will highlight cells 60 through 64 of channels 15 through 26.

5. From the Property Inspector window, type **455** into the Y field and then press the Enter key (Return on Macintosh). Director will update the selected sprites within the Stage window.

6. Click the Ink drop-down list and select the Background Transparent option. Director will remove the background from the selected sprites.

7. In the Score window, click cell 61 of channel 15. Director will highlight the Intro Link sprite.

8. Using the Property Inspector window, type **20** into the X field and then press the Enter key (Return on Macintosh). Director will update the Intro Link sprite within the Stage window.

9. Within the Score window, click cell 61 of channel 16. Director will highlight the 01 Link sprite.

10. Using the Property Inspector window, type **70** into the X field and then press the Enter key (Return on Macintosh). Director will update the 01 Link sprite within the Stage window.

11. In the Score window, click cell 61 of channel 17. Director will highlight the 02 Link sprite.

12. From the Property Inspector window, type **120** into the X field and then press the Enter key (Return on Macintosh). Director will update the 02 Link sprite within the Stage window.

13. In the Score window, click cell 61 of channel 18. Director will highlight the 03 Link sprite.

14. From the Property Inspector window, type **170** into the X field and then press the Enter key (Return on Macintosh). Director will update the 03 Link sprite within the Stage window.

15. Using the Score window, click cell 61 of channel 19. Director will highlight the 04 Link sprite.

16. In the Property Inspector window, type **220** into the X field and then press the Enter key (Return on Macintosh). Director will update the 04 Link sprite within the Stage window.

17. Within the Score window, click cell 61 of channel 20. Director will highlight the 05 Link sprite.

18. Within the Property Inspector window, type **270** into the X field and then press the Enter key (Return on Macintosh). Director will update the 05 Link sprite within the Stage window.

19. From the Score window, click cell 61 of channel 21. Director will highlight the 06 Link sprite.

20. In the Property Inspector window, type **320** into the X field and then press the Enter key (Return on Macintosh). Director will update the 06 Link sprite within the Stage window.

21. Using the Score window, click cell 61 of channel 22. Director will highlight the 07 Link sprite.

22. Within the Property Inspector window, type **370** into the X field and then press the Enter key (Return on Macintosh). Director will update the 07 Link sprite within the Stage window.

23. In the Score window, click cell 61 of channel 23. Director will highlight the 08 Link sprite.

24. Within the Property Inspector window, type **420** into the X field and then press the Enter key (Return on Macintosh). Director will update the 08 Link sprite within the Stage window.

25. Using the Score window, click cell 61 of channel 24. Director will highlight the 09 Link sprite.

26. From the Property Inspector window, type **470** into the X field and then press the Enter key (Return on Macintosh). Director will update the 09 Link sprite within the Stage window.

27. Within the Score window, click cell 61 of channel 25. Director will highlight the 10 Link sprite.

28. From the Property Inspector window, type **520** into the X field and then press the Enter key (Return on Macintosh). Director will update the 10 Link sprite within the Stage window.

29. In the Score window, click cell 61 of channel 26. Director will highlight the Help Link sprite.

30. Within the Property Inspector window, type **570** into the X field and then press the Enter key (Return on Macintosh). Director will update the Help Link sprite within the Stage window (see Figure 4.22).

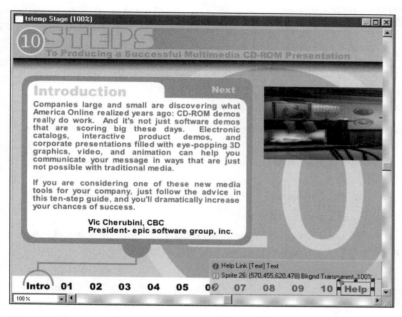

Figure 4.22 *The Help Link text.*

Now that the section links are all positioned as they should be, you can activate them by applying an appropriate behavior script. All the section links require only a single behavior because the labels of the frame markers directly correspond to the text of the links. Therefore, when the user clicks a link, its behavior script should just play the marker whose name matches the link's text. Not every link should contain the behavior in every frame, however. If the user is already in the Help section, the Help link should not respond to mouse interaction. Therefore, each link should be deactivated in its own section. The easiest way to accomplish this is by setting up the links for a single section complete with the Section Link behavior, copying and pasting those activated links into every remaining section, and then removing behaviors where necessary. To complete and apply the Section Link behavior script, follow the steps outlined in Procedure 4.8.

Procedure 4.8   Completing and Applying the Section Link Behavior

1. In the Cast window, click the Choose Cast button and select the Scripts option. Director will display the Scripts cast within the Cast window.

2. Click the Section Link member. Director will highlight the Section Link member.

3. Next click the Cast Member Script button. Director will display the Section Link script within the Script window.

4. Using the Script window, in the mouseDown handler, type the following code. Note that the following line plays the marker whose name matches the associated sprite's cast member's text:

```
play sprite(me.spriteNum).member.text
```

5. From the toolbar, click the Script Window button. Director will close the Script window.

6. In the Score window, click cell 60 of channel 15, press and hold the Shift key, and then click cell 64 of channel 26. Director will highlight the link sprites in cells 60 through 64 of channels 15 through 26.

7. Apply the Section Link behavior to the selected sprites as specified in Appendix A.

8. Click the Edit menu and select the Copy Sprites option. Director will hold a copy of the selected sprites in memory.

9. Within the Score window, click cell 65 of channel 15. Director will update the Stage window.

10. Click the Edit menu and select the Paste Sprites option. Director will paste a copy of the link sprites into cells 65 through 69 of channels 15 through 26 from memory.

11. Next click cell 70 of channel 15. Director will update the Stage window.

12. Click the Edit menu and select the Paste Sprites option. Director will paste a copy of the link sprites into cells 70 through 74 of channels 15 through 26 from memory.

13. Click cell 75 of channel 15. Director will update the Stage window.

14. Click the Edit menu and select the Paste Sprites option. Director will paste a copy of the link sprites into cells 75 through 79 of channels 15 through 26 from memory.

15. Click cell 80 of channel 15. Director will update the Stage window.

16. Click the Edit menu and select the Paste Sprites option. Director will paste a copy of the link sprites into cells 80 through 84 of channels 15 through 26 from memory.

17. Click cell 85 of channel 15. Director will update the Stage window.

18. Click the Edit menu and select the Paste Sprites option. Director will paste a copy of the link sprites into cells 85 through 89 of channels 15 through 26 from memory.

19. In the Score window, click cell 90 of channel 15. Director will update the Stage window.

20. Click the Edit menu and select the Paste Sprites option. Director will paste a copy of the link sprites into cells 90 through 94 of channels 15 through 26 from memory.

21. Click cell 95 of channel 15. Director will update the Stage window.

22. Click the Edit menu and select the Paste Sprites option. Director will paste a copy of the link sprites into cells 95 through 99 of channels 15 through 26 from memory.

23. Click cell 100 of channel 15. Director will update the Stage window.

24. Click the Edit menu and select the Paste Sprites option. Director will paste a copy of the link sprites into cells 100 through 104 of channels 15 through 26 from memory.

25. Click cell 105 of channel 15. Director will update the Stage window.

26. Click the Edit menu and select the Paste Sprites option. Director will paste a copy of the link sprites into cells 105 through 109 of channels 15 through 26 from memory.

27. Click cell 110 of channel 15. Director will update the Stage window.

28. Click the Edit menu and select the Paste Sprites option. Director will paste a copy of the link sprites into cells 110 through 114 of channels 15 through 26 from memory.

29. Click cell 115 of channel 15. Director will update the Stage window.

30. Click the Edit menu and select the Paste Sprites option. Director will paste a copy of the link sprites into cells 115 through 119 of channels 15 through 26 from memory.

31. Within the Score window, click cell 61 of channel 15, press and hold the Control key (Command key on Macintosh), click cell 66 of channel 16, cell 71 of channel 17, cell 76 of channel 18, cell 81 of channel 19, cell 86 of channel 20, cell 91 of channel 21, cell 96 of channel 22, cell 101 of channel 23, cell 106 of channel 24, cell 111 of channel 25, and then cell 116 of channel 26. Director will highlight the 12 selected sprites (see Figure 4.23).

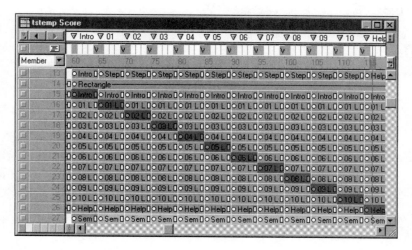

Figure 4.23 *The selected sprites.*

32. Using the Property Inspector window, click the Behavior tab. Director will display the Behavior sheet.

33. Click the Clear Behavior (minus sign) button and select the Remove All Behaviors option (see Figure 4.24). Director will remove the Section Link behavior from the selected sprites.

By now your interface should look exactly like the original Ten-Step Guide interface. The entire interface, with all its different links, requires only three Lingo scripts. Of course, another way to create the interface might prove just a bit more convenient. Instead of having each link behavior contain identical `mouseEnter` and `mouseLeave` handlers, you could create a generic link behavior with only these handlers and apply it to every link in the interface. In addition to this behavior, you would apply the Back Link, Next Link, and Section Link behaviors, but they would require only the `mouseDown` handler. The method would require less programming code in total but more behavior scripts.

MAKING ADJUSTMENTS

To customize the Ten-Step Guide interface, you need only to replace the section text and sample screen shots with your own. You also might want to change the color scheme of the interface. This could prove a bit more difficult. You can change the color of the text and vector shapes by just selecting a new foreground color for their sprites or cast members. The bitmap graphics, on the other hand, would have to be replaced entirely. Adding or removing sections from the interface would probably be more trouble than it is worth because of the way the sections are set up. In their current condition, the section links allow only for an introduction, a help screen, and of course ten steps.

Figure 4.24 *The Clear Behavior menu.*

Note:
As mentioned earlier, you are removing the Section Link behavior from these particular sprites to deactivate each navigation link in its own section.

"The only limits are, as always, those of vision."
—James Broughton

>>> **chapter 5**
television

Figures 5.1-5.4 *The Television interface in action.*

APPROACHING THE "TELEVISION" INTERFACE

The Television interface is a perfect example of a metaphor in action. By presenting the interface in the form of a familiar, physical object such as a television, most users know intuitively how to operate it. This does not work for everyone, however, because some people might never have owned an old-fashioned television, and some people might not know how to work a television at all. Therefore, you must always be sure to include a thorough help section in any interface that uses a metaphor. The Television interface displays two knobs that the user can twist to cycle through portfolio items and, of course, a power button.

UNDERSTANDING THE TELEVISION INTERFACE

Some parts of the Television interface, such as the screen's links, behave much like interfaces featured in this book so far. The feature that really makes the Television interface unique is its twistable knobs. The Media cast contains five knob images in different positions. Because these images are numbered in sequence, the Knob behavior script needs only to choose a new image that is numbered either one greater or one less than the current knob image to give the illusion that a knob is being twisted when it is clicked. To produce a smooth loop of knob images, the sequence should just cycle after the first five images have displayed. Notice that the last image in the sequence is in nearly the same position as the first image. To view the various Lingo scripts of the Scripts cast, follow these steps:

1. Open the `tv.dir` file from the 05 - Television folder as specified in Appendix A, "Guide to Common Tasks." The Scripts cast contains the 14 Lingo scripts shown in Table 5.1.

Table 5.1   The Scripts Cast Lingo Scripts

Script Name	Description
Global	Initializes the *section* variable and keeps the Section Text and Item Text members current.
Wait	Makes the movie repeat the current frame over and over until otherwise specified.
Play Main	Plays the Main marker when the playback head exits its associated frame.
Halt	Stops the movie entirely when the playback head exits its associated frame.
Portfolio Image	Keeps its associated sprite set to the current portfolio image based on the *section* variable.
Knob	Sets its associated sprite's cast member to look like a rotating knob when the user clicks or right-clicks it.
Section Knob	Sets the first item in the *section* list to a number based on mouse interaction with its associated sprite.
Item Knob	Sets the second item in the *section* list to a letter based on mouse interaction with its associated sprite.
Next Frame Link	Plays the frame directly to the right of the playback head when the user clicks its associated sprite.
Exit Link	Plays the Exit marker when the user clicks its associated sprite.
Main Link	Sets the *section* variable to ["Main", ""] and plays the Main marker when the user clicks its associated sprite.
Portfolio 1 Link	Sets the *section* variable to ["1", "A"] and plays the Portfolio marker when the user clicks its associated sprite.
Portfolio 2 Link	Sets the *section* variable to ["2", "A"] and plays the Portfolio marker when the user clicks its associated sprite.
Portfolio 3 Link	Sets the *section* variable to ["3", "A"] and plays the Portfolio marker when the user clicks its associated sprite.

2. Within the Cast window, double-click the Global member. Director will display the Global script within the Script window.

3. Within the Script window, use the Previous Cast Member and Next Cast Member buttons to view each of the Lingo scripts in the Scripts cast.

After browsing through the Television interface's scripts and taking a look at its organization in the Score, you should have a good understanding of the logic behind this interface. If some of its aspects are still not clear, you might want to refer to Appendix B, "Guide to Lingo Programming." Although understanding the innerworkings of the Television interface at this time is not completely necessary, it should make things easier for you as you re-create the interface throughout the rest of this chapter.

WRITING AND APPLYING THE PLAY MAIN AND HALT BEHAVIORS

The Television interface uses three behaviors that affect frames rather than sprites. You are already familiar with the Wait behavior from previous chapters, but the Play Main and Halt behaviors are new to you. Their names are actually rather self-explanatory. The Play Main behavior contains an exitFrame handler with a single line of code that tells Lingo to play the marker named Main. The Halt behavior consists of an exitFrame handler enclosing the halt command, which tells Lingo to stop the movie completely. To create and apply the Play Main and Halt behaviors, follow the steps outlined in Procedure 5.1.

Procedure 5.1   Creating the Play Main and Halt Behaviors

1. Open the tvtemp.dir file from the 05 - Television folder as specified in Appendix A.

2. Create a behavior script named Play Main as specified in Appendix A.

3. Within the Cast window, click the Play Main member. Director will highlight the Play Main member (see Figure 5.5).

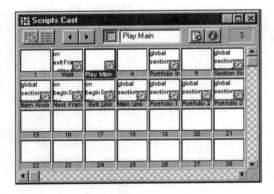

Figure 5.5   *The Play Main member.*

4. Click the Cast Member Script button. Director will display the Play Main script within the Script window.

5. From the Script window, type the following code. Note that following handler plays the marker named Main when the playback head exits the current frame:

```
on exitFrame
    play "Main"
end
```

6. Apply the Play Main behavior to frame 59 as specified in Appendix A.

7. Create a behavior script named Halt as specified in Appendix A.

8. In the Cast window, click the Halt member. Director will highlight the Halt member.

9. Click the Cast Member Script button. Director will display the Halt script within the Script window.

10. From the Script window, type the following code. Note that the following handler stops the movie entirely when the playback head exits the current frame:

```
on exitFrame
    halt
end
```

11. Apply the Halt behavior to frame 89 as specified in Appendix A.

12. Using the toolbar, click the Script Window button. Director will close the Script window.

Now that you have applied the Play Main and Halt behaviors to their appropriate frames, your interface should be functioning a bit more normally. If you were to preview your movie, you would find that the Help and Exit buttons are now fully functional. Without the Play Main behavior at the end of the animation that moves the help elements offscreen, the user would not be able to return to the Main section after viewing the Help section. Without the Halt behavior at the end of the exit animation, the movie might loop rather than stop.

WRITING THE GLOBAL SCRIPT

The Television interface is the first movie in this book to use a movie script. The reason is that most simple interfaces do not require events to be handled globally. Behavior scripts on sprites or frames can usually suit the programmer's needs. The major purpose of the Television interface's Global movie script is to initialize the *section* variable at the very beginning of the movie. The Global script also keeps the Section Text and Item Text members current throughout the run of the interface, but a movie script is not necessarily required for this task. To create the Global script, follow the steps outlined in Procedure 5.2.

Procedure 5.2 Writing the Global Script

1. Create a movie script named Global as specified in Appendix A.

2. Within the Cast window, double-click the Global member. Director will display the Global script within the Script window.

3. Use the Script window to type in the following code. Note that the following line tells Director that a global variable named *section* will be used at some point in this script:

```
global section
```

Note that the following handler initializes the *section* variable to a value of ["Main", ""] when the movie first begins. Because it was initialized to a list value, the *section* variable will hold two separate string values accessible through bracket notation:

```
on prepareMovie
   section = ["Main", ""]
end
```

Note that the following handler checks each frame to see whether the first item in the section list is equal to a string value of Main. If it is equal to Main, the text of the Section Text and Item Text members is set to a blank space. Otherwise, the Section Text member's text is set to the first item in the section list, and the Item Text member's text is set to the second item in the list:

```
on enterFrame
  if section[1] = "Main" then
    member("Section Text").text = " "
    member("Item Text").text = " "
  else
    member("Section Text").text = section[1]
    member("Item Text").text = section[2]
  end if
end
```

4. From the toolbar, click the Script Window button. Director will close the Script window.

The `section` variable is really the most important element of the Television interface. When the user is browsing through the portfolio images, the `section` variable keeps track of both the section number and item letter of the image you are viewing. Actually, you could accomplish the same task by creating two separate variables rather than `section`, which is a list containing two items. When the values serve such a similar purpose, however, a single variable is generally easier to deal with and better programming style.

SETTING UP THE TELEVISION COMPONENTS

The main body of the television is composed of two separate images. First, a complete television image is used as a background for the entire interface. Then, a second television image with the screen cut out is placed in the interface's foreground. All items that must appear onscreen are then sandwiched between the two television images. This way, the blank screen can show through when no screen items (such as navigation buttons) are visible and those that are visible are guaranteed to not appear outside of the television screen's borders. Any items positioned outside of the screen's borders will be either partially or completely covered by the foreground television image. To position the television components within the Score and the Stage, follow the steps outlined in Procedure 5.3.

Procedure 5.3   Positioning the Television Components

1. Within the Cast window, click the Choose Cast button and select the Media option. Director will display the Media cast within the Cast window.

2. Drag the Background member from the Cast window into cell 1 of channel 1 of the Score window. Director will display the Background sprite within the Stage window.

3. From the Score window, drag cell 28 of channel 1 to frame 89. Director will extend the Background sprite to frame 89 (see Figure 5.6).

4. Drag the Television member from the Cast window into cell 1 of channel 13 of the Score window. Director will display the Television sprite within the Stage window.

5. Drag cell 28 of channel 13 to frame 89. Director will extend the Television sprite to frame 89.

6. Click cell 2 of channel 13. Director will highlight the Television sprite.

7. Using the Property Inspector window, type **#0000FF** in the Background Color field and press the Enter key (Return on Macintosh). Director will set the background color of the Television sprite to blue.

8. Click the Ink drop-down list and select the Background Transparent option. Director will remove the blue background from the Television sprite.

9. Drag the Knob 1 member from the Cast window into cell 1 of channel 16 of the Score window. Director will display the Knob 1 sprite within the Stage window.

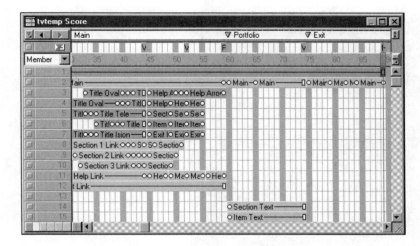

Figure 5.6 *Extending the Background sprite within the Score window.*

10. From the Score window, drag cell 28 of channel 16 to frame 59. Director will extend the Knob 1 sprite to frame 59.

11. Drag the Knob 1 member from the Cast window into cell 60 of channel 16 of the Score window. Director will display the Knob 1 sprite within the Stage window.

12. Drag the Knob 1 member from the Cast window into cell 75 of channel 16 of the Score window. Director will display the Knob 1 sprite within the Stage window.

13. Next drag cell 102 of channel 16 to frame 89. Director will curtail the Knob 1 sprite to frame 89.

14. Click cell 1 of channel 16, press and hold the Shift key, and then click cell 89 of channel 16. Director will highlight cells 1 through 89 of channel 16.

15. In the Property Inspector window, type **581** into the X field, **98** into the Y field, and then press the Enter key (Return on Macintosh). Director will update the Knob 1 sprite within the Stage window (see Figure 5.7).

16. In the Property Inspector window, in the Background Color field, type **#0000FF** and press the Enter key (Return on Macintosh). Director will set the background color of the Knob 1 sprite to blue.

17. Next click the Ink drop-down list and select the Background Transparent option. Director will remove the blue background from the Knob 1 sprite.

18. Click the Edit menu and select the Copy Sprites option. Director will hold a copy of the selected sprites in memory.

19. Within the Score window, click cell 1 of channel 17. Director will update the Stage window.

20. Click the Edit menu and select the Paste Sprites option. Director will paste a copy of the Knob 1 sprites into cells 1 through 89 of channel 17 from memory (see Figure 5.8).

>>>

Figure 5.7 *The Knob 1 sprite.*

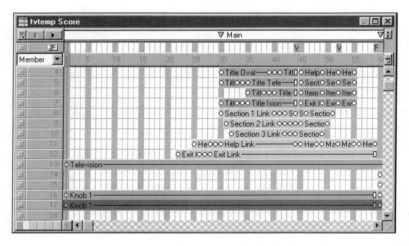

Figure 5.8 *The new Knob 1 sprites.*

21. From the Property Inspector window, type **579** into the X field, **189** into the Y field, and then press the Enter key (Return on Macintosh). Director will update the Knob 1 sprite within the Stage window.

22. Drag the Exit Button Down member from the Cast window into cell 1 of channel 18 of the Score window. Director will display the Exit Button Down sprite within the Stage window.

23. Drag cell 28 of channel 18 to frame 9. Director will curtail the Exit Button Down sprite to frame 9.

24. Drag the Exit Button Up member from the Cast window into cell 10 of channel 18 of the Score window. Director will display the Exit Button Up sprite within the Stage window.

25. In the Score window, drag cell 29 of channel 18 to frame 74. Director will extend the Exit Button Up sprite to frame 74.

26. Drag the Exit Button Down member from the Cast window into cell 75 of channel 18 of the Score window. Director will display the Exit Button Down sprite within the Stage window.

27. Drag cell 102 of channel 18 to frame 89. Director will curtail the Exit Button Down sprite to frame 89 (see Figure 5.9).

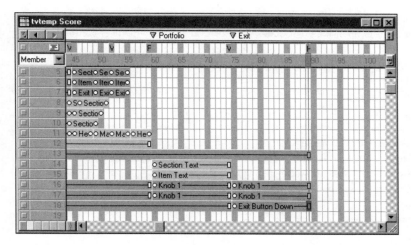

Figure 5.9 *Curtailing the Exit Button Down sprite.*

28. Click cell 1 of channel 18, press and hold the Shift key, and then click cell 89 of channel 18. Director will highlight cells 1 through 89 of channel 18.

29. Within the Property Inspector window, type **594** into the X field, **419** into the Y field, and then press the Enter key (Return on Macintosh). Director will update the selected sprites within the Stage window.

As mentioned earlier, all screen elements must be sandwiched between the background and foreground television images. The actual knobs and buttons of the television, however, must appear in front of the foreground television image because they are positioned outside of the screen's borders. Think of the Score as an actual television. The television has a back wall and a front wall. The images occur inside the television and show through the screen. The physical controls are fastened to the television's front surface. It's really very simple.

ACTIVATING THE KNOBS AND POWER BUTTON

The television's two knobs require three behaviors. You must apply the Knob behavior to both knobs. It changes the way a knob looks when the user clicks or right-clicks its sprite and gives the illusion that the knob is actually being twisted. The other two behaviors contain code specific to each knob. The top knob controls the Portfolio section, and the bottom knob controls the section's item. To create the three knob behaviors and apply them and the Exit Link behavior to their appropriate sprites, follow the steps outlined in Procedure 5.4.

Procedure 5.4   Activating the Knobs and Power Button

1. In the Cast window, click the Choose Cast button and select the Scripts option. Director will display the Scripts cast within the Cast window.

2. Create a behavior script named Knob as specified in Appendix A.

3. Click the Knob member. Director will highlight the Knob member.

4. Click the Cast Member Script button. Director will display the Knob script within the Script window.

5. In the Script window, type the following code. Note that he following line tells Director that a property variable named *my* will be used at some point in this script:

```
property my
```

Note that the following handler sets the *my* property equal to the behavior's associated sprite and then sets that sprite's cursor to a cursor made up of the Point Cursor and Point Cursor Mask members of the Media cast:

```
on beginSprite me
   my = sprite(me.spriteNum)
   my.cursor = [member("Point Cursor"), member("Point Cursor Mask")]
end
```

Note that the following handler plays the Click sound in the first sound channel when the user clicks its associated sprite. Then the handler uses a local variable named *knobNumber* to store the value of the current knob's number plus one. If the *knobNumber* variable is greater than five at this point, it is set back to one because there are only five knob images in the Media cast. Finally, the associated sprite's cast member is set to a knob image that is numbered the same as the *knobNumber* variable:

```
on mouseDown
   puppetSound(1, "Click")

   knobNumber = integer(my.member.name.word[2]) + 1
   if knobNumber > 5 then knobNumber = 1
   my.member = member("Knob" && knobNumber)
end
```

Note that the following handler behaves exactly like the mouseDown handler except it subtracts one from current knob's number instead of adding one. If the *knobNumber* variable is less than one, it must be set to five because the lowest numbered knob is named Knob 1:

```
on rightMouseDown
   puppetSound(1, "Click")

   knobNumber = integer(my.member.name.word[2]) - 1
   if knobNumber < 1 then knobNumber = 5
   my.member = member("Knob" && knobNumber)
end
```

6. Using the Score window, click cell 1 of channel 16, press and hold the Shift key, and then click cell 89 of channel 17. Director will highlight cells 1 through 89 of channels 16 through 17.

7. Apply the Knob behavior to the selected sprites as specified in Appendix A.

8. From the Cast window, click the Section Knob member. Director will highlight the Section Knob member.

9. Click the Cast Member Script button. Director will display the Section Knob script within the Script window.

10. In the Script window, in the `mouseDown` handler, type the following code:

```
knobNumber = integer(section[1]) + 1
if knobNumber > 3 then knobNumber = 1
section[1] = string(knobNumber)
section[2] = "A"

play "Portfolio"
```

Note that the preceding lines set a local variable named *knobNumber* to the integer value of the first item in the `section` list plus one. If the *knobNumber* variable is greater than three, it must be set back to one because the portfolio contains only three sections. The first item in the `section` list is then set to the string value of *knobNumber*, and the second item is set to A.

11. Apply the Section Knob behavior to the Knob 1 sprite that begins in cell 60 of channel 16 as specified in Appendix A.

12. In the Cast window, click the Item Knob member. Director will highlight the Item Knob member.

13. Click the Cast Member Script button. Director will display the Item Knob script within the Script window.

14. From the Script window, in the `mouseDown` handler, type the following code:

```
maxNumber = charToNum("E")
knobNumber = charToNum(section[2]) + 1
if knobNumber > maxNumber then knobNumber = charToNum("A")
section[2] = numToChar(knobNumber)

play "Portfolio"
```

Note that the preceding lines set a local variable named *maxNumber* to the ASCII number value of E and a local variable named *knobNumber* to the ASCII number value of the second item in the `section` list plus one. If *knobNumber* is then a bigger number than *maxNumber*, it is set to the ASCII number value of A because A is the minimum possible value that *knobNumber* should have. The second item in the `section` list is then set to the character value of the *knobNumber* variable. Possible values of the second item in the `section` list range anywhere from A to E.

15. Apply the Item Knob behavior to the Knob 1 sprite that begins in cell 60 of channel 17 as specified in Appendix A.

16. Using the toolbar, click the Script Window button. Director will close the Script window.

17. Apply the Exit Link behavior to the Exit Button Up sprite that begins in cell 10 of channel 18 as specified in Appendix A.

You may be wondering why the power button's Exit Link behavior was already built for you, whereas the knob behaviors were not. The answer is that all the commands contained within the Exit Link behavior have previously been explained. Basically, the only function of the power button's behavior is to play the Exit marker when the user clicks its associated sprite.

ACTIVATING THE TELEVISION SCREEN

After the user has entered the Portfolio section of the interface, the television screen no longer contains any navigation links. It is completely full with the current portfolio image. Therefore, if the user wants to return to the Main section, she should be able to click anywhere on the television screen. Nevertheless, how will Lingo recognize which portion of the Stage contains the actual screen? You could apply the Main Link behavior directly to the portfolio image if not for one problem: The foreground television image appears in front of the portfolio image. Therefore, when the user clicks the portfolio image, she is really clicking the transparent area of the foreground television image. To remedy this problem, you must create an invisible rectangle sprite whose sole purpose is to define the clickable area of the television's screen. To position the Rectangle shape within the Score and the Stage and apply the Main Link behavior to it, follow the steps outlined in Procedure 5.5.

Procedure 5.5 Positioning the Rectangle Shape

1. In the Cast window, click the Choose Cast button and select the Media option. Director will display the Media cast within the Cast window.

2. Drag the Rectangle member from the Cast window into cell 60 of channel 19 of the Score window. Director will display the Rectangle sprite within the Stage window.

3. Using the Score window, click cell 61 of channel 19. Director will highlight the Rectangle sprite (see Figure 5.10).

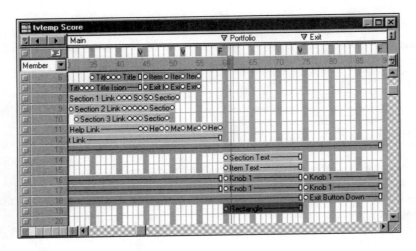

Figure 5.10 *The Rectangle sprite.*

4. In the Property Inspector window, type **52** into the X field, **69** into the Y field, **426** into the W field, **338** into the H field, and then press the Enter key (Return on Macintosh). Director will update the Rectangle sprite within the Stage window (see Figure 5.11).

5. In the Blend drop-down list, type **0** and press the Enter key (Return on Macintosh). Director will set the opacity of the Rectangle sprite to zero percent.

6. Using the Cast window, click the Choose Cast button and select the Scripts option. Director will display the Scripts cast within the Cast window.

7. Apply the Main Link behavior to the Rectangle sprite that begins in cell 60 of channel 19 as specified in Appendix A.

Figure 5.11 *The Rectangle sprite.*

Now that the user has a way to return to the Main section after viewing the portfolio, the Television interface is nearly complete. The only step that remains is to make the portfolio image display the image indicated by the *section* variable and change itself as the *section* variable changes. To avoid any chance of error, the portfolio image should assign its cast member to the member indicated by the section list at the beginning of each frame. The first item of the list indicates the Portfolio section, and the second indicates that section's item to be displayed. To complete the Portfolio Image behavior, follow the steps outlined in Procedure 5.6.

Procedure 5.6   Completing the Portfolio Image Behavior

1. In the Cast window, click the Portfolio Image member. Director will highlight the Portfolio Image member.

2. Click the Cast Member Script button. Director will display the Portfolio Image script within the Script window.

3. From the Script window, in the prepareFrame handler, type the following code:

```
sprite(me.spriteNum).member = member(section[1] & section[2])
```

   Note that the preceding line sets the cast member of the associated sprite to a member with a name equal to the string value of the section list's items combined. Because of the possible values of the *section* variable, the outcome will be only one of the members of the Portfolio cast or the Main member of the Media cast.

4. From the toolbar, click the Script Window button. Director will close the Script window.

If you preview your movie at this point, it should appear exactly like the original Television interface. Of course, when you watch the navigation links build on the screen or the portfolio image change this time, you might have a better idea of how this is all taking place. As you develop more and more interfaces in Director, you will begin to gain a sense of how different multimedia interfaces can be constructed. You just might start to notice how all sorts of applications, games, and even operating systems are actually functioning behind the scenes.

MAKING ADJUSTMENTS

The Television interface is actually quite flexible as a means of displaying a library of images. You can easily modify the number of Portfolio sections and the number of items in each section through Lingo. To change the number of sections, you just replace the numeral 3 with whatever positive integer you choose in both the `mouseDown` and `rightMouseDown` handlers of the Section Knob behavior. To change the number of section items, replace the letter *E* in the Item Knob behavior with the maximum letter value of your images. If you want the different sections to contain different numbers of items, you can include a conditional at the beginning of the Item Knob behavior's `mouseDown` and `rightMouseDown` handlers to set the value of *maxNumber* based on the current Portfolio section.

Simple Interfaces

< 94 >

"No idea is so antiquated that it was not once modern. No idea is so modern that it will not someday be antiquated."
—Ellen Glasgow

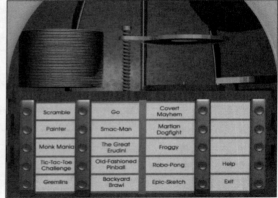

Figures 6.1-6.4   *The Classic Jukebox interface in action.*

APPROACHING THE "CLASSIC JUKEBOX" INTERFACE

The Classic Jukebox interface is another example of an interface metaphor. Much like the Television interface, the layout resembles a common appliance with which most users are already familiar. Of course, the jukebox interface is nothing more than a matrix of clearly labeled buttons. Therefore, even users who have no idea how to operate a jukebox should have no trouble with the Classic Jukebox interface.

Even though the interface's navigation buttons appear to be self-explanatory, it is still a good idea to include an easily accessible Help section. Some users like to visit interface Help sections just to make sure they're not missing any hidden features. Incidentally, the Help section is the only place where the user can learn how to toggle the background music. Because this is a nonessential feature of the interface, it really requires no explanation up front. The user can always adjust his speakers if he desires.

UNDERSTANDING THE CLASSIC JUKEBOX INTERFACE

Much like the Television interface, the Classic Jukebox interface relies on a global variable named *section* to keep track of navigation. This interface's *section* variable can equal either the string Main or a two-letter abbreviation of the current section. The section background images also are given two letter abbreviations so that several different sections can appear in a single keyframe. The Changing Background behavior uses the *section* variable to keep its associated sprite perpetually current. If this sort of behavior were not used, the Classic Jukebox interface would require 17 keyframes rather than only 4. You can accomplish many tasks without the use of Lingo, but using scripts will generally make things easier for you in the long run. To view the various Lingo scripts of the Scripts cast, follow these steps:

1. Open the cj.dir file from the 06 - Classic Jukebox folder as specified in Appendix A, "Guide to Common Tasks." The Scripts cast contains the 13 Lingo scripts shown in Table 6.1.

Table 6.1   The Scripts Cast Lingo Scripts

Script Name	Description
Global	Initializes global variables, controls music toggling, and contains the stopAllSounds function.
Wait	Makes the movie repeat the current frame over and over until otherwise specified.
Play Random Music	Stops all sounds and plays a random member of the Music cast when the playback head enters its associated frame.
Play Main	Plays the Main marker when the playback head exits its associated frame.
Check Exit	Checks the *exitConfirmation* variable when the playback head exits its associated frame to see whether it should play the next frame or the Main marker.
Halt	Stops the movie entirely when the playback head exits its associated frame.
Button	Creates smooth transitions between its button's Over, Down, and transparent states based on mouse interaction and its name property.
Changing Background	Sets its associated sprite's cast member to the current section's background image at the beginning of each frame.
Game Button	Sets the *section* variable to its button's name and plays the Game marker when the user clicks its associated sprite.
Help Button	Sets the *section* variable to HE and plays the Help marker when the user clicks its associated sprite.
Exit Button	Sets the *section* variable to EX and plays the Exit marker when the user clicks its associated sprite.

>>>

Table 6.1 Continued

Script Name	Description
Main Button	Plays the frame that is one frame to the right of the playback head when the user clicks its associated sprite.
Yes Button	Calls the `stopAllSounds` function, sets the *exitConfirmation* variable to true, and plays the frame that is one frame to the right of the playback head when the user clicks its associated sprite.

2. In the Cast window, double-click the Global member. Director displays the Global script within the Script window.

3. In the Script window, use the Previous Cast Member and Next Cast Member buttons to view each of the Lingo scripts in the Scripts cast.

After browsing through the Classic Jukebox interface's scripts and taking a look at its organization in the Score, you should have a good understanding of the logic behind this interface. If some of its aspects are still not clear, you may want to refer to Appendix B, "Guide to Lingo Programming." Although understanding the innerworkings of the Classic Jukebox interface at this time is not completely necessary, it should make things easier for you as you re-create the interface throughout the rest this chapter.

COMPLETING THE BUTTON BEHAVIOR

One major element of most interfaces is the push button. To create a push-button effect, each button should have an Up state, a Down state, and if desired, an Over state. By changing the appearance of the button as the user moves or clicks her mouse, the illusion of a physical button being pushed is created.

The Button behavior of the Classic Jukebox interface is unique in that its Up state is nothing more than being transparent. Because the Main section's background image contains the Up states of all its buttons, a transparent button shows the section's background and appears to be in its Up state. One advantage of using this somewhat confusing method is that the user can make buttons partially visible to create smooth transitions between button states. To complete the Button behavior, follow the steps outlined in Procedure 6.1.

Procedure 6.1 Completing the Button Behavior

1. Open the `cjtemp.dir` file from the 06 - Classic Jukebox folder as specified in Appendix A.

2. Within the Cast window, click the Button member. Director highlights the Button member (see Figure 6.5).

Figure 6.5 *The Button member within the Cast window.*

*from all the characters at
epic software group, inc.*

*We're all about making
you look great!*

For the past twelve years, the artists, animators, and programmers at **epic software group, inc.**™ have been helping their clients use the power of the computer to tell their stories in ways that are not possible with traditional media. epic creates applications such as multimedia presentations, electronic catalogs, computer-based training, interactive brochures, and touch-screen kiosks. Their work is distributed on CD-ROM, DVD, and the Internet.

In 1997, epic entered the world of publishing when the company was chosen to create over 100 3D illustrations for the Happy and Max series of children's books. In 2000, epic authored *Macromedia Flash 5—From Concept to Creation*, followed by *Macromedia Director Game Development—from Concept to Creation*. In 2001, epic produced *LightWave 6.5 & 7 Applied* and *Excel 2002 Plain & Simple*. Book projects currently in the works by epic include two titles for Flash, and *The World's Greatest 3D Graphics*, scheduled for release at Siggraph 2002.

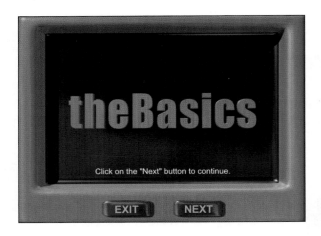

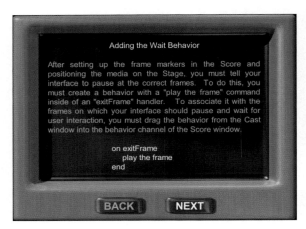

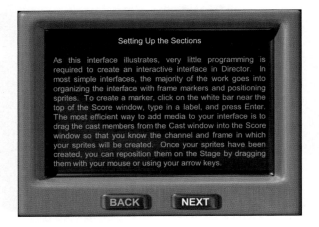

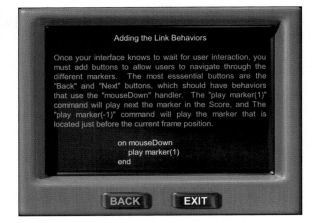

Chapter 3—"The Basics" interface. Walks you through the basic techniques involved in creating a simple interface application.

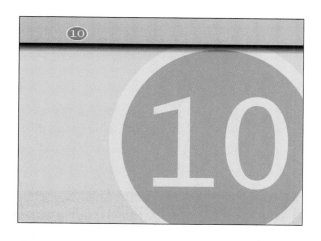

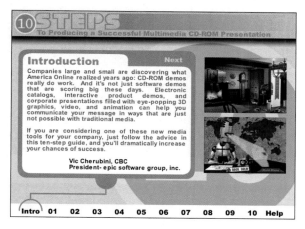

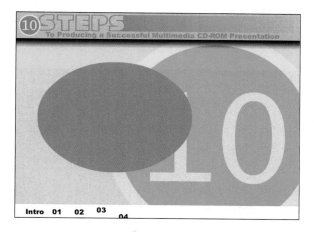

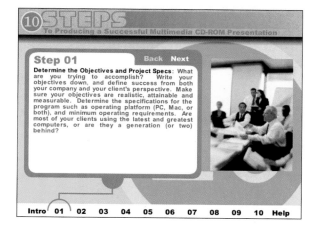

Chapter 4—"Ten-Step Guide" interface. Illustrates the advantages of offering the user two navigation options.

Chapter 5—"Television" interface. Introduces global variables and frame behaviors.

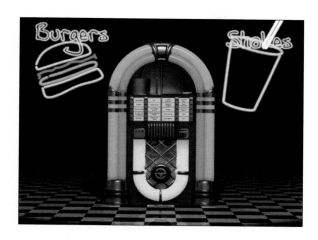

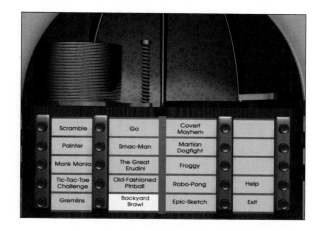

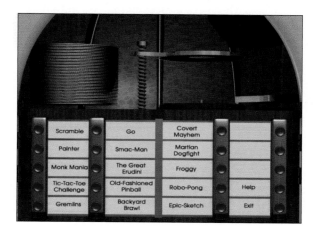

Chapter 6—"Classic Jukebox" interface. Walks you through the creation of a complex button behavior.

Chapter 7—"epic Model Library" interface. Illustrates the use of behavior parameters.

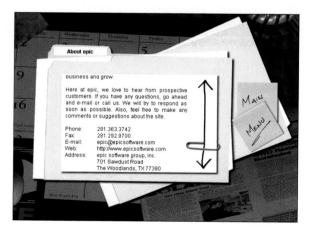

Chapter 8—"Cluttered Desktop" interface. Demonstrates the use of rollover status messages and dynamic background images.

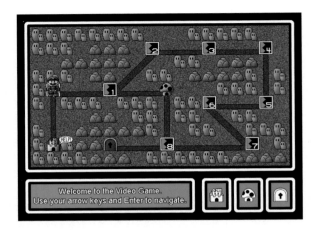

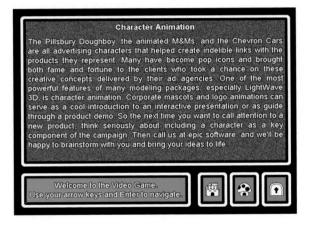

Character Animation

The Pillsbury Doughboy, the animated M&Ms, and the Chevron Cars are all advertising characters that helped create indelible links with the products they represent. Many have become pop icons and brought both fame and fortune to the clients who took a chance on these creative concepts delivered by their ad agencies. One of the most powerful features of many modeling packages, especially LightWave 3D, is character animation. Corporate mascots and logo animations can serve as a cool introduction to an interactive presentation or as guide through a product demo. So the next time you want to call attention to a new product, think seriously about including a character as a key component of the campaign. Then call us at epic software, and we'll be happy to brainstorm with you and bring your ideas to life.

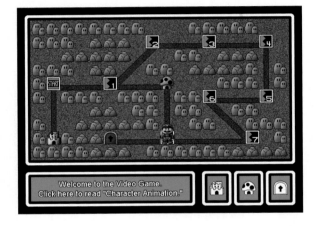

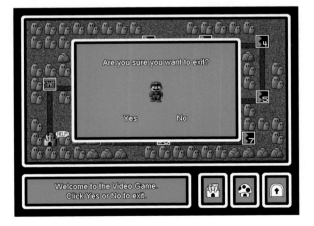

Chapter 9—"Video Game" interface. Introduces the creation and implementation of film loops.

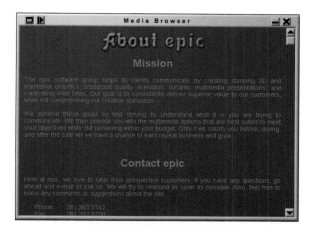

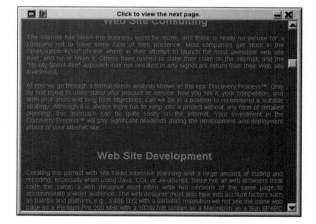

Chapter 10—"Media Browser" interface. Illustrates the basics of creating graphical, resizable windows for your Director interfaces.

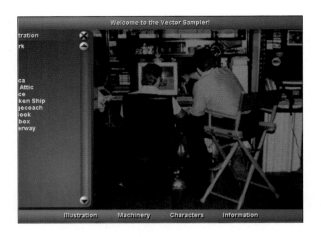

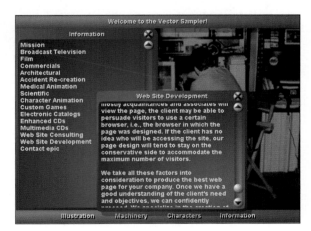

Chapter 11—"Vector Sampler" interface. Discusses the use of complex vector graphics within Director interfaces.

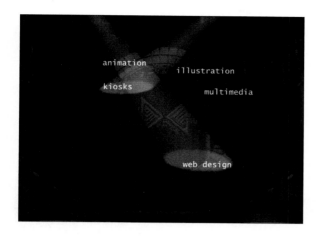

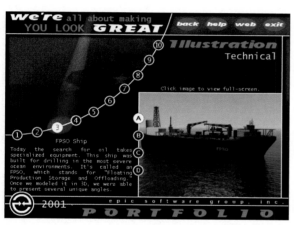

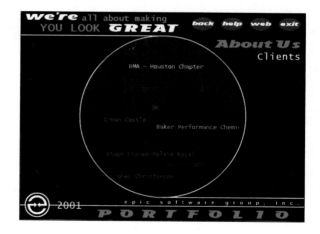

Chapter 12—"epic Portfolio" interface. Explains how to create complex image overlays and dynamic menu buttons.

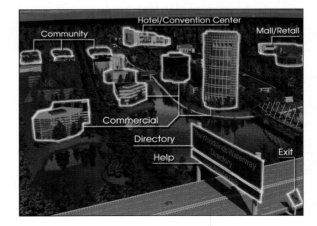

Chapter 13—"Woodlands Waterway" interface. Walks you through the creation and implementation of rollover caption messages.

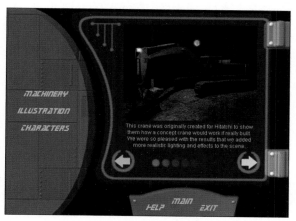

Chapter 14—"Chopper-Bot" interface. Explains how to manipulate the volume of sound channels through Lingo.

Chapter 15—"Holiday House" interface. Discusses the creation of various interactive animations.

Chapter 16—"Company Headquarters" interface. Explains how to incorporate QuickTime VR movies into your Director interfaces.

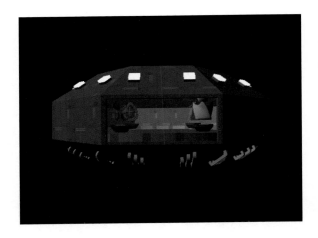

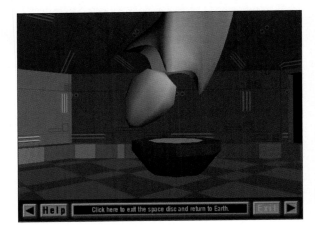

Chapter 17—"3D Gallery" interface. Introduces Shockwave 3D and explains how to affect 3D sprites through Lingo.

3. Click the Cast Member Script button. Director displays the Button script within the Script window.

4. In the `enterFrame` handler, type the following code:

```
if my.blend > 0 then
  if my.blend + 25 < 100 then
    my.blend = my.blend + 25
  else
    my.blend = 100
  end if
end if
```

Note that the preceding conditional checks the associated sprite to see whether it is more than zero percent opaque. Unless the sprite is completely transparent, a nested conditional then checks to see whether the value of the `blend` property would still be less than 100 if 25 were added to it. If so, the `blend` property is increased by 25. Otherwise, it is set to 100 because a sprite cannot have more than 100 percent opacity. In effect, this means that the sprite will fade in and become opaque unless it is completely transparent.

5. In the `mouseDown` handler, type the following code:

```
my.member = member(name && "Down", "Buttons")
```

Note that the preceding line sets the cast member of the associated sprite to its Down state.

6. In the `mouseUp` handler, type the following code:

```
if the rollOver <> the clickOn then exit

my.member = member(name && "Over", "Buttons")
my.blend = 100
```

Note that the preceding three lines make sure that the associated sprite was actually clicked, and then set the cast member of the associated sprite to its Over state and the sprite's opacity to 100 percent.

7. In the Script window, in the `mouseEnter` handler, type the following code:

```
if the mouseDown and the rollOver = the clickOn then
  my.member = member(name && "Down", "Buttons")
else
  my.member = member(name && "Over", "Buttons")
end if

my.blend = 1
```

Note that the preceding conditional checks to see whether the user's mouse button is pressed and the user has actually clicked the associated sprite. If so, the associated sprite's cast member is set to its Down state. Otherwise, the sprite's cast member is set to its Over state.

8. Within the Script window, in the `mouseLeave` handler, type the following code:

```
my.blend = 0
```

9. From the toolbar, click the Script Window button. Director closes the Script window.

Now that the navigation buttons appear to be in working order, your interface is starting to come into focus. Because the same Button behavior is used for all buttons, however, no actual navigation code can be included in it. The Button behavior is just for appearance. The work is really done by a few behavior scripts that tell Lingo which marker should be played when the user clicks a button.

ACTIVATING THE NAVIGATION BUTTONS

The Classic Jukebox interface's Game Button behavior makes full use of the *section* variable. Because all the game sections have the same layout, they can all be stored in a single keyframe. When that keyframe begins to play, the Changing Background behavior goes to work and the correct background image appears. Technically, the *section* variable could enable you to place all the sections in only one keyframe, but more Lingo code would have to be written so that Lingo would know which elements should appear in the current section and which should be hidden. To create the Game Button behavior and activate the navigation buttons of the main menu, follow the steps outlined in Procedure 6.2.

Procedure 6.2   Activating the Navigation Buttons

1. Create a behavior script named Game Button as specified in Appendix A.

2. Within the Cast window, click the Game Button member. Director will highlight the Game Button member (see Figure 6.6).

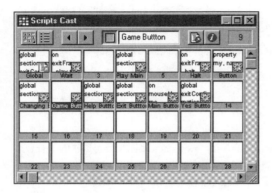

Figure 6.6   *The Game Button member.*

3. Click the Cast Member Script button. Director will display the Game Button script within the Script window.

4. In the Script window, type the following code:

```
on mouseUp me
  if the rollOver <> the clickOn then exit

  play the frame + 1
end
```

Note that the preceding handler makes sure that the associated sprite was actually clicked and then plays the frame directly to the right of the playback head.

5. From the toolbar, click the Script Window button. Director will close the Script window.

6. Within the Score window, click cell 15 of channel 2, press and hold the Shift key, and then click cell 29 of channel 16. Director will highlight cells 15 through 29 of channels 2 through 16 (see Figure 6.7).

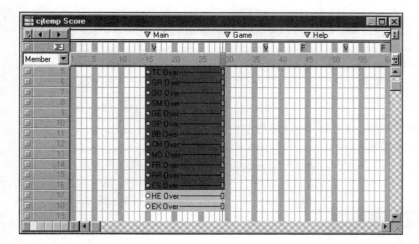

Figure 6.7 *The selected sprites.*

7. Apply the Game Button behavior to the selected sprites as specified in Appendix A.

8. Apply the Help Button behavior to the HE Over sprite that begins in cell 15 of channel 17 as specified in Appendix A.

9. Apply the Exit Button behavior to the EX Over sprite that begins in cell 15 of channel 18 as specified in Appendix A.

The Main button occurs most often in the Classic Jukebox interface because each section must provide a way back to the main menu. Even in the case of exit confirmation, the No button is really just a link back to the main menu. The Yes button, on the other hand, is a bit different. When the user clicks the Yes button, Lingo sets the *exitConfirmation* variable to true and then plays the next frame of the interface. The *exitConfirmation* variable will prove incredibly useful when you create the Check Exit behavior. To apply the Main Button and Yes Button behaviors to their appropriate sprites, follow the steps outlined in Procedure 6.3.

Procedure 6.3 Applying the Main Button and Yes Button Behaviors

1. Apply the Main Button behavior to the Main Over sprite that begins in cell 37 of channel 3 as specified in Appendix A.

2. Apply the Main Button behavior to the Main Over sprite that begins in cell 52 of channel 3 as specified in Appendix A.

3. Apply the Main Button behavior to the No Over sprite that begins in cell 67 of channel 4 as specified in Appendix A.

4. Apply the Yes Button behavior to the Yes Over sprite that begins in cell 67 of channel 3 as specified in Appendix A.

When the user clicks the Yes button, its behavior sets the *exitConfirmation* variable to true and plays the interface's next frame. This leads into the Exit section's closing animation and then into a special frame that checks whether the user has chosen to exit the interface. The behavior used to determine this will be named Check Exit. When the playback head exits this frame, it will either return to the Main marker or continue until it reaches the Halt behaviors and stops the interface entirely. To create and apply the Check Exit behavior, follow the steps outlined in Procedure 6.4.

Procedure 6.4   Creating and Applying the Check Exit Behavior

1. Create a behavior script named Check Exit as specified in Appendix A.

2. Within the Cast window, click the Check Exit member. Director highlights the Check Exit member (see Figure 6.8).

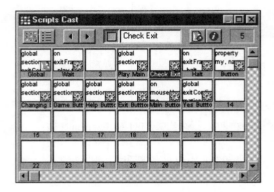

Figure 6.8   *The Check Exit member within the Cast window.*

3. Click the Cast Member Script button. Director displays the Check Exit script within the Script window.

4. From the Script window, type the following code:

```
global exitConfirmation
```

Note that the following handler checks to see whether the *exitConfirmation* variable has been set to true. If so, it plays the frame directly to the right of the playback head. Otherwise, it plays the Main marker.

```
on exitFrame
  if exitConfirmation then
    play the frame + 1
  else
    play "Main"
  end if
end
```

5. Apply the Check Exit behavior to frame 74 as specified in Appendix A.

6. From the toolbar, click the Script Window button. Director will close the Script window.

You should now have a complete, functioning interface. All the navigation buttons work like they should, and the user can always return to the main menu no matter where he goes. The problem is the interface is just a bit too simple. There is no reason to give the user a chance to get bored when Director makes it so easy to add all kinds of media to your interface. You should add animations to the beginning and end of the interface to give the user a good view of the jukebox and to create a more immersive atmosphere.

SETTING UP THE QUICKTIME MOVIES

QuickTime is perhaps the all-around best way to compress digital video. Aside from producing incredibly small file sizes with little compromise in video quality, QuickTime movies are viewable by almost anyone, regardless of his operating system. If you were to try to arrange the frames of a full-screen animation directly within Director's Score, it would be not only time-consuming but also completely impractical. The individual frames of an animation might take up hundreds of cells in the Score window. Also the animation would play back at a much slower speed than that of a QuickTime movie. When it comes to long or high-resolution animation sequences, QuickTime is probably your best bet. To position the QuickTime movies within the Score and the Stage, follow the steps outlined in Procedure 6.5.

Procedure 6.5   Positioning QuickTime Movies

1. Within the Cast window, click the Choose Cast button and select the Media option. Director will display the Media cast within the Cast window.

2. Drag the Introduction Movie member from the Cast window into cell 1 of channel 1 of the Score window. Director will display the first frame of the Introduction Movie sprite within the Stage window (see Figure 6.9).

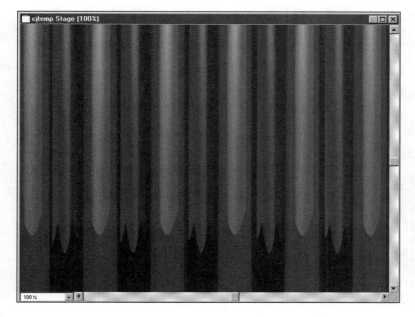

Figure 6.9   *The Introduction Movie sprite.*

3. Drag the Exit Movie member from the Cast window into cell 75 of channel 2 of the Score window. Director will display the first frame of the Exit Movie sprite within the Stage window.

4. Within the Score window, drag cell 102 of channel 2 to frame 90. Director will curtail the Exit Movie sprite to frame 90.

5. Click the Hide/Show Effects Channels button (see Figure 6.10). Director will show the effects channels within the Score window.

>>>

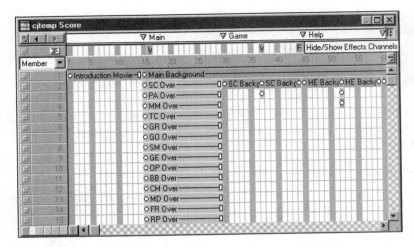

Figure 6.10   *The Hide/Show Effects Channels button.*

6. Double-click cell 14 of the Tempo (stopwatch icon) channel (see Figure 6.11). Director will display the Frame Properties: Tempo dialog box.

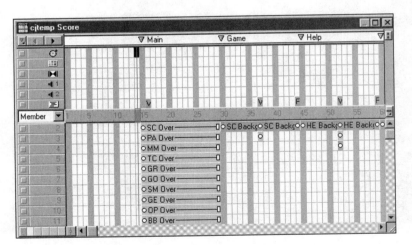

Note:
The effects channels provide a way for the programmer to create effects such as transitions and sounds without the use of Lingo code. They are (from top to bottom) the Tempo channel, the Palette channel, the Transition channel, the first and second Sound channels, and the Behavior channel. Director provides eight Sound channels, but only two are accessible through the Score window.

Figure 6.11   *Cell 14 of the Tempo channel.*

7. From the Tempo dialog box, click the Wait for Cue Point radio button. Director will update the Frame Properties: Tempo dialog box (see Figure 6.12).

8. Click the Cue Point drop-down list and select the { End } option. Director will set the current frame to pause the Director movie until the Introduction Movie sprite has completely finished playing.

9. Click the OK button. Director will apply your changes to frame 14.

10. In the Score window, double-click cell 90 of the Tempo (stopwatch icon) channel. Director will display the Frame Properties: Tempo dialog box.

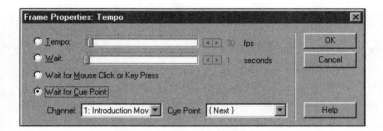

Figure 6.12 *The Frame Properties: Tempo dialog box.*

11. From the Tempo dialog box, click the Wait for Cue Point radio button. Director will update the Frame Properties: Tempo dialog box.

12. Click the Cue Point drop-down list and select the { End } option. Director will set the current frame to pause the Director movie until the Exit Movie sprite is completely finished playing.

13. Click the OK button. Director will apply your changes to frame 90.

14. Within the Score window, click the Hide/Show Effects Channels button. Director will hide the effects channels within the Score window.

You added the `Wait for Cue Point` properties to the last frames of the QuickTime sprites to make sure that the user can see the animation sequences in their entirety. If a QuickTime movie's sprite takes up only 15 cells in the Score, Director will take only about one second to play through it. If the QuickTime movie is longer than one second, then, obviously, something must be done. The Tempo channel provides a way to pause the entire Director movie until the QuickTime movie has completed.

ADDING MUSIC TO THE INTERFACE

A generic function that can often prove quite useful when dealing with sound is the `stopAllSounds` function. Its only purpose is to cycle through the eight Sound channels and stop any sounds currently playing. Its main purpose in the Classic Jukebox interface is to stop the background music before the exit animation plays. If the interface were to play external Director movies and then return to the main menu, the `stopAllSounds` function would be needed to silence any sounds being played by the external movies. For the purposes of this chapter, however, the Classic Jukebox interface does not need to play any external Director movies. To create a global `stopAllSounds` function and update the Yes Button behavior accordingly, follow the steps outlined in Procedure 6.6.

Procedure 6.6   Creating a Global *stopAllSounds* Function

1. From the Cast window, click the Choose Cast button and select the Scripts option. Director will display the Scripts cast within the Cast window.

2. Double-click the Global member. Director will display the Global script within the Script window.

3. In the Script window, at the end of the Global script, type the following code:

```
on stopAllSounds
  repeat with i = 1 to 8
    sound(i).stop()
  end repeat
end
```

>>>

Classic Jukebox

Note that the preceding function uses a local variable named i to stop any sounds playing in Sound channels one through eight.

4. Use the Cast window to click the Yes Button member. Director will highlight the Yes Button member (see Figure 6.13).

5. Click the Cast Member Script button. Director will display the Yes Button script within the Script window.

6. From the Script window, in the `mouseDown` handler, click the `stopAllSounds` command.

7. Within the Script window, click the Uncomment button, as shown in Figure 6.13. Director will remove the comment marks from the line that contains the `stopAllSounds` command.

Figure 6.13 *The Uncomment button within the Script window.*

The background music of the Classic Jukebox interface behaves differently than that of most interfaces. Each time the user visits a new section of the interface, the music changes randomly. The Music cast contains 10 sounds, each set to loop infinitely. Therefore, all the Play Random Music behavior must do is stop any sounds that might already be playing and then play a random member of the Music cast. To create and apply the Play Random Music behavior, follow the steps outlined in Procedure 6.7.

Procedure 6.7   Creating and Applying the Play Random Music Behavior

1. Create a behavior script named Play Random Music as specified in Appendix A.

2. Within the Cast window, click the Play Random Music member. Director will highlight the Play Random Music member.

3. Click the Cast Member Script button. Director will display the Play Random Music script within the Script window.

4. From the Script window, type the following code:

```
on prepareFrame
  stopAllSounds
  sound(1).play(member(random(10), "Music"))
end
```

Note that the preceding handler calls the `stopAllSounds` function, and then plays a random member of the Music cast in the first Sound channel.

5. Apply the Play Random Music behavior to frames 15, 30, 45, and 60 as specified in Appendix A.

6. From the toolbar, click the Script Window button. Director will close the Script window.

Because you applied the Play Random Music behavior to the beginning frame of each section, the user will notice scene changes at exactly the same time as music changes. This gives the interface a much more cohesive feel than just changing the music every few seconds. The music is a very important part of this interface in particular because the interface is jukebox-themed. A jukebox without music is just wrong.

MAKING ADJUSTMENTS

Creating your own unique version of the Classic Jukebox might prove more difficult than you expect. Because images rather than text are used for the navigation buttons, you would have to bring each button image into an external paint application and edit its text label. Furthermore, you would need to replace each section's background image with a completely new graphic to better suit your new sections. Of course, the QuickTime animation sequences would be virtually impossible to use without rendering completely new animations from the jukebox's 3D scene. If you were to create your own jukebox (or any appliance for that matter) in an external 3D editor, however, you could render completely new animations, buttons, and backgrounds. You can use similar Lingo code to create a variety of interfaces by changing little more than the Media cast members.

"There isn't a person anywhere that isn't capable of doing more than he thinks he can."
—Henry Ford

▼▼▼ **chapter 7**
epic model library

Figures 7.1-7.4 *The epic Model Library interface in action.*

APPROACHING THE "EPIC MODEL LIBRARY" INTERFACE

The epic Model Library interface differs quite a bit from the interfaces you have studied in previous chapters. The most obvious difference is that this interface uses only one keyframe. Only one is required because the epic Model Library is driven almost entirely by Lingo code. Interfaces driven by Lingo generally appear less like linear presentations and more like interactive browsers. Because the epic Model Library interface is more for practical purposes than aesthetic appeal, animation effects are not necessary and might even get in the user's way. When designing an interface, you should always keep its purpose in mind.

UNDERSTANDING THE EPIC MODEL LIBRARY INTERFACE

The interface uses a global list variable named *section* to keep track of both the current section and the item of that section currently displayed. You have seen all this before in previous chapters. The feature that makes the epic Model Library unique is the method it provides for browsing through the model images. Each section contains a text field that lists all the items of that section. When the user clicks this text field, a Lingo script determines which line of the field was clicked and displays the appropriate model. This method makes things more convenient for the programmer because a few text fields are much easier to manage than dozens and dozens of links. Because each section's text field, model images, and text descriptions are stored in a separate cast, the model images can be accessed directly by number. The first line of the text list corresponds to the first item in the current section's cast, and so on, and so on. To view the various Lingo scripts of the Scripts cast, follow these steps:

1. Open the `em.dir` file from the 07 - epic Model Library folder as specified in Appendix A, "Guide to Common Tasks." The Scripts cast contains the 20 Lingo scripts shown in Table 7.1.

Table 7.1 The Scripts Cast Lingo Scripts

Script Name	Description
Global	Initializes the interface's global variables.
Wait	Makes the movie repeat the current frame over and over until otherwise specified.
Button	Makes its associated sprite become visible while the user's mouse is clicking it.
Link	Makes its associated sprite become visible while the user's mouse is within its bounds.
Section Button	Sets the *section* variable to a value indicated by an input parameter.
Up Button	Sets the `scrollTop` property of the current section's List Text member to scroll the list upward.
Down Button	Sets the `scrollTop` property of the current section's List Text member to scroll the list downward.
Model Image	Sets its associated sprite's cast member to an image indicated by the global *section* variable.
Model Text	Sets its associated sprite's cast member to text indicated by the global *section* variable.
Model List	Changes the *section* variable based on mouse interaction.
Help Button	Toggles the *helpMode* variable when clicked and keeps its associated sprite visible only when *helpMode* is `true`.
Options Button	Toggles the *optionsMode* variable when clicked and keeps its associated sprite visible only when *optionsMode* is `true`.
Exit Button	Toggles the *exitMode* variable when clicked and keeps its associated sprite visible only when *exitMode* is `true`.
Help Component	Keeps its associated sprite visible only when *helpMode* is `true`.
Options Component	Keeps its associated sprite visible only when *optionsMode* is `true`.
Exit Component	Keeps its associated sprite visible only when *exitMode* is `true`.
Sound On	Makes its associated sprite visible, makes the sprite in the next channel invisible, and sets the volume of the first sound channel to 255 when the user clicks its associated sprite.
Sound Off	Makes its associated sprite visible, makes the sprite in the previous channel invisible, and sets the volume of the first Sound channel to zero when the user clicks its associated sprite.
Yes Link	Stops the movie entirely when the user clicks its associated sprite.
No Link	Sets the *exitMode* variable to `false` and the Exit Button sprite to `invisible` when the user clicks its associated sprite.

2. Within the Cast window, double-click the Global member. Director will display the Global script within the Script window.

3. Within the Script window, use the Previous Cast Member and Next Cast Member buttons to view each of the Lingo scripts in the Scripts cast.

After browsing through the epic Model Library interface's scripts and taking a look at its organization in the Score, you should have a good understanding of the logic behind this interface. If some of its aspects are still not clear, you may want to refer to Appendix B, "Guide to Lingo Programming." Although understanding the innerworkings of the epic Model Library interface at this time is not completely necessary, it should make things easier for you as you re-create the interface throughout the rest of this chapter.

WRITING AND APPLYING THE SECTION BUTTON BEHAVIOR

The Section Button behavior is a single script that works for each of the section buttons in the epic Model Library interface. When the user releases a mouse click on a sprite associated with this behavior, Lingo will set the first item in the global `section` list equal to the behavior's `sectionName` property and the second item equal to the number one. You have seen similar Lingo code in previous chapters. The part that you haven't seen is the `getPropertyDescriptionList` handler. This handler's sole purpose is to initialize property variables by accepting their values as parameters. This means that when the programmer applies the behavior to a sprite, she will be prompted to enter a value for the `sectionName` property. To create and apply the Section Button behavior, follow the steps outlined in Procedure 7.1.

Procedure 7.1   Creating and Applying the Section Button Behavior

1. Open the `emtemp.dir` file from the 07 - epic Model Library folder as specified in Appendix A.

2. Create a behavior script named Section Button as specified in Appendix A.

3. In the Cast window, click the Section Button member. Director will highlight the Section Button member (see Figure 7.5).

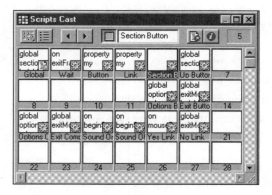

Figure 7.5   *The Section Button member.*

4. Click the Cast Member Script button. Director will display the Section Button script within the Script window.

5. From the Script window, type the following code:

```
global section
property sectionName
```

< 112 >

Note that the following handler sets the *section* variable equal to a list consisting of the value of sectionName and the number one when the user releases a mouse click the associated sprite:

```
on mouseUp
    section = [sectionName, 1]
end
```

Note that the following handler tells Director that the current behavior script accepts one string parameter named sectionName that uses Office as a default value. When the programmer is prompted to enter a value for sectionName, the text field will be labeled Section: as is specified by the returned list's sectionName item's comment item. This will work only if the programmer defines sectionName as a property variable in the current script:

```
on getPropertyDescriptionList
    return [#sectionName: [#comment:"Section:", #format:#string, #default:"Office"]
]
end
```

6. Click the Script Window button. Director will close the Script window.

7. Apply the Section Button behavior to the Office Button sprite that begins in cell 1 of channel 5 as specified in Appendix A.

8. When the Parameters dialog box prompts you for a value, type **Office** into the Section field and then press the Enter key (Return on Macintosh), as shown in Figure 7.6. Director will apply the Section Button behavior to the Office Button sprite.

Figure 7.6   *The Section field.*

9. Apply the Section Button behavior to the Household Button sprite that begins in cell 1 of channel 6 as specified in Appendix A.

10. When the Parameters dialog box prompts you for a value, type **Household** into the Section field and then press the Enter key (Return on Macintosh). Director will apply the Section Button behavior to the Household Button sprite.

11. Apply the Section Button behavior to the Characters Button sprite that begins in cell 1 of channel 7 as specified in Appendix A.

12. When the Parameters dialog box prompts you for a value, type **Characters** into the Section field and then press the Enter key (Return on Macintosh). Director will apply the Section Button behavior to the Characters Button sprite.

13. Apply the Section Button behavior to the Tools Button sprite that begins in cell 1 of channel 8 as specified in Appendix A.

14. When the Parameters dialog box prompts you for a value, type **Tools** into the Section field and then press the Enter key (Return on Macintosh). Director will apply the Section Button behavior to the Tools Button sprite.

15. Apply the Section Button behavior to the Holidays Button sprite that begins in cell 1 of channel 9 as specified in Appendix A.

>>>

16. When the Parameters dialog box prompts you for a value, type **Holidays** into the Section field and then press the Enter key (Return on Macintosh). Director will apply the Section Button behavior to the Holidays Button sprite.

17. Apply the Section Button behavior to the Interfaces Button sprite that begins in cell 1 of channel 10 as specified in Appendix A.

18. When the Parameters dialog box prompts you for a value, type **Interfaces** into the Section field and then press the Enter key (Return on Macintosh). Director will apply the Section Button behavior to the Interfaces Button sprite.

19. Apply the Section Button behavior to the Animals Button sprite that begins in cell 1 of channel 11 as specified in Appendix A.

20. When the Parameters dialog box prompts you for a value, type **Animals** into the Section field and then press the Enter key (Return on Macintosh). Director will apply the Section Button behavior to the Animals Button sprite.

21. Apply the Section Button behavior to the Vehicles Button sprite that begins in cell 1 of channel 12 as specified in Appendix A.

22. When the Parameters dialog box prompts you for a value, type **Vehicles** into the Section field and then press the Enter key (Return on Macintosh). Director will apply the Section Button behavior to the Vehicles Button sprite.

23. Apply the Section Button behavior to the Sci-Fi Button sprite that begins in cell 1 of channel 13 as specified in Appendix A.

24. When the Parameters dialog box prompts you for a value, type **Sci-Fi** into the Section field and then press the Enter key (Return on Macintosh). Director will apply the Section Button behavior to the Sci-Fi Button sprite.

25. Apply the Section Button behavior to the Urban Button sprite that begins in cell 1 of channel 14 as specified in Appendix A.

26. When the Parameters dialog box prompts you for a value, type **Urban** into the Section field and then press the Enter key (Return on Macintosh). Director will apply the Section Button behavior to the Urban Button sprite.

Now that you have applied the Section Button behavior with an appropriate parameter value to each of the section buttons, the buttons are complete. You may have noticed, however, that the Section Button behavior contains only code to modify the *section* variable. Just changing a variable's value will produce no visible results at runtime. Not until you activate the model image, description, and list will the *section* variable be used to its full potential.

ACTIVATING THE MODEL IMAGE AND DESCRIPTION

Throughout the run of the epic Model Library interface, the user's attention remains focused on the current model image and its description. Although the user never directly interacts with either item, the model image and description require behavior scripts to display the current model based on the values of the *section* list. When the *section* variable changes, the model image and description must be updated before the next frame appears on the Stage. To create and apply the Model Image and Model Text behaviors, follow the steps outlined in Procedure 7.2.

Procedure 7.2   Creating and Applying the Model Image and Model Text Behaviors

1. Create a behavior script named Model Image as specified in Appendix A.

2. Within the Cast window, click the Model Image member. Director will highlight the Model Image member (see Figure 7.7).

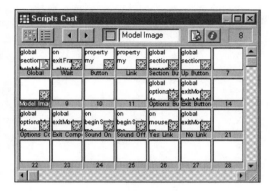

Figure 7.7   *The Model Image member within the Cast window.*

3. Within the Cast window, click the Cast Member Script button. Director will display the Model Image script within the Script window.

4. Within the Script window, type the following code:

```
global section
property my
```

Note that the following handler sets the `my` property equal to the associated sprite and then sets that sprite's opacity to 100 percent. The sprite's opacity must be set to 100 percent through Lingo because it is set to an initial value of zero percent in the Score to prevent it from appearing while the interface is loading:

```
on beginSprite me
   my = sprite(me.spriteNum)
   my.blend = 100
end
```

Note that the following handler makes sure that the `section` list does not contain a blank string in its first item or the number zero in its second item and then sets its associated sprite's cast member based on the `section` list:

```
on prepareFrame
   if section[1] = "" or section[2] = 0 then exit

   my.member = member(section[2], section[1])
end
```

5. Apply the Model Image behavior to the model image sprite that begins in cell 1 of channel 17 as specified in Appendix A.

6. Create a behavior script named Model Text as specified in Appendix A.

7. Within the Cast window, click the Model Text member. Director will highlight the Model Text member (see Figure 7.8).

>>>

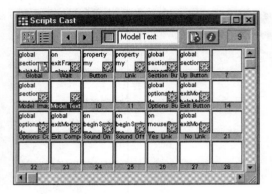

Figure 7.8 *The Model Text member.*

8. Within the Cast window, click the Cast Member Script button. Director will display the Model Text script within the Script window.

9. Within the Script window, type the following code:

```
global section
property my

on beginSprite me
  my = sprite(me.spriteNum)
  my.blend = 100
end
```

Note that the following handler makes the associated sprite invisible if the section list contains a blank string in its first item or the number zero in its second item. Otherwise, it uses a local variable named *offset* to store the number of model items in the current section, sets the associated sprite's cast member based on the section list, and then makes the associated sprite visible:

```
on prepareFrame
  if section[1] = "" or section[2] = 0 then
    my.visible = false
  else
    offset = member("List Text", section[1]).line.count
    my.member = member(section[2]+offset, section[1])
    my.visible = true
  end if
end
```

10. Apply the Model Text behavior to the model text sprite that begins in cell 1 of channel 18 as specified in Appendix A.

11. From the toolbar, click the Script Window button. Director will close the Script window.

When the user chooses a section by clicking a section button, the model image and description update themselves to display the first model in that section. If the user wants to see another model of the section, however, he will be unable to do so because the model list has not yet been activated. Much as the section buttons affect the section list's first item, the section list will affect the second item. The section list's second item allows for control over the current section's model actually being displayed.

CREATING THE SCROLLING MODEL LIST

Perhaps you are wondering why you are using a text field to give the user control over the current model instead of just using a few buttons. Buttons require less complicated Lingo code and are fairly easy to deal with. One major advantage of a text field is the ability to modify the text easily. This way, you can add or remove items from the model list with very little effort. Perhaps the most important reason to use a text field is that one scrolling text field can take the place of a nearly infinite number of buttons. Each line of the field will function as if it is a unique button after the Model List behavior has been applied. To create and apply the Model List behavior, follow the steps outlined in Procedure 7.3.

Procedure 7.3   Creating and Applying the Model List Behavior

1. Create a behavior script named Model List as specified in Appendix A.

2. Within the Cast window, click the Model List member. Director will highlight the Model List member (see Figure 7.9).

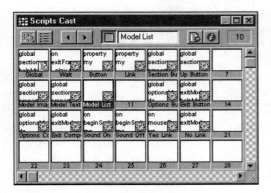

Figure 7.9   *The Model List member.*

3. In the Cast window, click the Cast Member Script button. Director will display the Model List script within the Script window.

4. From the Script window, type the following code:

```
global section
property my, oldSection
```

Note that the following handler sets the `my` property equal to the associated sprite, sets the `oldSection` property to the value of `section`, sets the sprite's opacity to 100 percent, and then sets the sprite's `cursor` property to a list containing the Point Cursor and Point Cursor Mask members. The `cursor` property tells Lingo to change the user's mouse cursor to the specified image (with a specified mask) when the mouse cursor is within the bounds of the associated sprite:

```
on beginSprite me
  my = sprite(me.spriteNum)
  oldSection = section
  my.blend = 100
  my.cursor = [member("Point Cursor"), member("Point Cursor Mask")]
end
```

>>>

Note that the following handler sets the second item of the `section` list to the number of the paragraph that the user's cursor is currently over when the user clicks the associated sprite. Because each line of the associated sprite's text ends with a hard return, each line is technically its own paragraph:

```
on mouseDown
   section[2] = my.pointToParagraph(the mouseLoc)
end
```

Note that the following handler tells Lingo to execute the `mouseDown` handler when the user's mouse is pressed and its cursor is within the bounds of the associated sprite. This enables the user to click and drag within the `model` list to scroll through the list items:

```
on mouseWithin
   if the mouseDown then mouseDown()
end
```

Note that the following handler makes the associated sprite invisible if the `section` list contains a blank string in its first item or the number zero in its second item. Otherwise, as long as the *section* variable has recently changed, the handler sets the associated sprite's cast member to the List Text member of the current section cast, sets that member's text to be scrolled to the very top of its field, and then makes the associated sprite visible. Then, the handler updates the `oldSection` property, which is used to detect changes in the *section* variable:

```
on prepareFrame
   if section[1] = "" or section[2] = 0 then
      my.visible = false
   else if oldSection <> section then
      my.member = member("List Text", section[1])
      my.member.scrollTop = 0
      my.visible = true
   end if

   oldSection = section
end
```

Note that the following handler sets the associated sprite's `cursor` property back to the default cursor just before the sprite ends. This prevents other sprites that might occur in the same channel from inheriting the current sprite's cursor:

```
on endSprite
   my.cursor = 0
end
```

5. Apply the Model List behavior to the List Text sprite that begins in cell 1 of channel 19 as specified in Appendix A.

Now that you have activated the `model` list, it should function perfectly and enable the user to change the current model with nothing more than a mouse click. This works just fine so long as the number of models in the current section does not exceed the number of lines that can be displayed within the List Text sprite. To create room for infinite models in a section, you must provide the user with a means of scrolling the `model` list text up and down. To create the Down Button behavior and apply it as well as the Up Button behavior to their appropriate sprites, follow the steps outlined in Procedure 7.4.

Procedure 7.4   Creating and Applying the Up Button and Down Button Behaviors

1. Create a behavior script named Down Button as specified in Appendix A.

2. Within the Cast window, click the Down Button member. Director will highlight the Down Button member (see Figure 7.10).

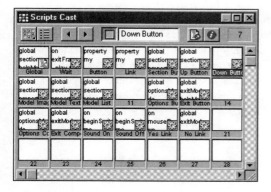

Figure 7.10   *The Down Button member.*

3. Click the Cast Member Script button. Director will display the Down Button script within the Script window.

4. From the Script window, type the following code:

```
global section
```

Note that the following handler sets the scrollTop property of the List Text member of the current section's cast to 20 more than its current value. The scrollTop property determines the number of pixels at the top of a text field that are not visible because they been scrolled higher than the top border of the field. In other words, it determines the number of the row of pixels that is currently located at the top border of the text field. Adding to the scrollTop property moves the text upward and therefore exposes text at the bottom of the field:

```
on mouseDown
    member("List Text", section[1]).scrollTop = member("List Text",
section[1]).scrollTop + 20
end

on mouseWithin
    if the mouseDown then mouseDown()
end
```

5. Apply the Down Button behavior to the Down Button sprite that begins in cell 1 of channel 16 as specified in Appendix A.

6. Apply the Up Button behavior to the Up Button sprite that begins in cell 1 of channel 15 as specified in Appendix A.

If you were to preview your epic Model Library interface at this point, you would discover that it is now completely functional. The user may choose a section by clicking a button on the left side of the Stage and then choose a model by clicking the model list on the right side of the Stage. Both the model image and its description will update themselves based on these controls. If you wanted, you could leave the interface exactly as it appears now. As a courtesy, however, you should provide the user with easy access to a Help section, the ability to adjust the background music, and an Exit button complete with a confirmation screen.

CREATING THE HELP, OPTIONS, AND EXIT SECTIONS

When the user clicks the Help, Options, or Exit button, the current model image in the middle of the Stage should be replaced with the text and/or controls of that section. The Help section consists solely of an image that explains how to use the interface. When the user decides to view the Help section, this image just replaces the current model image. The Options and Exit sections, on the other hand, contain buttons that enable the user to adjust the background music or exit the interface. To keep these buttons from displaying at the wrong time, they contain behaviors that make them visible only when a global variable indicates they should be. To position the elements of the Help, Options, and Exit sections in the Stage and the Score, follow the steps outlined in Procedure 7.5.

Procedure 7.5   Positioning Elements on the Stage

1. Within the Cast window, click the Choose Cast button and select the Media option. Director will display the Media cast within the Cast window.

2. Drag the Help Screen member from the Cast window into cell 1 of channel 20 of the Score window. Director will display the Help Screen sprite within the Stage window (see Figure 7.11).

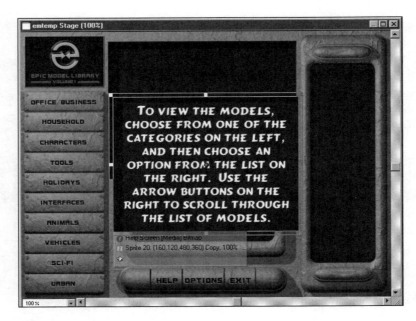

Figure 7.11   *The Help Screen sprite.*

3. Within the Score window, click cell 2 of channel 20. Director will highlight the Help Screen sprite.

4. From the Property Inspector window, type **314** into the X field, **143** into the Y field, and then press the Enter key (Return on Macintosh). Director will update the Help Screen sprite within the Stage window (see Figure 7.12).

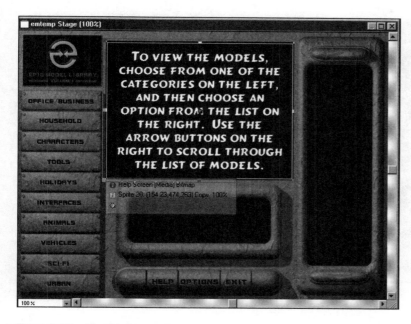

Figure 7.12 *The Help Screen sprite.*

5. Drag the Options Screen member from the Cast window into cell 1 of channel 21 of the Score window. Director will display the Options Screen sprite within the Stage window.

6. In the Score window, click cell 2 of channel 21. Director will highlight the Options Screen sprite.

7. Within the Property Inspector window, type **314** into the X field, **143** into the Y field, and then press the Enter key (Return on Macintosh). Director will update the Options Screen sprite within the Stage window.

8. Drag the Sound On member from the Cast window into cell 1 of channel 22 of the Score window. Director will display the Sound On sprite within the Stage window.

9. Within the Score window, click cell 2 of channel 22. Director will highlight the Sound On sprite.

10. In the Property Inspector window, type **315** into the X field, **125** into the Y field, and then press the Enter key (Return on Macintosh). Director will update the Sound On sprite within the Stage window.

11. Drag the Sound Off member from the Cast window into cell 1 of channel 23 of the Score window. Director will display the Sound Off sprite within the Stage window.

12. From the Score window, click cell 2 of channel 23. Director will highlight the Sound Off sprite.

13. Within the Property Inspector window, type **170** into the Y field and then press the Enter key (Return on Macintosh). Director will update the Sound Off sprite within the Stage window (see Figure 7.13).

14. Drag the Exit Screen member from the Cast window into cell 1 of channel 24 of the Score window. Director will display the Exit Screen sprite within the Stage window.

15. In the Score window, click cell 2 of channel 24. Director will highlight the Exit Screen sprite.

16. Within the Property Inspector window, type **314** into the X field, **143** into the Y field, and then press the Enter key (Return on Macintosh). Director will update the Exit Screen sprite within the Stage window.

17. Drag the Yes Link member from the Cast window into cell 1 of channel 25 of the Score window. Director will display the Yes Link sprite within the Stage window.

>>>

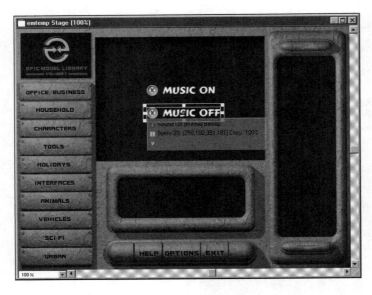

Figure 7.13 *The Sound Off sprite.*

18. Within the Score window, click cell 2 of channel 25. Director will highlight the Yes Link sprite.

19. From the Property Inspector window, type **250** into the X field, **185** into the Y field, and then press the Enter key (Return on Macintosh). Director will update the Yes Link sprite within the Stage window.

20. Drag the No Link member from the Cast window into cell 1 of channel 26 of the Score window. Director will display the No Link sprite within the Stage window.

21. Within the Score window, click cell 2 of channel 26. Director will highlight the No Link sprite.

22. In the Property Inspector window, type **390** into the X field, **185** into the Y field, and then press the Enter key (Return on Macintosh). Director will update the No Link sprite within the Stage window (see Figure 7.14).

Figure 7.14 *The No Link sprite.*

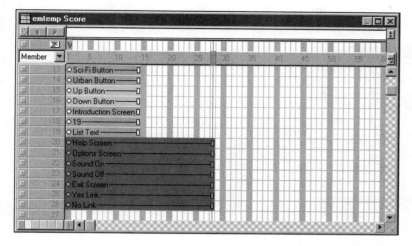

Figure 7.15 *The selected sprites.*

23. Within the Score window, click cell 1 of channel 20, press and hold the Shift key, and then click cell 28 of channel 26. Director will highlight cells 1 through 28 of channels 20 through 26 (see Figure 7.15).

24. From the Property Inspector window, in the Blend drop-down list, type **0** and press the Enter key (Return on Macintosh). Director will set the opacity of the selected sprites to zero percent.

    Note that the opacities of the Help, Options, and Exit components must be set to zero percent initially so that the user will not see any of them at the start of the interface before Lingo makes them invisible.

25. Within the Property Inspector window, in the End Frame field, type **14** and press the Enter key (Return on Macintosh), as shown in Figure 7.16. Director will curtail the selected sprites to frame 14.

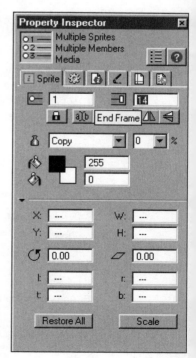

Figure 7.16 *The End Frame field.*

Each of the Help, Options, and Exit sections must have its own button and component behaviors. The purpose of the button behavior is to set the *helpMode*, *optionsMode*, and *exitMode* variables. It also must adjust the opacities of all three buttons to create a toggle effect. When one of the buttons is down, the other two must be up. A button should remain down for as long as its section is being displayed. The component behavior displays only the appropriate sprites by setting each sprite's visible property to the value of *helpMode*, *optionsMode*, or *exitMode*. The component behavior's beginSprite handler also must set the associated sprite's opacity to 100 percent because you set it to zero percent in the Score. To create the Help Button and Help Component behaviors, and activate the elements of the Help, Options, and Exit sections, follow the steps outlined in Procedure 7.6.

Procedure 7.6   Creating the Help Button and Help Component Behaviors

1. In the Cast window, click the Choose Cast button and select the Scripts option. Director will display the Scripts cast within the Cast window.

2. Create a behavior script named Help Button as specified in Appendix A.

>>>

3. Click the Help Button member. Director will highlight the Help Button member (see Figure 7.17).

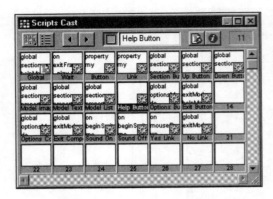

Figure 7.17   *The Help Button member.*

4. Click the Cast Member Script button. Director will display the Help Button script within the Script window.

5. From the Script window, type the following code:

```
global helpMode, optionsMode, exitMode
```

Note that the following handler sets the *helpMode* variable to the opposite of its current Boolean value when the user releases a click the associated sprite. Then, it sets both *optionsMode* and *exitMode* to false and sets the opacities of the Options Button and Exit Button sprites to zero percent:

```
on mouseUp me
  helpMode = not helpMode
  optionsMode = false
  exitMode = false
  sprite(me.spriteNum+1).blend = 0
  sprite(me.spriteNum+2).blend = 0
end
```

Note that the following handler sets its associated sprite's opacity to 100 percent if the *helpMode* variable equals true:

```
on prepareFrame me
  if helpMode then sprite(me.spriteNum).blend = 100
end
```

6. Apply the Help Button behavior to the Help Button sprite that begins in cell 1 of channel 2 as specified in Appendix A.

7. Apply the Options Button behavior to the Options Button sprite that begins in cell 1 of channel 3 as specified in Appendix A.

8. Apply the Exit Button behavior to the Exit Button sprite that begins in cell 1 of channel 4 as specified in Appendix A.

9. Create a behavior script named Help Component as specified in Appendix A.

10. Within the Cast window, click the Help Component member. Director will highlight the Help Component member (see Figure 7.18).

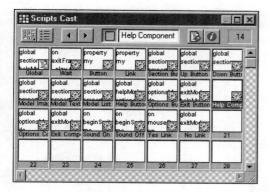

Figure 7.18 *The Help Component member.*

11. Click the Cast Member Script button. Director will display the Help Component script within the Script window.

12. From the Script window, type the following code:

```
global helpMode
```

Note that the following handler sets its associated sprite's visibility to the value of *helpMode* and sets the sprite's opacity to 100 percent:

```
on beginSprite me
    sprite(me.spriteNum).visible = helpMode
    sprite(me.spriteNum).blend = 100
end
```

Note that the following handler sets its associated sprite's visibility to the value of *helpMode*:

```
on prepareFrame me
    sprite(me.spriteNum).visible = helpMode
end
```

13. Apply the Help Component behavior to the Help Screen sprite that begins in cell 1 of channel 20 as specified in Appendix A.

14. In the Score window, click cell 1 of channel 21, press and hold the Shift key, and then click cell 14 of channel 23. Director will highlight cells 1 through 14 of channels 21 through 23 (see Figure 7.19).

15. Apply the Options Component behavior to the selected sprites as specified in Appendix A.

16. Click cell 1 of channel 24, press and hold the Shift key, and then click cell 14 of channel 26. Director will highlight cells 1 through 14 of channels 24 through 26.

17. Apply the Exit Component behavior to the selected sprites as specified in Appendix A.

18. Apply the Sound On behavior to the Sound On sprite that begins in cell 1 of channel 22 as specified in Appendix A.

19. Apply the Sound Off behavior to the Sound Off sprite that begins in cell 1 of channel 23 as specified in Appendix A.

20. Apply the Link behavior and the Yes Link behavior to the Yes Link sprite that begins in cell 1 of channel 25 as specified in Appendix A.

>>>

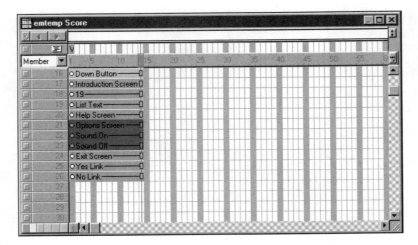

Figure 7.19 *The selected sprites.*

21. Apply the Link behavior and the No Link behavior to the No Link sprite that begins in cell 1 of channel 26 as specified in Appendix A.

Now that the Help, Options, and Exit sections are complete, your epic Model Library interface is complete. Not only can the user access the model of her choice, but if the user needs to understand, modify, or exit the interface, she should have no problem doing so. When developing interfaces, keep in mind that all people are different and avoid assuming things about the user. Any time music is involved in an interface, try to give the user the option to mute it if she desires. The user might actually be playing other music on her computer at the time. In such a situation, an interface's background music might be nothing more than an unnecessary annoyance.

MAKING ADJUSTMENTS

Because of the epic Model Library's minimalist style, it is actually quite easy to update. To add an item to a particular section, you must start by viewing that section's cast. Then, edit the List Text member and add the new model's name to the list. You must pay very close attention to the order that you add new items. When you add new images and text descriptions to a section's cast, they must occur in exactly the same order that the new items appear in the List Text member. Updating the epic Model Library is easy; but if you want to actually add or remove sections from the interface, you will have to re-create the button images. Instead of trying to make new button images that match the current interface, you might want to re-create all the interface's graphics and give the interface your own unique feel.

>> **part 3**
complex interfaces

"Be nice to nerds. Chances are you'll end up working for one."
—Charles Sykes

▼▼▼ **chapter 8**
cluttered desktop

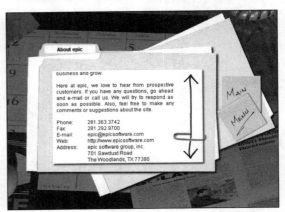

Figures 8.1-8.4 *The Cluttered Desktop interface in action.*

APPROACHING THE "CLUTTERED DESKTOP" INTERFACE

The Cluttered Desktop interface may appear simple at first glance, but as you look deeper into it, you will notice that it has several features not yet covered in this book. Aside from the obvious image mapping, the interface also uses rollover status message text, scrollable text, and scrollable images. When the user clicks one of these images, it will fill the entire Stage and give the user a close-up view of itself. To return to the interface, the user must simply click the enlarged image anywhere on the Stage. Like the Classic Jukebox interface, the Cluttered Desktop uses a separate keyframe to display the sections' content. However, the sections of the Cluttered Desktop interface are more interactive and just a bit more difficult to build than those of the Classic Jukebox.

UNDERSTANDING THE CLUTTERED DESKTOP INTERFACE

The feature of the Cluttered Desktop interface that immediately jumps out at the user is the changing background image. As the user moves his mouse over the various items on the desk, the items do not glow or change color as the user might expect. Instead, the background image (including all the other desk items) turns gray and blurry. This forces the user's attention to the highlighted item without actually changing the appearance of the item at all. The highlighted item now appears brighter and in sharper focus than the rest of the Stage. This backward rollover technique may not suit every interface you build, but it certainly serves to break up the monotony of boring, predictable interfaces. To view the various Lingo scripts of the Scripts cast, follow these steps:

1. Open the `cd.dir` file from the 08 - Cluttered Desktop folder as specified in Appendix A "Guide to Common Tasks." The Scripts cast contains the 15 Lingo scripts shown in Table 8.1.

Table 8.1   The Scripts Cast Lingo Scripts

Script Name	Description
Wait	Makes the movie repeat the current frame over and over until otherwise specified.
Use Cursor	Sets its associated sprite's cursor to a cursor made up of the Point Cursor and Point Cursor Mask members of the Media cast.
Set Message	Sets the text of the Status Text member to a specified string when the user's mouse enters the bounds of its associated sprite and back to normal when the mouse leaves.
Desk Item	Sets the background image to the Background Gray member and the associated sprite's opacity to 100 percent when the user's mouse enters the bounds of its associated sprite and back to normal when the mouse leaves.
Screen Saver	Makes its associated sprite bounce around the bounds of the background image's monitor screen and randomly shifts its foreground color.
Main Link	Plays the Main marker when the user clicks its associated sprite.
Help Link	Plays the Help marker when the user clicks its associated sprite.
Exit Link	Stops the movie entirely when the user clicks its associated sprite.
Section Link	Sets the $section$ variable to a specified string and plays the Section marker when the user clicks its associated sprite.
Up Arrow	Moves the Paperclip sprite up 10 pixels when the user clicks its associated sprite.
Down Arrow	Moves the Paperclip sprite down 10 pixels when the user clicks its associated sprite.
Paperclip	Enables the user to drag its associated sprite vertically within a set area.
Section Title	Sets its associated sprite's cast member's text to the value of the $section$ variable when the sprite begins.
Section Text	Sets its associated sprite's cast member based on the $section$ variable and scrolls its text based on the location of the Paperclip sprite.
Section Image	Sets its associated sprite's cast member based on the $section$ variable and the location of the Paperclip sprite and enables the user to enlarge its associated sprite by clicking it.

2. In the Cast window, double-click the Global member. Director will display the Global script within the Script window.

3. Within the Script window, use the Previous Cast Member and Next Cast Member buttons to view each of the Lingo scripts in the Scripts cast.

After browsing through the Cluttered Desktop interface's scripts and taking a look at its organization in the Score, you should have a good understanding of the logic behind this interface. If some of its aspects are still not clear, you may want to refer to Appendix B "Guide to Lingo Programming." Although understanding the innerworkings of the Cluttered Desktop interface at this time is not completely necessary, it should make things easier for you as you recreate the interface throughout the rest of this chapter.

DISPLAYING A ROLLOVER STATUS MESSAGE

The rollover status message is an extraordinarily common element of interface design that allows for an almost unlimited amount of variation. Because the desk items of the Cluttered Desktop interface do not contain text labels, some form of rollover message is required to indicate the section to which each item points. One way to incorporate status text into the interface that is both obvious and entertaining is by creating a mock screen saver. The Screen Saver behavior causes the status text to bounce around the background image's monitor screen and continuously shift colors. Users immediately recognize the bouncing, color-shifting text as a screen saver, and therefore, the continuity of the desktop image is not broken. The purpose of the Set Message behavior is to affect the screen saver's text. To complete the Set Message behavior, follow the steps outlined in Procedure 8.1.

Procedure 8.1   Completing the Set Message Behavior

1. Open the `cdtemp.dir` file from the 08 - Cluttered Desktop folder as specified in Appendix A.

2. From the Cast window, click the Set Message member. Director will highlight the Set Message member (see Figure 8.5).

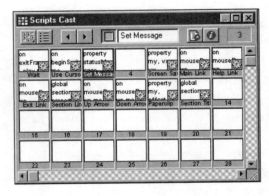

Figure 8.5   *The Set Message member.*

3. Click the Cast Member Script button. Director will display the Set Message script within the Script window.

4. In the Script window, in the `mouseEnter` handler, type the following code:

```
member("Status Text").text = statusMessage
```

Note that the preceding line sets the Status Text member's text equal to the `statusMessage` property.

5. In the `mouseLeave` handler, type the following code:

```
member("Status Text").text = "Cluttered Desktop"
```

Note that the preceding line sets the Status Text member's text equal to "Cluttered Desktop," the default status message.

6. In the `endSprite` handler, type the following code:

```
mouseLeave
```

Note that the preceding line calls the associated sprite's `mouseLeave` handler, which sets the Status Text member's text equal to the default status message.

7. From the toolbar, click the Script Window button. Director will close the Script window.

With the rollover status message text now completely active, the main menu is nearly complete. When the user moves her mouse over a desk item, she can now see where that item leads. The user might still feel uneasy clicking a desk item because the item's clickable area is not clearly outlined. To make the user more comfortable, you must give her a clear indication of which desk item, if any, is currently selected.

CREATING THE DESK ITEM BEHAVIOR

The rollover item highlighting effect is achieved with surprisingly little effort. Each of the desk items is copied from the colored background image and pasted in the foreground in their appropriate spots. Then, the opacity of each of the desk items is set to zero percent. When the user moves his mouse over one of these invisible desk items, it becomes visible and the background image changes to a blurred, grayscale version of itself. When the user's mouse leaves the bounds of the desk item, the Stage returns to normal. To create and apply the Desk Item behavior, follow the steps outlined in Procedure 8.2.

Procedure 8.2   Creating and Applying the Desk Item Behavior

1. Create a behavior script named Desk Item as specified in Appendix A.

2. Within the Cast window, click the Desk Item member. Director will highlight the Desk Item member (see Figure 8.6).

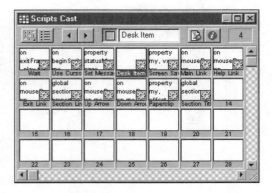

Figure 8.6   *The Desk Item member.*

3. Click the Cast Member Script button. Director will display the Desk Item script within the Script window.

4. From the Script window, type the following code:

```
property my

on beginSprite me
  my = sprite(me.spriteNum)
end
```

>>>

Note that the following handler sets the cast member of sprite 2 to the Gray Background member and sets the opacity of the associated sprite to 100 percent. This creates the effect of turning the entire Stage gray except for the associated sprite:

```
on mouseEnter
  sprite(2).member = "Gray Background"
  my.blend = 100
end
```

Note that the following handler sets the cast member of sprite 2 to the Background member and sets the opacity of the associated sprite to zero percent. This returns the Stage to normal:

```
on mouseLeave
  sprite(2).member = "Background"
  my.blend = 0
end
```

5. On the toolbar, click the Script Window button. Director will close the Script window.

6. In the Score window, click cell 1 of channel 4, press and hold the Shift key, and then click cell 14 of channel 11. Director will highlight cells 1 through 14 of channels 4 through 11 (see Figure 8.7).

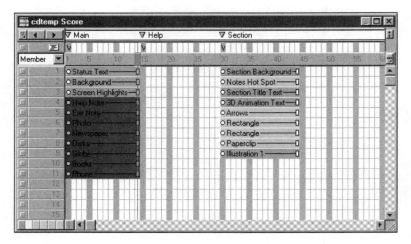

Figure 8.7 *The selected sprites.*

7. Apply the Desk Item behavior to the selected sprites as specified in Appendix A.

At this point, the main menu of your Cluttered Desktop interface should function exactly as that of the original Cluttered Desktop. By moving the mouse cursor around the Stage, the user can figure out which desk items are active and to which section each item leads. This should be just fine for most users exploring the interface, but some people might not feel like exploring. For the user who knows exactly where he wants to go and doesn't feel like searching for a way to get there, you must provide a Help section.

BUILDING THE HELP SECTION

The most important attribute of the user's link to the Help section is that it must be clearly labeled. For the type of user who will be looking for a Help section, a confusing link might as well not exist at all. Another control that should always be obvious to the user is the Exit button. Some users might run the interface by accident, or they might want to just look at its layout for a moment and then exit immediately. To accommodate these types of users, the Help and Exit links are both clearly labeled. To maintain the realism of the interface's atmosphere, the two links appear as notes stuck onto the face of the background image's desk. To position the elements of the Help section in the Stage and the Score, follow the steps outlined in Procedure 8.3.

Procedure 8.3   Positioning the Help Section in the Stage and Score

1. In the Score window, click cell 1 of channel 5, press and hold the Shift key, and then click cell 14 of channel 11. Director will highlight cells 1 through 14 of channels 5 through 11.

2. Click the Edit menu and select the Copy Sprites option. Director will hold a copy of the selected sprites in memory.

3. Click cell 15 of channel 5. Director will update the Stage window.

4. Click the Edit menu and select the Paste Sprites option. Director will paste a copy of the desk item sprites into cells 15 through 28 of channels 5 through 11 from memory (see Figure 8.8).

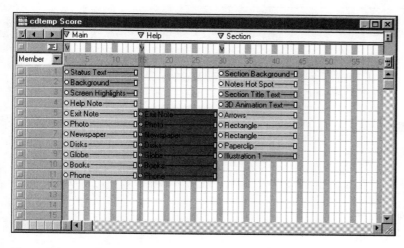

Figure 8.8   *The new sprites within the Score window.*

5. In the Property Inspector window, in the End Frame field, type **29** and press the Enter key (Return on Macintosh). Director will extend the selected sprites to frame 29.

6. Click the Blend drop-down list and select the 100 option. Director will set the opacity of the selected sprites to 100 percent (see Figure 8.9).

>>>

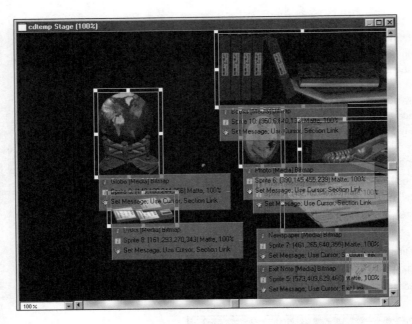

Figure 8.9   *The new sprites within the Stage window.*

7. Click the Behavior tab. Director will display the Behavior sheet within the Property Inspector window.

8. Click the Desk Item behavior. Director will highlight the Desk Item behavior (see Figure 8.10).

Figure 8.10   *The Desk Item behavior within the Property Inspector window.*

9. Click the Clear Behavior (minus sign) button and select the Remove Behavior option. Director will remove the Desk Item behavior from the selected sprites.

10. Within the Score window, drag cell 14 of channel 1 to frame 29. Director will extend the Status Text sprite to frame 29.

11. Drag cell 14 of channel 3 to frame 29. Director will extend the Screen Highlights sprite to frame 29.

12. In the Cast window, click the Choose Cast button and select the Media option. Director will display the Media cast within the Cast window.

13. Drag the Gray Background member from the Cast window into cell 15 of channel 2 of the Score window. Director will display the Gray Background sprite within the Stage window (see Figure 8.11).

Figure 8.11   *The Gray Background sprite within the Stage window.*

Note that in the Gray Background bitmap, the computer monitor's screen appears green so that when the color green is set to be transparent, the Status Text sprite will show through.

14. In the Score window, click cell 16 of channel 2. Director will highlight the Gray Background sprite.

15. From the Property Inspector window, in the Background Color field, type **#00FF00** and press the Enter key (Return on Macintosh). Director will set the background color of the Gray Background sprite to green.

16. Next click the Ink drop-down list and select the Background Transparent option. Director will remove the green background from the Gray Background sprite.

17. Drag the Main Note member from the Cast window into cell 15 of channel 4 of the Score window. Director will display the Main Note sprite within the Stage window.

18. In the Score window, click cell 16 of channel 4. Director will highlight the Main Note sprite.

19. Within the Property Inspector window, click the Ink drop-down list and select the Matte option. Director will remove the white border from the Main Note sprite.

>>>

20. Apply the Set Message behavior to the Main Note sprite that begins in cell 15 of channel 4 as specified in Appendix A.

21. When the Parameters dialog box prompts you for a value, type **Main Menu** into the Status Message field and then press the Enter key (Return on Macintosh). Director will apply the Set Message behavior to the Main Note sprite.

22. Apply the Use Cursor and Main Link behaviors to the Main Note sprite that begins in cell 15 of channel 4 as specified in Appendix A.

If you were to preview your movie right now, you would find that the main menu and Help section of your interface appear as they should and work together smoothly. You can now move back and forth between the main menu and the Help section just by clicking the Help/Main link. From either section, in fact, you can click the various desk items and view their respective sections. Because the scrollable section text and section image sprites have not yet been activated, however, the sections' media items will be completely inactive and will not respond to your attempts to scroll through them. To remedy this problem, you must create behaviors for the section text and section image sprites.

CREATING THE SECTION TEXT BEHAVIOR

Although Director enables programmers to create scrolling text fields automatically, learning to scroll a text field through Lingo is an important skill you must master. The appearance of automatic scrolling text fields is dependent on the user's operating system, and their scrollbars always appear on top of the other elements of your interface. This lack of control might be enough to seriously interfere with your artistic vision. By scrolling the text fields through Lingo, as in the Section Text behavior, you can give the user complete control over a text field without disrupting your interface's appearance. To create and apply the Section Text behavior, follow the steps outlined in Procedure 8.4.

Procedure 8.4 Creating and Applying the Section Text Behavior

1. Using the Cast window, click the Choose Cast button and select the Scripts option. Director will display the Scripts cast within the Cast window.

2. Create a behavior script named Section Text as specified in Appendix A.

3. Next click the Section Text member. Director will highlight the Section Text member (see Figure 8.12).

4. Click the Cast Member Script button. Director will display the Section Text script within the Script window.

5. From the Script window, type the following code:

```
global section
property my
```

Note that the following handler sets the my property equal to the associated sprite and that sprite's cast member's scrollTop property to zero. Because the cast member is a text field, this sets the text to scroll up to its very beginning:

```
on beginSprite me
   my = sprite(me.spriteNum)
   my.member.scrollTop = 0
end
```

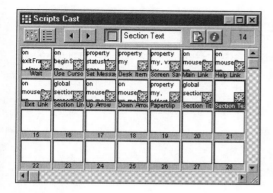

Figure 8.12 *The Section Text member.*

Note that the following handler sets the associated sprite's opacity to 100 percent, sets its cast member based on the *section* variable, and sets its member's `scrollTop` property based on the position of the Paperclip sprite if the *section* variable indicates a text field should be displayed. Otherwise, the handler sets the associated sprite's opacity to zero percent:

```
on prepareFrame
   if section = "3D Animation" or section = "Web Development" or section = "Other
Services" or section = "About epic" then
      my.blend = 100
      my.member = section && "Text"
      percentage = float(sprite(my.spriteNum+4).locV-205)/100
      my.member.scrollTop = (my.member.height-220)*percentage
   else
      my.blend = 0
   end if
end
```

6. From the toolbar, click the Script Window button. Director will close the Script window.

7. Apply the Section Text behavior to the 3D Animation Text sprite that begins in cell 30 of channel 4 as specified in Appendix A.

Even though your section text sprite should now function properly, it will remain blocked out by the inactive section image sprite. The section image does not yet know which cast member should be displayed or even when it should and should not be visible. Until you create a behavior for the section image sprite as well, your section text might as well still be inactive.

CREATING THE SECTION IMAGE BEHAVIOR

By far the easiest way to enable the user to scroll through a gallery of images is to set the image sprite's cast member based on the position of the scrollbar's slider. This method will not provide a smooth transition from one image to the next, but it will give both you and the user a clear indication of the gallery image currently being displayed. If you were to actually display smooth scrolling images, you would need at least two active section image sprites and a great deal more Lingo code. To create and apply the Section Image behavior, follow the steps outlined in Procedure 8.5.

Procedure 8.5   Creating the Section Image Behavior

1. Create a behavior script named Section Image as specified in Appendix A.

2. Within the Cast window, click the Section Image member. Director will highlight the Section Image member (see Figure 8.13).

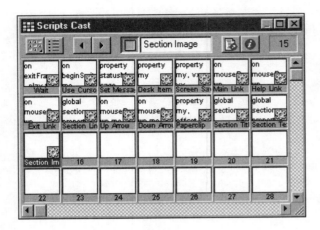

Figure 8.13   *The Section Image member.*

3. Click the Cast Member Script button. Director will display the Section Image script within the Script window.

4. From the Script window, type the following code:

```
global section
property my, zooming
```

Note that the following handler sets the my property equal to the associated sprite and the zooming property equal to zero. The purpose of the zooming property is to indicate the zooming status of the section image. A value of 1 means that it is enlarging, 2 means that it is shrinking, and 0 means that it is resting in its default position:

```
on beginSprite me
  my = sprite(me.spriteNum)
  zooming = 0
end
```

Note that the following five lines set the associated sprite's opacity to 100 percent and set its cast member based on the *section* variable and the position of the Paperclip sprite if the value of section is "Illustration" or "Technical":

```
on prepareFrame
  if section = "Illustration" or section = "Technical" then
    my.blend = 100
    tempNum = integer((sprite(my.spriteNum-1).locV-205)/10) + 1
    my.member = section && tempNum
```

Note that the following line checks whether the value of the zooming property is 1. A value of 1 indicates that the image should be increasing in size:

```
if zooming = 1 then
```

Note that the following conditional adjusts the associated sprite's dimensions and position to be closer to full-screen.

```
if abs(640-my.width) < 5 and abs(480-my.height) < 5 then
   my.width = 640
   my.height = 480
   my.locH = 320
   my.locV = 240
else
   my.width = (640 + my.width)/2
   my.height = (480 + my.height)/2
   my.locH = (320 + my.locH)/2
   my.locV = (240 + my.locV)/2
end if
```

Note that the following checks whether the value of the `zooming` property is 2. A value of 2 indicates that the image should be decreasing in size:

```
else if zooming = 2 then
```

Note that the following conditional adjusts the associated sprite's dimensions and position to be closer to their original values:

```
if abs(266-my.width) < 5 and abs(198-my.height) < 5 then
   my.width = 266
   my.height = 198
   my.locH = 255
   my.locV = 255
   zooming = 0
else
   my.width = (266 + my.width)/2 + 1
   my.height = (198 + my.height)/2 + 1
   my.locH = (255 + my.locH)/2
   my.locV = (255 + my.locV)/2
end if
```

Note that the following five lines set the associated sprite's opacity to zero percent if the earlier condition was not met (if the value of section was not "Illustration" or "Technical"):

```
      end if
   else
      my.blend = 0
   end if
end
```

Note that the following handler sets the `zooming` property to a value of 2 if the section image is already in Enlarging mode. Otherwise, the handler sets the `zooming` property to a value of 1. This enables the user to click the associated sprite to toggle the zooming of the section image:

```
on mouseDown
   if zooming = 1 then
      zooming = 2
   else
      zooming = 1
   end if
end
```

5. From the toolbar, click the Script Window button. Director will close the Script window.

>>>

6. Apply the Section Image behavior to the Illustration 1 sprite that begins in cell 30 of channel 9 as specified in Appendix A.

Now that all the sections of your Cluttered Desktop interface function as they should, you are free to preview the interface in its entirety. If you plan to use this interface as a template for one of your own projects, keep your intended audience in mind and make note of any adjustments you might need to make. The Cluttered Desktop interface is a bit less self-explanatory than the other interfaces you have studied so far because it was designed more to let the user explore than to quickly retrieve information. If your audience might need to move quickly through your interface, you should probably consider adding text labels to the desk items.

MAKING ADJUSTMENTS

Adjusting the Cluttered Desktop interface may seem like an unpleasant chore at first, but after you have a solid understanding of how the application works, you should be able to change media elements, rename sections, and even activate or deactivate desk items to add or remove sections from the interface. To add a new desk item sprite to the stage, you must start with the Background member of the Media cast. Copy its image and paste it into a new cast member or external paint application. Edit this new image by painting everything white except the item you want to activate. Your brush must have absolutely no anti-aliasing or smoothing. Everything that you paint absolutely white will appear transparent on the Stage. After you have finished editing the image, name its cast member appropriately and drag it onto the Stage. Because you just edited the Background image, the new sprite should appear exactly in place when it is located at 320 pixels horizontally and 240 pixels vertically. Set the sprite's ink to Matte, apply the appropriate behaviors, and your new section should be up and running in no time.

*"Man does not cease to play because he grows old;
he grows old because he ceases to play."*
—Drew Lachey

▼▼▼ chapter 9
video game

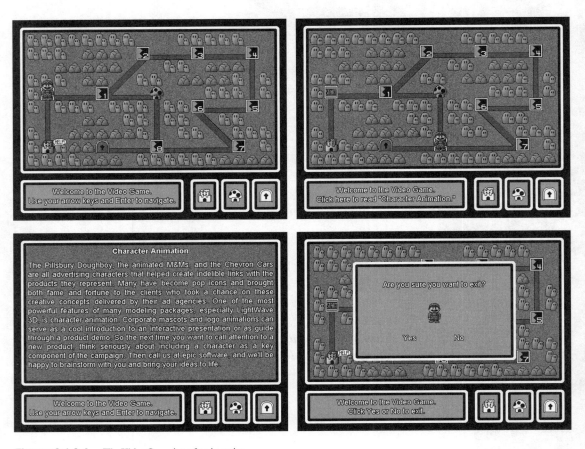

Figures 9.1-9.4 *The Video Game interface in action.*

APPROACHING THE "VIDEO GAME" INTERFACE

The Video Game interface attempts to give off a campy, nostalgic feeling that can be accomplished only through keyboard interaction. Thanks to a bit of Lingo code, the user can move the video game character around the Stage and use the Enter key (Return on Macintosh) to move back and forth between sections. Although keyboard interaction better serves to transport the user back into the early days of home entertainment systems, the mouse is still generally the preferred input device. Therefore, to keep the user happy, you must provide a means of navigation in which the user can input either keyboard or mouse commands. Although this may seem unnecessary and even redundant, you must remember that a little extra time spent on your part might save your audience a great deal of confusion.

UNDERSTANDING THE VIDEO GAME INTERFACE

Accepting keyboard input is fairly simple. The tricky part of the Video Game interface is getting the character to walk from spot to spot based on that keyboard input. To keep track of the character's possible locations, or stations, a list variable named `station` is used to store the coordinates of each of the stations. The character's behavior uses the `global` variable's location and destination to store the number of the current station and the station toward which the character is walking. If the two variables are equal, the character is not moving and the Enter key (Return on Macintosh) can be used to access the section indicated by the character's location. To view the various Lingo scripts of the Scripts cast, follow these steps:

1. Open the `vg.dir` file from the 09 - Video Game folder as specified in Appendix A, "Guide to Common Tasks." The Scripts cast contains the 14 Lingo Scripts shown in Table 9.1.

Table 9.1   The Scripts Cast Lingo Scripts

Script Name	Description
Global	Initializes *global* variables and handles keyboard input.
Wait	Makes the movie repeat the current frame over and over until otherwise specified.
Set Message	Sets the text of the Status member based on a specified string when the user's mouse enters the bounds of its associated sprite and back to normal when the mouse leaves.
Player	Moves its associated sprite from the location item of the *station* list to the destination item.
Station	Initializes its item of the *station* list to the location of its associated sprite when the sprite begins and instructs the character sprite to move instantly to the associated sprite when the user clicks it.
Help Bubble	Changes the opacity of its associated sprite based on its *animation* property to create a blinking effect.
Section Text	Sets the cast member of its associated sprite based on the *location* variable.
Section Link	Sets the Status member to its default value and plays the Text marker with a transition when the user clicks its associated sprite.
Help Link	Sets the Status member to its default value and plays the Help marker with a transition when the user clicks its associated sprite.
Web Link	Sets the Status member to its default value and opens http://www.epicsoftware.com in a web browser when the user clicks its associated sprite.
Exit Link	Sets the Status member for exit confirmation and plays the Exit marker when the user clicks its associated sprite.
Main Link	Sets the Status member to its default value and plays the Main marker with a transition when the user clicks its associated sprite.
Yes Link	Stops the movie completely when the user clicks its associated sprite.
No Link	Sets the Status member to its default value and plays the Main marker when the user clicks its associated sprite.

2. Within the Cast window, double-click the Global member. Director will display the Global script within the Script window.

3. In the Script window, use the Previous Cast Member and Next Cast Member buttons to view each of the Lingo scripts in the Scripts cast.

After browsing through the Video Game interface's scripts and taking a look at its organization in the Score, you should have a good understanding of the logic behind this interface. If some of its aspects are still not clear, you may want to refer to Appendix B, "Guide to Lingo Programming." Although understanding the innerworkings of the

Video Game interface at this time is not completely necessary, it should make things easier for you as you re-create the interface throughout the rest of this chapter.

CREATING AND IMPLEMENTING FILM LOOPS

In Director, a film loop is a type of cast member that consists of a group of sprites that have been combined to save space in the Score or to produce a repeating animation. You might think of a film loop as a miniature Director movie. Film loops use their own playback heads that advance independent of the Director movie's Score. Sprites within a film loop can use their own behavior scripts and ink effects just as they would normally. However, you cannot apply ink effects to a film loop as a whole. You must be sure to have your sprites looking the way you want them to look before compiling them into a film loop. To create the Player film loop and position it within the Score and the Stage, follow the steps outlined in Procedure 9.1.

Procedure 9.1 Creating and Implementing Film Loops

1. Open the `vgtemp.dir` file from the 09 - Video Game folder as specified in Appendix A.

2. In the Cast window, click the Choose Cast button and select the Media option. Director will display the Media cast within the Cast window.

3. Next, from the Score window, click cell 1 of channel 32, press and hold the Shift key, and then click cell 8 of channel 32. Director will highlight cells 1 through 8 of channel 32 (see Figure 9.5).

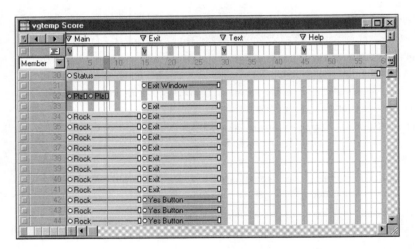

Figure 9.5 *The selected sprites.*

4. Click the Insert menu and select the Film Loop option. Director will display the Create Film Loop dialog box.

   You can achieve the same effect by dragging the selected sprites into the Cast window. Director will create the new film loop in whatever spot you drag the sprites.

5. In the Name field, type **Player** and then press the Enter key (Return on Macintosh). Director will create a film loop named Player within the Cast window (see Figure 9.6).

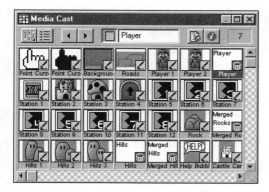

Figure 9.6 *The Player member of the Media cast.*

6. Drag the Player member from the Cast window into cell 15 of channel 32 of the Score window. Director will display the Player loop within the Stage window.

7. In the Score window, click cell 16 of channel 32. Director will highlight the Player loop.

8. Using the Property Inspector window, type **196** into the Y field and then press the Enter key (Return on Macintosh). Director will update the Player loop within the Stage window (see Figure 9.7).

Figure 9.7 *The Player loop.*

9. In the Score window, click cell 1 of channel 32, press and hold the Shift key, and then click cell 8 of channel 32. Director will highlight cells 1 through 8 of channel 32.

>>>

Because you have already created a film loop using the selected sprites, you no longer need them in the Score window. You can split a film loop back into its original sprites at any time by copying the film loop cast member from the Cast window and pasting it into the Score window.

10. Press the Delete key to remove the selected sprites from the Score window.

Not all film loops are used for the purpose of animation. Without the use of a film loop, the rocks of the Video Game's background would require 33 sprite channels. This may seem only a minor inconvenience until you consider that the hill animations would require an additional 65 channels. By just combining similar sprites to create film loops, you save nearly 100 sprite channels. To create the Merged Rocks film loop and position it within the Score and the Stage, follow the steps outlined in Procedure 9.2.

Procedure 9.2   **Creating and Positioning a Film Loop in the Score and the Stage**

1. In the Score window, click cell 1 of channel 34, press and hold the Shift key, and then click cell 14 of channel 66. Director will highlight cells 1 through 14 of channels 34 through 66 (see Figure 9.8).

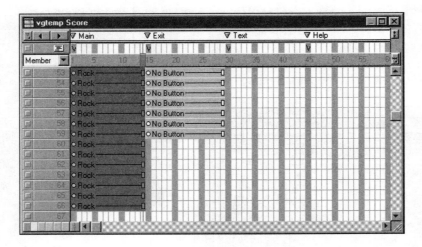

Figure 9.8   *The selected sprites.*

2. Click the Insert menu and select the Film Loop option. Director will display the Create Film Loop dialog box.

3. In the Name field, type **Merged Rocks** and then press the Enter key (Return on Macintosh). Director will create a film loop named Merged Rocks within the Cast window (see Figure 9.9).

4. Drag the Merged Rocks member from the Cast window into cell 1 of channel 3 of the Score window. Director will display the Merged Rocks loop within the Stage window.

5. In the Score window, drag cell 14 of channel 3 to frame 29. Director will extend the Merged Rocks loop to frame 29.

6. Click cell 2 of channel 3. Director will highlight the Merged Rocks loop.

7. In the Property Inspector window, type **352** into the X field, **208** into the Y field, and then press the Enter key (Return on Macintosh). Director will update the Merged Rocks loop within the Stage window.

8. Click cell 1 of channel 34 in the Score window and press and hold the Shift key, and then click cell 14 of channel 66. Director will highlight cells 1 through 14 of channels 34 through 66.

9. Press the Delete key to remove the selected sprites from the Score window.

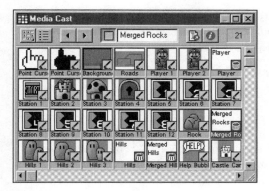

Figure 9.9 *The Merged Rocks member of the Media cast.*

Although combining the Rock sprites into a Merged Rocks film loop was not completely necessary, you will most likely find the resulting sprite much easier to deal with than the 33 original sprites. It is true that the user would never be able to tell the difference, but you should try to keep your Director source files as neat and orderly as possible to prevent other programmers from running into problems if they need to edit or expand your work.

COMPLETING THE PLAYER BEHAVIOR

The Player behavior creates the unique effect of a character that can walk around the screen. Although this may seem fairly simple when compared to today's complex video games, it is enough to amuse the reader as he browses through the information contained within the interface. Remember that the purpose of an interface is generally to provide some sort of information, but that doesn't mean that it must be purely utilitarian. To complete the Player behavior, follow the steps outlined in Procedure 9.3.

Procedure 9.3 Completing the Player Behavior

1. In the Cast window, click the Choose Cast button and select the Scripts option. Director will display the Scripts cast within the Cast window.

2. Click the Player member. Director will highlight the Player member.

3. Next click the Cast Member Script button. Director will display the Player script within the Script window.

4. Within the Script window, in the `prepareFrame` handler, type the following code:

```
if location = destination then
   my.member = member("Player 1", "Media")
   my.locH = station[destination].locH
   my.locV = station[destination].locV - 8
else
```

Note that the preceding five lines set the associated sprite's cast member to the Player 1 bitmap and its location on the Stage to the destination item of the `station` list if the character sprite is currently located at its final destination.

Note that the following line sets the associated sprite's cast member to the Player film loop to create a walking effect:

```
my.member = member("Player", "Media")
```

>>>

Note that the following conditional moves the associated sprite eight pixels horizontally closer to its intended destination. If the associated sprite is close enough, it moves directly to its final horizontal destination:

```
if my.locH + 8 < station[destination].locH then
    my.locH = my.locH + 8
else if my.locH - 8 > station[destination].locH then
    my.locH = my.locH - 8
else
    my.locH = station[destination].locH
end if
```

Note that the following conditional moves the associated sprite eight pixels vertically closer to its intended destination. If the associated sprite is close enough, it moves directly to its final vertical destination:

```
if my.locV + 8 < station[destination].locV - 8 then
    my.locV = my.locV + 8
else if my.locV - 8 > station[destination].locV - 8 then
    my.locV = my.locV - 8
else
    my.locV = station[destination].locV - 8
end if
```

Note that the following conditional sets the *location* variable equal to the *destination* variable if the associated sprite is currently located at its final destination:

```
if station[destination] = point(my.locH, my.locV+8) then
    location = destination
end if
end if
```

5. From the toolbar, click the Script Window button. Director will close the Script window.

Until you modify the Global script to accept keyboard input, you will not be able to make the character walk around the screen. You can, however, click the stations to access their sections and the character will be located at the appropriate station when you return to the Main section. The video game character is now fully able to walk. You need only to set the *destination* variable to an appropriate station number.

ACCEPTING KEYBOARD INPUT

The most important part of the Global script's keyDown handler is its first line. This short conditional tells Lingo not to accept any sort of keyboard input while the character is in the process of walking to its destination. This eliminates confusion as to which section should display when the Enter key (Return on Macintosh) is pressed and prevents the character from leaving its indicated pathways. The handler uses other conditionals to react to the keyboard press based on the current frame and the key that is pressed. Remember that the key property indicates the string value of the last key pressed, and the keyCode property indicates its numeric ASCII value. To complete the Global script, follow the steps outlined in Procedure 9.4.

Procedure 9.4   Accepting Keyboard Input

1. Within the Cast window, double-click the Global member. Director will display the Global script within the Script window.

2. In the keyDown handler, type the following code:

```
if location <> destination then exit
```

Note that the preceding line exits the current handler if the value of the *location* variable is not equal to destination.

Note that the following conditional ensures that the current frame is not frame 1, and then plays the Main marker with a transition if the user has pressed the Enter key (Return on Macintosh) and is not in the Exit section (frame 15). If a different key was pressed or the current frame is frame 15, the conditional exits the current handler. This is because the only key the user should press outside of the Video Game interface's Main section is the Enter key (Return on Macintosh):

```
if the frame <> 1 then
  if the key = return and the frame <> 15 then
    puppetTransition("Square Transition")
    play "Main"
  else
    exit
  end if
end if
```

Note that the following 11 lines set the *destination* variable based on the *location* variable if the user has pressed the left-arrow key:

```
if the keyCode = 123 then
  case location of
    3: destination = 5
    5: destination = 1
    6: destination = 5
    7: destination = 6
    8: destination = 7
    9: destination = 10
    11: destination = 12
    12: destination = 4
  end case
```

Note that the following 10 lines set the *destination* variable based on the *location* variable if the user has pressed the right-arrow key:

```
else if the keyCode = 124 then
  case location of
    1: destination = 5
    4: destination = 12
    5: destination = 3
    6: destination = 7
    7: destination = 8
    10: destination = 9
    12: destination = 11
  end case
```

Note that the following eight lines set the *destination* variable based on the *location* variable if the user has pressed the up-arrow key:

```
else if the keyCode = 126 then
  case location of
    2: destination = 1
    5: destination = 6
    9: destination = 8
    11: destination = 10
    12: destination = 3
  end case
```

>>>

Note that the following eight lines set the *destination* variable based on the *location* variable if the user has pressed the down-arrow key:

```
else if the keyCode = 125 then
  case location of
     1: destination = 2
     3: destination = 12
     6: destination = 5
     8: destination = 9
    10: destination = 11
  end case
```

Note that the following lines check whether the user has pressed the Enter key (Return on Macintosh), and then play the Help marker with a transition if the location is 2, open the Web site http://www.epicsoftware.com if the location is 3, play the Exit marker (and set the status text appropriately) if the location is 4, or play the Text marker with a transition if the location is 1. This gives the user the option of pressing the Enter key (Return on Macintosh) to enter the highlighted section instead of clicking it:

```
else if the key = return then
  if location = 2 then
    puppetTransition("Square Transition")
    play "Help"
  else if location = 3 then
    goToNetPage("http://www.epicsoftware.com")
  else if location = 4 then
    member("Status", "Text").text = member("Status", "Text").text.line[1] &
return & "Click Yes or No to exit."
    play "Exit"
  else if location <> 1 then
    puppetTransition("Square Transition")
    play "Text"
  end if
end if
```

3. In the toolbar, click the Script Window button. Director will close the Script window.

At this point, you should have a fully functional Video Game interface that can be controlled by the mouse or the keyboard. Try previewing your interface and making sure that everything works as it should. You might not notice any problems, but someone less familiar with computers might. The Help section is just not easy enough to access. If you move your mouse cursor over it, you can tell by the status text to click the castle; but the type of user who would access the Help section probably wouldn't want to drag her mouse around and read status text. Therefore, you should add a clear-text label to accommodate this type of user. As a general rule, the Help button should be among the most obvious of your interface's controls.

ADDING A BLINKING HELP BUBBLE

One way to label the interface's Help button without disrupting the interface's video game theme is to create a speech bubble coming from the castle. In an actual video game, this speech bubble might indicate that you must save a trapped princess, but in the Video Game interface, the user is the one really asking for help. The bubble should not immediately jump out at the average user, but it should be obvious to the user who is looking for help. To position the Help Bubble sprite within the Score and the Stage, follow the steps outlined Procedure 9.5.

Procedure 9.5   Adding a Blinking Help Bubble

1. Within the Cast window, click the Choose Cast button and select the Media option. Director will display the Media cast within the Cast window.

2. Drag the Help Bubble member from the Cast window into cell 1 of channel 17 of the Score window. Director will display the Help Bubble sprite within the Stage window.

3. In the Score window, drag cell 14 of channel 17 to frame 29. Director will extend the Help Bubble sprite to frame 29.

4. Click cell 2 of channel 17. Director will highlight the Help Bubble sprite.

5. From the Property Inspector window, type **108** into the X field, **300** into the Y field, and then press the Enter key (Return on Macintosh). Director will update the Help Bubble sprite within the Stage window (see Figure 9.10).

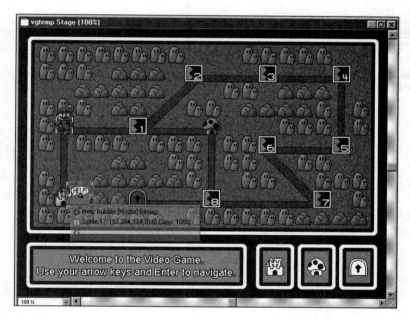

Figure 9.10   *The Help Bubble sprite.*

6. In the Background Color field, type **#FF00FF** and press the Enter key (Return on Macintosh). Director will set the background color of the Help Bubble sprite to magenta.

7. Within the Property Inspector window, click the Ink drop-down list and select the Background Transparent option. Director will remove the magenta background from the Help Bubble sprite (see Figure 9.11).

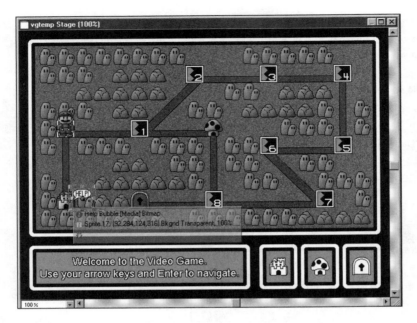

Figure 9.11 *The Help Bubble sprite.*

Having the speech bubble blink serves to both accentuate its importance and separate it from the interface's static background elements. The Video Game interface is so full of items such as hills and rocks that an inactive speech bubble could easily be overlooked. The intermittent blinking also adds to the campy appeal of the interface by indicating that an unseen victim trapped in the castle has nothing better to do than repeatedly yell the word "help." To create and apply the Help Bubble behavior, follow the steps outlined in Procedure 9.6.

Procedure 9.6   Creating and Applying the Help Bubble Behavior

1. In the Cast window, click the Choose Cast button and select the Scripts option. Director will display the Scripts cast within the Cast window.
2. Create a behavior script named Help Bubble as specified in Appendix A.
3. Click the Help Bubble member. Director will highlight the Help Bubble member (see Figure 9.12).
4. Click the Cast Member Script button. Director will display the Help Bubble script within the Script window.
5. Within the Script window, type the following code:

```
property my, animation

on beginSprite me
   my = sprite(me.spriteNum)
   animation = 0
end
```

Note that the following handler uses the `animation` property to toggle the associated sprite's opacity between 0 and 100 percent every 16th, 18th, and 20th frame. The `animation` property keeps track of the frame number by incrementing, or adding 1 to itself each time the `enterFrame` handler executes:

```
on enterFrame
   if animation mod 20 = 0 or animation mod 20 = 16 or animation mod 20 = 18 then
```

```
       if my.blend = 0 then
          my.blend = 100
       else
          my.blend = 0
       end if
    end if

       animation = animation + 1
    end
```

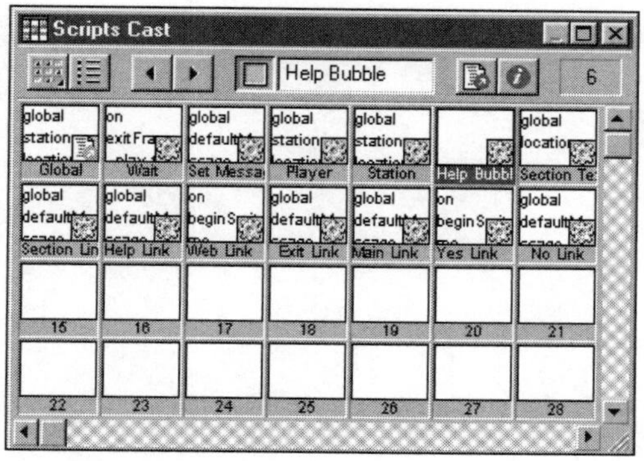

Figure 9.12   *The Help Bubble member of the Scripts cast.*

6. From the toolbar, click the Script Window button. Director will close the Script window.

7. Apply the Help Bubble behavior to the Help Bubble sprite that begins in cell 1 of channel 17 as specified in Appendix A.

If you preview your Video Game interface now, it should appear exactly like the original Video Game. When testing an interface that accepts keyboard input, you should always make sure to have the Stage window highlighted. Your keyboard commands should work whether or not you have another window highlighted, but they might trigger additional actions within Director. Be especially careful when testing interfaces that work with the Alt key (Option on Macintosh) or the Control key (Command on Macintosh).

MAKING ADJUSTMENTS

If you want to edit the content of the Video Game interface, you need to edit only the various members of the Text cast. Adding or removing sections from the interface, however, might prove exceedingly difficult. Unless you think that you fully understand the workings of the Video Game interface and are comfortable re-creating the Roads bitmap and reorganizing the Stage, you should adjust your desired content to fit into eight sections. Remember to keep track of how much Stage area your text fields are using and keep text from leaking out of the green background rectangle. You can change the font sizes of the text fields to fit more or less information in each section.

"Examine what you believe to be impossible, then change your belief."
—Dr. Wayne Dyer

▼▼▼ **chapter 10**
media browser

Figures 10.1-10.4   *The Media Browser interface in action.*

APPROACHING THE "MEDIA BROWSER" INTERFACE

Unlike most applications built with Director, the Media Browser contains its own graphical title bar, scrollbar, and window borders. When the interface is compiled into an executable projector with the In a Window option selected and the Show Title Bar check box unchecked, it can be moved, resized, minimized, and even maximized just like a normal window. Although it is true that such basic windows functions have already been built for you by your operating system, you will discover that learning to control the dimensions and coordinates of your Director movies manually can give you the freedom you need to create truly impressive interfaces.

UNDERSTANDING THE MEDIA BROWSER INTERFACE

Although the idea of changing the position of your interface through Lingo may seem a little difficult, it really all boils down to one command. You can set both the dimensions and the coordinates of the Stage by setting the `rect` property of the `activeWindow` system property. System properties are denoted by the use of the keyword `the`, so the `activeWindow` property can be accessed by typing **the activeWindow**. In some situations, you must enclose the `the` keyword and its system property in parentheses to ensure that Lingo sees the two words as a single item. You can change the `rect` property of `activeWindow` by typing **(the activeWindow).rect =** and then a rectangle value. If you are not yet familiar with rectangle values, do not worry. You will be. To view the various Lingo scripts of the Scripts cast, follow these steps:

1. Open the `mb.dir` file from the 10 - Media Browser folder as specified in Appendix A, "Guide to Common Tasks." The Scripts cast contains the 29 Lingo scripts shown in Table 10.1.

Table 10.1 The Scripts Cast Lingo Scripts

Script Name	Description
Global	Initializes $global$ variables, refreshes sprites, and sets the Stage dimensions and coordinates.
Wait	Makes the movie repeat the current frame over and over until otherwise specified.
Play First Frame	Plays frame 1 when the playback head exits its associated frame.
Set Last Item	Sets the $global$ variable $lastItem$ to a specified value and $pageY$ to zero.
Set Layer	Sets its associated sprite's layer to a specified value.
Set Cursor	Sets its associated sprite's cursor to a specified value.
Set Message	Sets the text of the Title Text member to a specified string when the user's mouse enters the bounds of its associated sprite and back to normal when the mouse leaves.
Button	Sets its associated sprite's cast member based on mouse interaction and its `name` property.
Draggable	Makes its associated sprite draggable horizontally and/or vertically.
Background	Makes its associated sprite stretch to fill the Stage each time its `refresh` function is called.
Title Bar	Makes its associated sprite update the position of the Stage each time its `refresh` function is called.
Bottom Bar	Makes its associated sprite update the height of the Stage each time its `refresh` function is called.
Left Bar	Makes its associated sprite update the width and horizontal location of the Stage each time its `refresh` function is called.
Right Bar	Makes its associated sprite update the width of the Stage each time its `refresh` function is called.
Top-Left Corner	Makes its associated sprite update the dimensions and location of the Stage each time its `refresh` function is called.
Top-Right Corner	Makes its associated sprite update the dimensions and vertical location of the Stage each time its `refresh` function is called.
Bottom-Left Corner	Makes its associated sprite update the dimensions and horizontal location of the Stage each time its `refresh` function is called.
Bottom-Right Corner	Makes its associated sprite update the dimensions of the Stage each time its `refresh` function is called.
Title Text	Sets its associated sprite's width and location each time its `refresh` function is called.
Scroll Bar	Sets its associated sprite's location each time its `refresh` function is called and adjusts the $pageY$ variable each time the user clicks it.

>>>

Table 10.1 Continued

Script Name	Description
Up Button	Sets its associated sprite's location each time its `refresh` function is called and adjusts the `pageY` variable each time the user clicks it.
Down Button	Sets its associated sprite's location each time its `refresh` function is called and adjusts the `pageY` variable each time the user clicks it.
Scroll Slider	Sets either its associated sprite's vertical location based on the `pageY` variable or the `pageY` variable based on the sprite's vertical location each time its `refresh` function is called. Also sets the sprite's visibility and location when `refresh` is called.
Maximize Button	Sets its associated sprite's location each time its `refresh` function is called and set the dimensions and coordinates of the Stage based on its `maximized` property each time the user clicks it.
Next Button	Sets its associated sprite's location each time its `refresh` function is called and plays the next frame each time the user clicks it.
Minimize Button	Sets its associated sprite's location each time its `refresh` function is called and executes the `appMinimize` command each time the user clicks it.
Close Button	Sets its associated sprite's location each time its `refresh` function is called and stops the movie entirely when the user clicks it.
Graphic Item	Sets its associated sprite's dimensions and location based on its sprite channel and parameters each time its `refresh` function is called.
Text Item	Sets its associated sprite's dimensions and location based on its sprite channel and parameters each time its `refresh` function is called.

2. Within the Cast window, double-click the Global member. Director will display the Global script within the Script window.

3. In the Script window, use the Previous Cast Member and Next Cast Member buttons to view each of the Lingo scripts in the Scripts cast.

After browsing through the Media Browser interface's scripts and taking a look at its organization in the Score, you should have a good understanding of the logic behind this interface. If some of its aspects are still not clear, you may want to refer to Appendix B, "Guide to Lingo Programming." Although understanding the innerworkings of the Media Browser interface at this time is not completely necessary, it should make things easier for you as you re-create the interface throughout the rest of this chapter.

COMPLETING THE GLOBAL SCRIPT

The trickiest part of allowing the user to move and resize the Stage is making sure that all the elements update themselves in the proper order. If the user is dragging the window's corner to resize the Stage, for example, the corner being dragged should set the new Stage dimensions before the other elements of the window position themselves based on those Stage dimensions. Updating window elements out of order can result in sloppy-looking delays in the movement of certain elements. The easiest way to gain control over the order in which the window elements update themselves is to give each element a custom function that updates its properties and, in some cases, the properties of related elements. Instead of calling this function (called here `refresh`) from one of the sprite's event handlers such as `prepareFrame`, you should place its call in the `prepareFrame` handler of the Global movie script (along with all the calls to the `refresh` functions of other window elements). To complete the Global script, follow the steps outlined in Procedure 10.1.

Procedure 10.1   Completing the Global Script

1. Open the `mbtemp.dir` file from the 10 - Media Browser folder as specified in Appendix A.

2. In the Cast window, double-click the Global member. Director will display the Global script within the Script window.

3. In the `prepareFrame` handler, type the following code:

```
if the frame = 1 then exit
```

Note that the preceding line exits the current handler if the playback head is currently on frame 1.

Note that the following loop calls the `refresh` functions of any sprite in channels two through nine currently being dragged.

```
repeat with i = 2 to 9
   if sprite(i).dragging then sendSprite(i, #refresh)
end repeat
```

Note that the following loop calls the `refresh` functions of any sprite in channels two through nine currently not being dragged. This ensures that all sprites two through nine will be refreshed starting with the one that the user is currently dragging:

```
repeat with i = 2 to 9
   if not sprite(i).dragging then sendSprite(i, #refresh)
end repeat
```

Note that the following loop calls the `refresh` functions of all sprites 10 through 18:

```
repeat with i = 10 to 18
   sendSprite(i, #refresh)
end repeat
```

Note that the following conditional sets the *pageY* variable to its minimum value if it is currently less than it should be:

```
if pageY < stageH - 40 - pageH then pageY = stageH - 40 - pageH
```

Note that the following conditional sets the *pageY* variable to its maximum value if it is currently more than it should be:

```
if pageY > 0 then pageY = 0
```

Note that the following seven lines update the `mediaTop` properties and call the `refresh` functions of the page items, and then update the *pageH* variable based on the position of the last page item:

```
sprite(19).mediaTop = pageY + 40
sendSprite(19, #refresh)
repeat with i = 20 to lastItem
   sprite(i).mediaTop = sprite(i-1).mediaTop + sprite(i-1).height + 10
   sendSprite(i, #refresh)
end repeat
pageH = sprite(lastItem).mediaTop + sprite(lastItem).height - pageY - 20
```

Note that the following lines call the `refresh` function of sprite 1 and then update the dimensions and coordinates of the Stage based on *global* variables:

```
sendSprite(1, #refresh)
(the stage).rect = rect(stageX, stageY, stageX+stageW, stageY+stageH)
```

>>>

Note that the `rect` function accepts four integers as arguments and returns a rectangle value. The first two arguments are used for the coordinates of the top-left corner of the rectangle. The second two make up the bottom-right corner.

4. Within the toolbar, click the Script Window button. Director will close the Script window.

Now that you have completed the Global script, the `refresh` function of each of the window elements should execute exactly once every frame. If you were to preview your movie at this point, most of the elements would fall right into place. Of course, the actual content of the interface has not yet been activated, but the window itself should look about right. One major flaw is glaring, however. None of the elements, such as the title bar and window borders, can be dragged by the user. You must complete the Draggable behavior before you can be sure that your interface is working correctly.

COMPLETING THE DRAGGABLE BEHAVIOR

You might already be aware of Director's built-in methods of allowing the user to drag sprites around the Stage. To make a sprite draggable, all you really need to do is highlight it and click the Moveable button within the Property Inspector window. Alternatively, you can accomplish this in Lingo by setting a sprite's `moveableSprite` property to `true`. You must learn how to make a sprite draggable manually, however, because the `moveableSprite` property does not work in all situations. For the purposes of the Media Browser interface, the Draggable behavior must not edit the sprite's actual location. It must instead edit the sprite's x and y properties so that the sprite's location will not change until the Global script calls the sprite's `refresh` function. Another reason the `moveableSprite` property would not work in this situation is that the `dragging` property is needed to let the Global script know when a sprite is actually being dragged. To complete the Draggable behavior, follow the steps outlined in Procedure 10.2.

Procedure 10.2   Completing the Draggable Behavior

1. Within the Cast window, click the Draggable member. Director will highlight the Draggable member (see Figure 10.5).

2. In the Cast window, click the Cast Member Script button. Director will display the Draggable script within the Script window.

3. In the `enterFrame` handler, type the following code:

```
if the mouseUp then dragging = false
```

Note that the preceding line sets the `dragging` property to `false` if the user is not currently pressing the mouse button.

Note that the following conditional sets the x property based on the horizontal location of the mouse if the associated sprite is currently being dragged horizontally. Otherwise, it sets the x property based on the horizontal location of the associated sprite:

```
if dragging and dragX then
    x = the mouseH + offsetX
else
    x = my.locH
end if
```

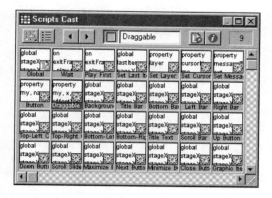

Figure 10.5 *The Draggable member within the Cast window.*

Note that the following conditional sets the y property based on the vertical location of the mouse if the associated sprite is currently being dragged vertically. Otherwise, it sets the y property based on the vertical location of the associated sprite:

```
if dragging and dragY then
    y = the mouseV + offsetY
else
    y = my.locV
end if
```

4. In the `mouseDown` handler, type the following code:

```
dragging = true
offsetX = my.locH - the mouseH
offsetY = my.locV - the mouseV
```

Note that the preceding three lines set the `dragging` property to `true`, set the `offsetX` property to the difference in pixels between the horizontal locations of the associated sprite and the mouse, and set the `offsetY` property to the difference in pixels between the vertical locations of the associated sprite and the mouse.

5. From the toolbar, click the Script Window button. Director will close the Script window.

If you preview your movie at this point, it should be fairly obvious that something is wrong with both the window's title bar and its bottom-right corner. You should be able to resize the window by dragging its borders; but if you attempt to drag the title bar or the bottom-right corner, nothing will happen. This is because the Draggable behavior only enables you to change a sprite's x and y properties, not actually change its location. In the Media Browser template, the `refresh` functions of the Title Bar and Bottom-Right Corner behaviors have been left blank. Therefore, the Global script has no way to move the sprites based on their x and y properties.

AFFECTING THE STAGE THROUGH DRAGGABLE SPRITES

Think about what your operating system actually does when you maximize a window. Basically, the window becomes slightly bigger than your screen (big enough to hide the window's borders), and the title bar ceases to be draggable. Because of how the Draggable behavior is set up, toggling a sprite's draggability through its `refresh` function is actually quite simple. When the maximized variable indicates that the window is maximized, the `refresh` function should change the sprite's cursor from Drag to Normal. Only when the window is not maximized should `refresh` adjust the Stage coordinates based on the sprite's x and y properties. To complete the Title Bar and Bottom-Right Corner behaviors, follow the steps outlined in Procedure 10.3.

Procedure 10.3   Completing the Title Bar and Bottom-Right Corner Behaviors

1. In the Cast window, click the Title Bar member. Director will highlight the Title Bar member (see Figure 10.6).

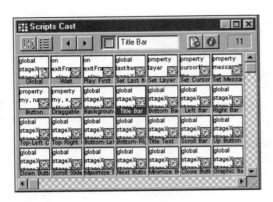

Figure 10.6   *The Title Bar member.*

2. Click the Cast Member Script button. Director will display the Title Bar script within the Script window.

3. In the `refresh` function, type the following code:

```
if maximized then
    my.cursor = [member("Normal", "Cursors"), member("Normal Mask", "Cursors")]
else
    my.cursor = [member("Drag", "Cursors"), member("Drag Mask", "Cursors")]
    if my.dragging then
        stageX = the activeWindow.rect.left + (my.x-my.width/2) - 10
        stageY = the activeWindow.rect.top + (my.y-my.height/2)
    end if
end if
```

Note that the preceding conditional sets the associated sprite's cursor to Normal if the maximized property has a value of `true`. Otherwise, it sets the sprite's cursor to Drag and adjusts the location of the Stage if the user is currently dragging the associated sprite.

Note that the following line stretches the associated sprite based on the width of the Stage:

```
my.rect = rect(10, 0, stageW-10, 30)
```

4. In the Cast window, click the Bottom-Right Corner member. Director will highlight the Bottom-Right Corner member (see Figure 10.7).

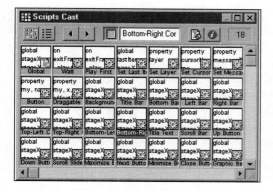

Figure 10.7 *The Bottom-Right Corner member.*

5. Click the Cast Member Script button. Director will display the Bottom-Right Corner script within the Script window.

6. In the `refresh` function, type the following code:

```
if my.dragging then
  stageW = (my.x+my.width/2)
  stageH = (my.y+my.height/2)
```

Note that the preceding three lines set the dimensions of the Stage based on the location of the associated sprite if the sprite is currently being dragged.

Note that the following conditional sets the Stage width to its minimum value if it is currently less than it should be:

```
if stageW < minW then
  my.x = my.x + (minW-stageW)
  stageW = minW
end if
```

Note that the following conditional sets the Stage height to its minimum value if it is currently less than it should be:

```
  if stageH < minH then
    my.y = my.y + (minH-stageH)
    stageH = minH
  end if
end if
```

Note that the following line positions the associated sprite based on the dimensions of the Stage:

```
my.rect = rect(stageW-10, stageH-10, stageW, stageH)
```

7. From the toolbar, click the Script Window button. Director will close the Script window.

At this point, the window of your Media Browser interface should be fully functional. However, Director really isn't the best place to test an interface that manipulates the location of the Stage. If you really want to make sure it works, you should create an executable projector file (as specified in Appendix A). Make sure that you select the In a Window option and uncheck the Show Title Bar check box of the Projector Options dialog box. When Director finishes, run the EXE file that was produced. Try dragging it around, resizing it, and maximizing it. You should definitely not have any problem with the Minimize button because `appMinimize` is a built-in Lingo command.

ACTIVATING THE PAGE ITEMS

A graphical window is fine, but for your interface to become useful, you must fill it with content. The Media Browser interface works sort of like a web browser that positions its images and text items one after another down the page by default. Think of each page item as actually being a media element and a line break. No two-page items can appear side-by-side in a section. When writing the `refresh` functions for the page items, do not worry about calculating the right vertical locations. The `mediaTop` properties of the page items are set to appropriate values in the `prepareFrame` handler of the Global script. Therefore, you can just assume that `mediaTop` represents an appropriate location for the top of the associated sprite when writing the `refresh` functions of the Graphic Item and Text Item behaviors. To complete the Graphic Item and Text Item behaviors, follow the steps outlined in Procedure 10.4.

Procedure 10.4   Activating the Page Items

1. Within the Cast window, click the Graphic Item member. Director will highlight the Graphic Item member (see Figure 10.8).

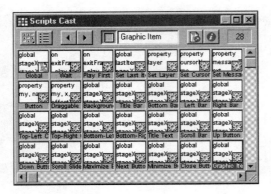

Figure 10.8   *The Graphic Item member.*

2. Click the Cast Member Script button. Director will display the Graphic Item script within the Script window.

3. In the `refresh` function, type the following code:

```
if mediaWidth.char[mediaWidth.char.count] = "%" then
   w = integer(mediaWidth.char[1..mediaWidth.char.count-1])
   w = integer(w*(stageW-60)/100)
else
   w = integer(mediaWidth)
end if
```

Note that the preceding conditional sets the `w` property to an appropriate width for the associated sprite based on the specified pixel or percentage value of `mediaWidth`.

Note that the following line sets the `h` property to an appropriate height for the associated sprite based on the `w` property:

```
h = integer(w*my.member.height/my.member.width)
```

Note that the following conditional positions the associated sprite based on the specified value of `mediaAlign`:

```
if mediaAlign = "Left" then
   my.rect = rect(20, mediaTop, 20+w, mediaTop+h)
```

```
else if mediaAlign = "Right" then
  my.rect = rect(stageW-40-w, mediaTop, stageW-40, mediaTop+h)
else
  my.rect = rect((stageW-20)/2-w/2, mediaTop, (stageW-20)/2+w/2, mediaTop+h)
end if
```

4. Click the Text Item member. Director will highlight the Text Item member (see Figure 10.9).

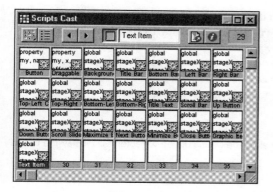

Figure 10.9   *The Text Item member.*

5. Click the Cast Member Script button. Director will display the Text Item script within the Script window.

6. In the Script window, in the `refresh` function, type the following code:

```
if mediaWidth.char[mediaWidth.char.count] = "%" then
  w = integer(mediaWidth.char[1..mediaWidth.char.count-1])
  w = integer(w*(stageW-60)/100)
else
  w = integer(mediaWidth)
end if
```

Note that the preceding conditional sets the `w` property to an appropriate width for the associated sprite based on the specified pixel or percentage value of `mediaWidth`.

Note that the following two lines set the dimensions of the associated sprite based on the `w` property and the sprite's cast member's height:

```
my.member.width = w
my.height = my.member.height
```

Note that the following conditional positions the associated sprite horizontally based on the specified value of `mediaAlign`:

```
if mediaAlign = "Left" then
  my.locH = 20
else if mediaAlign = "Right" then
  my.locH = stageW - 40 - w
else
  my.locH = (stageW-20)/2 - w/2
end if
```

Note that the following line positions the associated sprite vertically based on the `mediaTop` property:

```
my.locV = mediaTop
```

7. From the toolbar, click the Script Window button. Director will close the Script window.

By now, your Media Browser interface should behave almost exactly like the original. You should be able to cycle through the different sections and scroll through their media elements without any problem. However, you must master one more aspect of the Media Browser. Because you may want to fill the Media Browser interface with your own images and text, you must learn how to add and remove page items from the interface's sections.

ADDING A NEW PAGE ITEM

To add a new page item to a section, all the programmer must do is specify its width and horizontal alignment, and the Global script will position it vertically. The media elements you add to a section will appear on the page in the same order as they appear in the Score. You can have as many page items as you want in a section as long as you remember to specify the sprite channel in which the last page item is located to the frame's Set Last Item behavior. If the `lastItem` variable does not match up with the Score, it can result in errors or ignored page items. To add the Copyright Text member to the "About epic" section, follow the steps outlined in Procedure 10.5.

Procedure 10.5   Adding a New Page Item

1. In the Cast window, click the Choose Cast button and select the Media option. Director will display the Media cast within the Cast window.

2. Drag the Copyright Text member from the Cast window into cell 1 of channel 22 of the Score window. Director will display the Copyright Text sprite within the Stage window (see Figure 10.10).

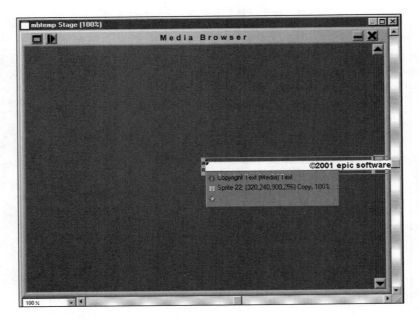

Figure 10.10   *The Copyright Text sprite.*

3. Within the Score window, click cell 2 of channel 22. Director will highlight the Copyright Text sprite.

4. In the Property Inspector window, type **-1000** into the X field, **-1000** into the Y field, and then press the Enter key (Return on Macintosh). Director will update the Copyright Text sprite within the Stage window.

5. Click and hold the button to the right of the Foreground Color icon and select the green swatch. Director will set the foreground color of the Copyright Text sprite to green.

6. Click the Ink drop-down list and select the Background Transparent option. Director will remove the background from the Copyright Text sprite.

7. Apply the Set Layer behavior to the Copyright Text sprite that begins in cell 1 of channel 22 as specified in Appendix A.

8. When the Parameters dialog box prompts you for a value, type **200** into the Layer Number field and then press the Enter key (Return on Macintosh). Director will apply the Set Layer behavior to the Copyright Text sprite.

9. Apply the Text Item behavior to the Copyright Text sprite that begins in cell 1 of channel 22 as specified in Appendix A.

10. When the Parameters dialog box prompts you for values, click the OK button (see Figure 10.11). Director will apply the Text Item behavior to the Copyright Text sprite.

11. In the Score window, click cell 1 of the Behavior channel. Director will highlight cell 1 of the Behavior channel (see Figure 10.12).

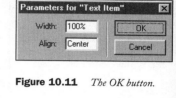

Figure 10.11 *The OK button.*

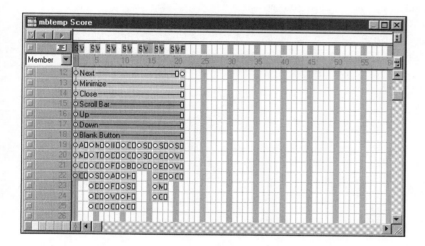

Figure 10.12 *Cell 1 of the Behavior channel within the Score window.*

12. Next click the Behavior tab in the Property Inspector window. Director will display the Behavior sheet.

13. Click the Parameters button (see Figure 10.13). Director will display the Parameters dialog box.

14. In the Last Item Number field, type **22** and press the Enter key (Return on Macintosh). Director will update the Set Last Item behavior's parameters.

Figure 10.13 *The Parameters button.*

At this point, you might want to preview your movie and test its various features to check for bugs. If you want to really see your Media Browser in action, however, you should create another executable projector file and run it. Look closely at your Media Browser and think about the Lingo code behind its construction. It may be that you will never use the Media Browser interface as a basis for future Director movies, but at the very least you have learned how to move and resize your interfaces through Lingo.

MAKING ADJUSTMENTS

In the preceding section, you learned how to add a page item to a section of the Media Browser interface. To remove a page item, just delete it from the Score and adjust the frame's Set Last Item behavior accordingly. For any new page items you create, you should apply the Set Layer behavior and enter a value of **200** in the Parameters dialog box's Layer Number field. Setting the layer to 200 ensures that the item will appear in front of the window's background but behind its borders. As for the Graphic Item and Text Item behaviors, you can enter any number or percentage you want in the Parameters dialog box Width field. Percentage values must end in a percent symbol (%) and are based on the width of the interface's window. In the Align field, you can enter a value of Left, Right, or Center. If you want to add or remove a section, you can add or delete page item sprites and adjust the lengths of the window sprites accordingly. Apply the Set Last Item and Wait behaviors exactly as they have been applied to the original section. If the length of your movie changes, you must be sure to drag the Play First Frame behavior of frame 21 to the movie's new ending frame.

"We shape our buildings; thereafter they shape us."
—Winston Churchill

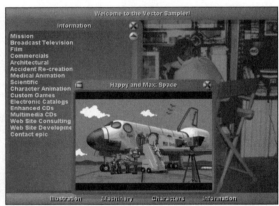

Figures 11.1-11.4 *The Vector Sampler interface in action.*

APPROACHING THE "VECTOR SAMPLER" INTERFACE

As mentioned in Chapter 4, "Ten-Step Guide," vector graphics differ from raster, or bitmap, graphics in that they are made up of curves and vertices rather than pixels. They are ideal for web design because they tend to download quickly and can be scaled and distorted with no loss of quality. Because Director is centered on the use of raster graphics, many programmers overlook its vector graphics capabilities. Although it is true that Director's vector drawing tools are somewhat limited, it is possible to build complex vector graphics within Director. You just may have to put forth a little more effort.

UNDERSTANDING THE VECTOR SAMPLER INTERFACE

The Vector Sampler interface was designed to accommodate developers who constantly need to update their interface's content. To add new media elements to the interface, the programmer must just add appropriately named files to the interface's folder and then modify the corresponding links text fields of the Text cast. Adding or removing media elements will not change the file size of the Vector Sampler interface because all media is stored in external files and imported only when needed. The interface uses each line of the Window Links text field to represent a numbered external media file. Therefore, you must always be sure that the number of lines in your links text field matches up with the number of its corresponding media files. To view the various Lingo scripts of the Scripts cast, follow these steps:

1. Open the vs.dir file from the 11 - Vector Sampler folder as specified in Appendix A., "Guide to Common Tasks." The Scripts cast contains the 19 Lingo scripts shown in Table 11.1.

Table 11.1 The Scripts Cast Lingo Scripts

Script Name	Description
Wait	Makes the movie repeat the current frame over and over until otherwise specified.
Set Layer	Sets its associated sprite's layer to a specified value.
Set Cursor	Sets its associated sprite's cursor to a specified value.
Set Message	Sets the text of the Status Text member to a specified string when the user's mouse enters the bounds of its associated sprite and back to normal when the mouse leaves.
Component	Sets its associated sprite's visibility to that of a specified sprite.
Follow Sprite	Sets its associated sprite's location to that of a specified sprite.
Button	Sets its associated sprite's cast member based on mouse interaction and its `name` property.
Section Button	Sets its associated sprite's text field cast member's `color` and `dropShadow` properties based on mouse interaction.
Scroll Bar	Adjusts the `textField` sprite's cast member's `scrollTop` property each time the user clicks its associated sprite.
Up Button	Adjusts the `textField` sprite's cast member's `scrollTop` property each time the user clicks its associated sprite.
Down Button	Adjusts the `textField` sprite's cast member's `scrollTop` property each time the user clicks its associated sprite.
Scroll Slider	Sets either its associated sprite's vertical location and the `textField` sprite's cast member's `scrollTop` property if the user is dragging the associated sprite or the sprite's vertical location based on the `textField` sprite's cast member's `scrollTop` property.
Window Links	Sets the viewer window's title text and imports and displays an image or text field for the viewer window when the user clicks its associated sprite and sets the text of the Status Text member to an appropriate string while the user's mouse is within its sprite's bounds.
Viewer Window	Sets its `viewerWindow` sprite's `visible` property to `false` and its location to its default value if the user drags the sprite outside the bounds of the Stage
Window Image	Sets its `windowImage` sprite's cursor and sets its dimensions to fill the Stage while the `fullScreen` property is `true`. Sets the `fullScreen` property to `false` and returns the sprite to its normal dimensions when the user clicks it when `fullScreen` is `true`.
Window Text	Sets its `windowText` sprite's visibility based on the visibility of the `viewerWindow` and `windowImage` sprites and catches mouse clicks so that nothing behind its sprite is clickable.

>>>

Table 11.1 Continued

Script Name	Description
Close Links Button	Plays the `Hide Links` marker when the user clicks its associated sprite.
Close Viewer Button	Sets the `viewerWindow` sprite's `visible` property to `false` when the user clicks its associated sprite.
Maximize Button	Sets the `windowImage` sprite's `fullScreen` property to `true` when the user clicks its associated sprite and sets its visibility based on that of the `windowImage` sprite.

2. In the Cast window, click the Wait member. Director will update the Cast window.

3. Next click the Cast Member Script button. Director will display the Wait script within the Script window.

4. From within the Script window, use the Previous Cast Member and Next Cast Member buttons to view each of the Lingo scripts in the Scripts cast.

After browsing through the Vector Sampler interface's scripts and taking a look at its organization in the Score, you should have a good understanding of the logic behind this interface. If some of its aspects are still not clear, you may want to refer to Appendix B, "Guide to Lingo Programming." Although understanding the innerworkings of the Vector Sampler interface at this time is not completely necessary, it should make things easier for you to re-create the interface throughout the rest of this chapter.

COMPILING VECTOR GRAPHICS ON THE STAGE

Unlike Macromedia Flash, Director's vector-drawing tools allow only one shape per cast member. (In Flash, cast members are called symbols.) This means that each vector cast member you create can have only a single fill style. If you want to create vector images with multiple colors, you must position several sprites on the Stage and then compile them into a film loop. Because of the superiority of Flash's vector-drawing tools, many programmers choose to create complex vectors in Flash and just import their SWF files into their Director movies. However, too much Flash content can bog down a Director movie and make things run slower than they should. Therefore, you should use Director's vector editor rather than Flash whenever possible. To create the Close Button, Close Button Over, and Close Button Down film loops, follow the steps outlined in Procedure 11.1.

Procedure 11.1   Compiling Vector Graphics on the Stage

1. Open the `vstemp.dir` file from the 11 - Vector Sampler folder as specified in Appendix A.

2. In the Cast window, click the Choose Cast button and select the Media option. Director will display the Media cast.

3. Drag the Black Circle member from the Cast window into cell 1 of channel 33 of the Score window. Director will display the Black Circle sprite within the Stage window (see Figure 11.5).

4. Drag the White Sphere member from the Cast window into cell 1 of channel 34 of the Score window. Director will display the White Sphere sprite within the Stage window.

5. In the Cast window, click the Choose Cast button and select the Buttons option. Director will display the Buttons cast within the Cast window.

6. Drag the Close member from the Cast window into cell 1 of channel 35 of the Score window. Director will display the Close sprite within the Stage window.

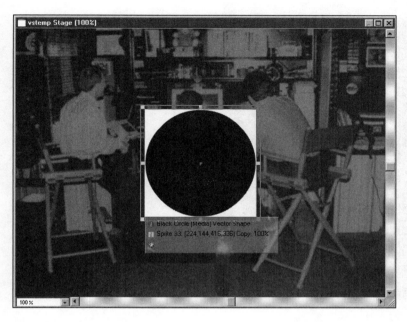

Figure 11.5 *The Black Circle sprite.*

7. In the Score window, click cell 2 of channel 33. Director will highlight the Black Circle sprite.

8. Using the Property Inspector window, type **322** into the X field, **242** into the Y field, **20** into the W field, **20** into the H field, and then press the Enter key (Return on Macintosh). Director will update the Black Circle sprite within the Stage window.

9. Click the Ink drop-down list, and select the Background Transparent option. Director will remove the background from the Black Circle sprite.

10. In the Blend drop-down list, type **25** and press the Enter key (Return on Macintosh). Director will set the opacity of the Black Circle sprite to 25 percent.

11. In the Score window, click cell 2 of channel 34. Director will highlight the White Sphere sprite.

12. Within the Property Inspector window, type **20** into the W field, **20** into the H field, and then press the Enter key (Return on Macintosh). Director will update the White Sphere sprite within the Stage window.

13. Next click the Ink drop-down list and select the Background Transparent option. Director will remove the background from the White Sphere sprite (see Figure 11.6).

14. Within the Score window, click cell 2 of channel 35. Director will highlight the Close sprite.

15. In the Property Inspector window, click the Ink drop-down list and select the Subtract Pin option (see Figure 11.7). Director will make the Close sprite subtract the RGB values of its pixels from the portion of the Stage it covers.

>>>

Figure 11.6 *The White Sphere sprite.*

Figure 11.7 *The Subtract Pin option.*

< 176 >

16. In the Score window, click cell 1 of channel 33, press and hold the Shift key, and then click cell 15 of channel 35. Director will highlight the button sprites in cells 1 through 15 of channels 33 through 35.

17. Click the Insert menu and select the Film Loop option. Director will display the Create Film Loop dialog box.

18. Using the Create Film Loop dialog box, in the Name field, type **Close Button** and then press the Enter key (Return on Macintosh). Director will create a film loop named Close Button within the Cast window (see Figure 11.8).

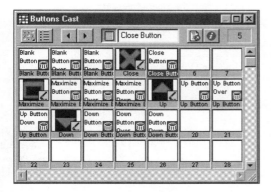

Figure 11.8 *The Close Button member of the Buttons cast within the Cast window.*

19. From the Score window, click cell 2 of channel 35. Director will highlight the Close sprite.

20. Next drag the selected Close sprite from cell 1 of channel 35 to cell 1 of channel 36 (see Figure 11.9).

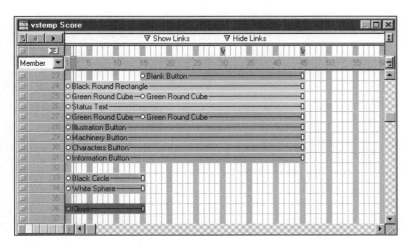

Figure 11.9 *The Close sprite within the Score window.*

21. Click cell 2 of channel 34. Director will highlight the White Sphere sprite.

22. Click the Edit menu and select the Copy Sprites option. Director will hold a copy of the White Sphere sprite in memory.

>>>

23. Next click cell 1 of channel 35. Director will update the Stage window.

24. Click the Edit menu and select the Paste Sprites option. Director will paste a copy of the White Sphere sprite into cells 1 through 15 of channel 35 from memory (see Figure 11.10).

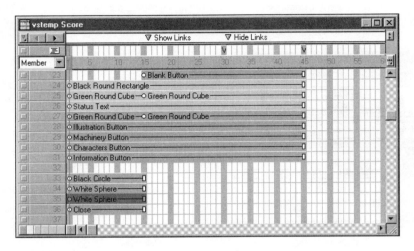

Figure 11.10   *The White Sphere sprite within the Score window.*

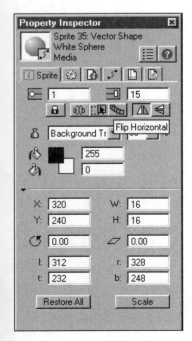

Figure 11.11   *The Flip Horizontal button within the Property Inspector window.*

25. In the Property Inspector window, type **16** into the W field, **16** into the H field, and then press the Enter key (Return on Macintosh). Director will update the White Sphere sprite within the Stage window.

26. Click the Blend drop-down list and select the 50 option. Director will set the opacity of the White Sphere sprite to 50 percent.

27. Next click the Flip Horizontal button (see Figure 11.11). Director will flip the White Sphere sprite horizontally.

28. Click the Flip Vertical button. Director will flip the White Sphere sprite vertically (see Figure 11.12).

    Note that the Flipping the White Sphere sprite both horizontally and vertically makes the shape appear concave as opposed to convex. This is because humans naturally expect light to come from above them. The standard light source for computer interfaces is in the upper-left corner of the screen.

29. In the Score window, click cell 1 of channel 33, press and hold the Shift key, and then click cell 15 of channel 36. Director will highlight the button sprites in cells 1 through 15 of channels 33 through 36.

30. Click the Insert menu and select the Film Loop option. Director will display the Create Film Loop dialog box.

31. In the Name field, type **Close Button Over** and then press the Enter key (Return on Macintosh). Director will create a film loop named Close Button Over within the Cast window.

Figure 11.12   *The White Sphere sprite within the Stage window.*

32. In the Score window, click cell 2 of channel 33. Director will highlight the Black Circle sprite.

33. Press the Delete key to remove the selected sprite from the Score window.

34. Click cell 2 of channel 35. Director will highlight the White Sphere sprite.

35. From the Property Inspector window, click the Blend drop-down list and select the 100 option. Director will set the opacity of the White Sphere sprite to 100 percent.

36. Using the Score window, click cell 1 of channel 34, press and hold the Shift key, and then click cell 15 of channel 36. Director will highlight the button sprites in cells 1 through 15 of channels 34 through 36 (see Figure 11.13).

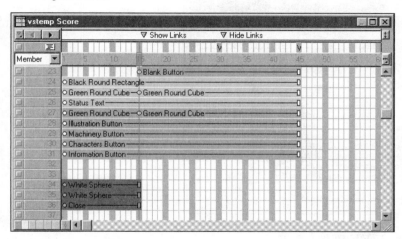

Figure 11.13   *The selected sprites within the Score window.*

37. Click the Insert menu and select the Film Loop option. Director will display the Create Film Loop dialog box.

38. In the Name field, in the Create Film Loop dialog box, type **Close Button Down** and then press the Enter key (Return on Macintosh). Director will create a film loop named Close Button Down within the Cast window.

39. Press the Delete key to remove the selected sprites from the Score window.

Now that you have created the three Close button film loops, you can treat them almost like ordinary bitmap images. When you create film loop sprites on the Stage, you can set their coordinates and dimensions just as you would any other sprite. However, film loops do not respond to certain sprite effects. You cannot rotate or flip film loops, for example, and they will ignore any ink applied to them. All ink effects must be applied directly to the original sprites before you compile them into a film loop.

ADDING THE CLOSE BUTTON

The Close button appears twice within the Vector Sampler interface. The button attached to the viewer window acts completely as expected. When the user clicks the viewer window's Close button, it makes the window (and all its components) invisible. The links window's Close button, however, behaves a bit differently. To create the effect of the links window sliding on and off the screen instead of appearing and disappearing, the Vector Sampler interface uses motion tweening in the Score. Therefore, instead of making the links window invisible, its Close button just plays the Hide Links marker. To position the Close Button loop within the Score and the Stage and apply its appropriate behaviors, follow the steps outlined in Procedure 11.2.

Procedure 11.2   Positioning the Close Button Loop Within the Score and the Stage

1. Drag the Close Button member from the Cast window into cell 15 of channel 6 of the Score window. Director will display the Close Button loop.

2. Drag the Close Button member from the Cast window into cell 15 of channel 17 of the Score window. Director will display the Close Button loop.

3. In the Score window, click cell 15 of channel 6, press and hold the Control key (Option on Macintosh), and then click cell 15 of channel 17. Director will highlight the Close Button sprites that begin in cell 15 of channel 6 and cell 15 of channel 17 (see Figure 11.14).

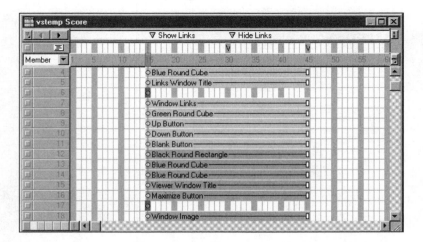

Figure 11.14   *The selected Close Button sprites within the Score window.*

4. Within the Property Inspector window, in the End Frame field, type **45** and then press the Enter key (Return on Macintosh). Director will extend the selected sprites to frame 45.

5. From the Score window, click cell 45 of channel 6, press and hold the Control key (Option on Macintosh), and then click cell 45 of channel 17. Director will highlight cell 45 of channels 6 and 17 (see Figure 11.15).

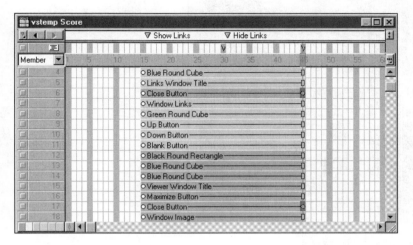

Figure 11.15   *The selected cells within the Score window.*

6. Click the Edit menu and select the Clear Keyframes option. Director will remove the keyframes from cell 45 of channels 6 and 17.

    Note that the only situation in which Director will create keyframes without being instructed to do so is when the programmer extends a sprite that is only one cell in length. Because the sprite has no ending cell, Director creates it and marks it as a keyframe.

7. Click cell 16 of channel 6. Director will highlight the Close Button loop.

8. Within the Property Inspector window, type **-30** into the X field, **45** into the Y field, and then press the Enter key (Return on Macintosh). Director will update the Close Button loop within the Stage window.

9. In the Score window, click cell 16 of channel 17. Director will highlight the Close Button loop.

10. Using the Property Inspector window, type **620** into the X field, **115** into the Y field, and then press the Enter key (Return on Macintosh). Director will update the Close Button loop within the Stage window (see Figure 11.16).

11. Apply the Button behavior to the Close Button sprite that begins in cell 15 of channel 6 as specified in Appendix A.

12. Apply the Follow Sprite behavior to the Close Button sprite that begins in cell 15 of channel 6 as specified in Appendix A.

13. When the Parameters dialog box prompts you for a value, type **3** into the Leader Number field, **300** into the X Offset field, **-195** into the Y Offset field, and then press the Enter key (Return on Macintosh). Director will apply the Follow Sprite behavior to the Close Button sprite.

14. Apply the Close Links Button behavior to the Close Button sprite that begins in cell 15 of channel 6 as specified in Appendix A.

>>>

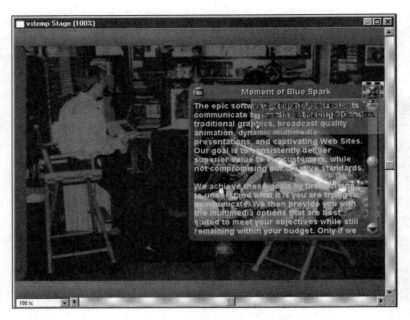

Figure 11.16 *The Close Button loop within the Stage window.*

15. Apply the Set Message behavior to the Close Button sprite that begins in cell 15 of channel 6 as specified in Appendix A.

16. When the Parameters dialog box prompts you for a value, type **Click to close the file list window**. into the Status Message field and then press the Enter key (Return on Macintosh). Director will apply the Set Message behavior to the Close Button sprite.

17. Apply the Button behavior to the Close Button sprite that begins in cell 15 of channel 17 as specified in Appendix A.

18. Apply the Follow Sprite behavior to the Close Button sprite that begins in cell 15 of channel 17 as specified in Appendix A.

19. When the Parameters dialog box prompts you for a value, type **13** into the Leader Number field, **150** into the X Offset field, **-125** into the Y Offset field, and then press the Enter key (Return on Macintosh). Director will apply the Follow Sprite behavior to the Close Button sprite.

20. Apply the Component behavior to the Close Button sprite that begins in cell 15 of channel 17 as specified in Appendix A.

21. When the Parameters dialog box prompts you for a value, type **13** into the Leader Number field and then press the Enter key (Return on Macintosh). Director will apply the Component behavior to the Close Button sprite.

22. Apply the Close Viewer Button behavior to the Close Button sprite that begins in cell 15 of channel 17 as specified in this Appendix A.

23. Apply the Set Message behavior to the Close Button sprite that begins in cell 15 of channel 17 as specified in Appendix A.

24. When the Parameters dialog box prompts you for a value, type **Click to close the viewing window.** into the Status Message field and then press the Enter key (Return on Macintosh). Director will apply the Set Message behavior to the Close Button sprite.

Of course the Set Message behavior is completely optional. You can apply it to as many or as few sprites as you want. If there is any question about whether a user might need a rollover status message to explain a particular element of your interface, you should go ahead and apply the Set Message behavior. Because rollover status messages do not unnecessarily affect the appearance of the interface, you are free to be as liberal with them as you choose.

COMPLETING THE WINDOW LINKS BEHAVIOR

The body text of the links window behaves very much like the scrolling model list of the epic Model Library interface. Both text fields use the line number clicked by the user to determine which media element to display. The Vector Sampler differs from the epic Model Library, however, in that it uses external media files rather than ordinary cast members. The simplest method of importing a media file through Lingo is to set the `fileName` property of a cast member. Director will immediately set the contents of the cast member that you specified to the external file. When importing text files, you must remember that Director will not keep any font or alignment formatting from the original cast member. Therefore, you should import text files into a temporary cast member and then assign the `text` property of whatever field you want to change to the contents of the that cast member. To complete the Window Links behavior, follow the steps outlined in Procedure 11.3.

Procedure 11.3 Completing the Window Links Behavior

1. In the Cast window, click the Choose Cast button and select the Scripts option. Director will display the Scripts cast within the Cast window.

2. Click the Window Links member. Director will highlight the Window Links member (see Figure 11.17).

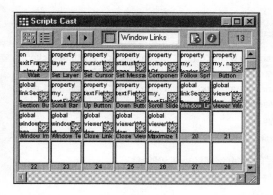

Figure 11.17 *The Window Links member within the Cast window.*

3. Next click the Cast Member Script button. Director will display the Window Links script within the Script window.

4. In the Script window, in the `prepareFrame` handler, type the following code:

```
if member("Links Window Title", "Text").text <> linkSection then
  member("Links Window Title", "Text").text = linkSection
  member("Window Links", "Text").text = member(linkSection && "Text",
"Text").text
end if
```

>>>

Note that the preceding conditional sets the links window's title text to the name of the current section and the links window's body text to a cast member based on the *linkSection* variable if the *linkSection* variable has recently changed.

5. In the `mouseDown` handler, type the following code:

```
if member("Status Text", "Text").text = "Welcome to the Vector Sampler!" then
  exit
```

Note that the preceding conditional exits the current handler if the status text is equal to its default value. The status text should only equal its default value if the user's mouse is over a part of the Window Links text that contains no text:

```
member("Viewer Window Title", "Text").text = member("Window Links",
"Text").text.line[lineNumber]
```

Note that the preceding line sets the viewer window's title text to the line of the Window Links member that the user just clicked:

```
if linkSection = "Information" then
  linkName = linkSection & lineNumber & ".txt"
  member("Window Text File", "Text").fileName = linkName
  windowText.member.text = member("Window Text File", "Text").text
  windowText.member.scrollTop = 0
  viewerWindow.visible = true
  windowImage.visible = false
  windowText.visible = true
else
  linkName = linkSection & lineNumber & ".jpg"
  windowImage.member.fileName = linkName
  viewerWindow.visible = true
  windowImage.visible = true
  windowText.visible = false
end if
```

Note that the preceding conditional sets the *linkName* variable based on the current section and link clicked, imports the `linkName` file into a temporary cast member, uses that cast member to set the viewer window's body text, and then sets the scrolling and visibilities of the viewer window to display the `linkName` file's text if the current section is the Information section. Otherwise, the conditional sets the *linkName* variable to the name of an image file, imports that file, and then displays it.

6. Next, in the `mouseWithin` handler, type the following code:

```
lineNumber = sprite(me.spriteNum).pointToParagraph(the mouseLoc)
```

Note that the preceding line sets the *lineNumber* variable to the number of the line of the associated sprite's text field to which the user's mouse is currently pointing.

```
if member("Window Links", "Text").text.line[lineNumber] = "" then
  member("Status Text", "Text").text = "Welcome to the Vector Sampler!"
else
  member("Status Text", "Text").text = "Click to view" && quote & member("Window
Links", "Text").text.line[lineNumber] & "." & quote
end if
```

Note that the preceding conditional sets the status text to its default value if the user's mouse is not currently over a line of text. Otherwise, it sets the status text to a prompt based on the line of text to which the mouse is pointing.

7. From the toolbar, click the Script Window button. Director will close the Script window.

By now, your Vector Sampler interface should be nearly complete. Preview your movie and test the behavior of the links window. Even though you have not yet completed the Window Image behavior, both text files and graphics files should be imported and displayed properly. The file importing is handled entirely within the Window Links script. The main purpose of the Window Image script is to enable the user to enlarge the viewer window's image to fill the Stage. Although the Maximize button is the designated control to enlarge the viewer window image, its only function is really to set the `fullScreen` property of the `windowImage` sprite to `true`. The window image itself must use the `fullScreen` property to set its own dimensions.

COMPLETING THE WINDOW IMAGE BEHAVIOR

The Window Image behavior is really quite simple. Each frame, the `windowImage` sprite checks to see whether the user has made its `fullScreen` property `true`. If `fullScreen` is `true`, the behavior sets the coordinates and dimensions of the image to fill the Stage. As a courtesy to the user, the behavior then changes the image's cursor to indicate that it has become clickable. Because the window image fills the entire Stage, the user can assume that clicking it somewhere will return it to normal. This is accomplished by setting `fullScreen` to `false` when the user clicks the image in `fullScreen` mode. The `mouseDown` handler must then set the images dimensions back to normal, but (so long as the Window Image behavior does not modify the image's location) the location of the window image is handled by its Follow Sprite behavior. To complete the Window Image behavior, follow the steps outlined in Procedure 11.4.

Procedure 11.4   Completing the Window Image Behavior

1. In the Cast window, click the Window Image member. Director will highlight the Window Image member (see Figure 11.18).

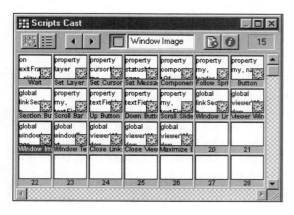

Figure 11.18   *The Window Image member.*

2. Click the Cast Member Script button. Director will display the Window Image script within the Script window.

3. Within the Script window, in the `prepareFrame` handler, type the following code:

```
if fullScreen then
   windowImage.width = 640
   windowImage.height = 480
   windowImage.locH = 320
   windowImage.locV = 240
   windowImage.cursor = [member("Point Cursor"), member("Point Cursor Mask")]
else
   windowImage.cursor = [member("Normal Cursor"), member("Normal Cursor Mask")]
end if
```

Note that the preceding conditional sets the viewer window's image to fill the Stage and its cursor to the Point cursor if the value of the `fullScreen` property is `true`. Otherwise, it sets the image's cursor back to normal.

4. In the `mouseDown` handler, type the following code:

```
if fullScreen then
   fullScreen = false
   windowImage.width = 320
   windowImage.height = 240
end if
```

Note that the preceding conditional sets `fullScreen` to `false` and the dimensions of the viewer window's image back to normal if the value of the `fullScreen` property is `true`. This enables the user to click the viewer window's image when it fills the Stage to return it to normal.

5. From the toolbar, click the Script Window button. Director will close the Script window.

Yet another advantage of vector graphics is their capability to be dynamically modified. If you decide that you would like a different color scheme for your Vector Sampler interface, you need only to edit the vector shapes of the Media cast and select new colors from the Vector Shape window. In fact, Director enables you to modify vector shapes entirely with Lingo code. Just change the `fillColor`, `strokeColor`, or `endColor` properties of a vector shape cast member to change its appearance instantly. You can even move and rotate vertices inside a shape as your movie is running. However, you may find that this is more trouble than it is worth.

MAKING ADJUSTMENTS

Because the Vector Sampler interface was designed with the idea of changing content in mind, adjusting the interface to suit your purposes is simpler than you might think. As mentioned earlier, the media files are all external, so you can edit them however you want and the Media Browser will update itself with them the next time it runs. To modify the names of the sections, just change the text in the appropriate Button members of the Text cast. Just be sure that each section has as many media files as it does lines in its Text member. The last line in each of the Text members should be blank. Do not count this line. It is just to let the interface know that there are no more links. Be certain to name your external media files properly or the Vector Sampler will not be able to find them. A filename should consist of the exact name of the section (the text in its Button member) and then a two-digit number indicating the line of the section's Text member where the file's description is located.

"*There are only two things in life: reasons and results.*
And reasons simply don't count."
—Robert Anthony

▼▼▼ chapter 12
epic portfolio

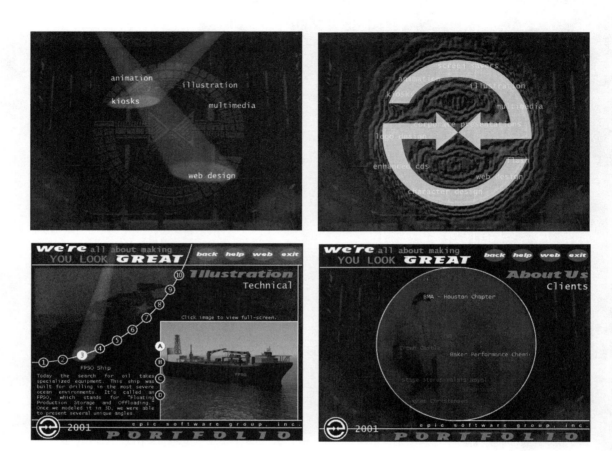

Figures 12.1-12.4 *The epic Portfolio interface in action.*

APPROACHING THE "EPIC PORTFOLIO" INTERFACE

The 2001 epic Portfolio interface is a revision of an interface that was originally created in Flash. Soon after creating the portfolio demo in Flash, epic software group, inc.™ decided that it wanted to add features to the demo that were available only through Director's Lingo and Xtras. To increase the capabilities of the existing Flash demo, epic compiled it into a single SWF movie and then imported it into Director. The new portfolio demo worked fine for a while, but when the time came to update its interface, epic decided to re-create the portfolio entirely in Director. Flash is fine for web design and animation, but when it comes to building powerful multimedia interfaces, nothing beats Director.

UNDERSTANDING THE EPIC PORTFOLIO INTERFACE

Although the epic Portfolio interface may seem overwhelmingly complex at first, if you look closely at its Score, you will see that most of the interface's animation is accomplished through simple tweening. When you understand the basic concepts of tweening in Director, all that remains is setting up the Score. Because you have already learned about tweening in Chapter 3, "The Basics," you will not need to concern yourself with the tween animations of the epic Portfolio interface. Moreover, most of the other effects, such as the spotlights, are easier than you might think. To view the various Lingo scripts of the Scripts cast, follow these steps:

1. Open the `ep.dir` file from the 12 - epic Portfolio folder as specified in Appendix A, "Guide to Common Tasks." The Scripts cast contains the 31 Lingo scripts shown in Table 12.1.

Table 12.1 The Scripts Cast Lingo Scripts

Script Name	Description
Global	Sets the global `section` list to an initial value of `["Main", "", ""]`.
Wait	Makes the movie repeat the current frame over and over until otherwise specified.
Illustration	Makes sure the `section` list is set to an appropriate value and then sets the section's background image based on the `section` list.
Animation	Makes sure the `section` list is set to an appropriate value and then sets the section's background image based on the `section` list.
Interactive	Makes sure the `section` list is set to an appropriate value and then sets the section's background image based on the `section` list.
About	Makes sure the `section` list is set to an appropriate value.
Halt	Stops the movie entirely when the playback head exits its associated frame.
Fade In	Gradually increases its associated sprite's opacity by a specified value until it reaches the specified value of its `maxValue` property unless the sprite's opacity is zero percent.
Blend Pulse	Gradually transitions its associated sprite's opacity between the specified values of its `maxValue` and `minValue` properties.
Visible if Section	Signals its associated sprite to fade in if the `section` list matches its specified section value. Otherwise, sets the sprite's opacity to zero percent.
Button	Sets its associated sprite's cast member based on mouse interaction and its `name` property and, if specified, plays a specified sound in a specified channel when the user clicks its associated sprite.
Blue Button	Sets its associated sprite's background color to white in its normal state and green in other states. For use with the Background Transparent ink.
Menu Button	Slides its associated sprite into place based on a specified `number` property.
Number Button	Sets its associated sprite's opacity based on the `section` list, adjusts the `spotlight` sprite based on mouse interaction, and sets the third item in the `section` list when the user clicks its associated sprite.
Letter Button	Sets its associated sprite's opacity based on the `section` list, adjusts the `spotlight` sprite based on mouse interaction, and sets the third item in the `section` list when the user clicks its associated sprite.
Hyperlink	Changes the color of its associated sprite based on mouse interaction and opens a specified web page when the user clicks its associated sprite.
Spotlight	Distorts its associated sprite to point at a specified sprite.
Number Spotlight	Distorts its associated sprite to point at a specified number or letter button sprite.
Intro Background	Plays the Build Main marker when the user clicks its associated sprite.
Overlay	Sets its associated sprite's layer to 1000 when the sprite begins.
Section Text	Sets its associated sprite's member's text to the second item of the `section` list when the sprite begins.

>>>

Table 12.1   Continued

Script Name	Description
Thumbnail	Gradually resizes its associated sprite to its default dimensions each time its `reset` function is called.
Thumbnail Full Screen	Sets its associated sprite's dimensions to fill the Stage while the `zooming` property is equal to one. Sets the `zooming` property to two and returns the sprite to its normal dimensions when the user clicks it when `zooming` is one.
Help Button	Sets its associated sprite's layer and plays the Help marker when the user clicks its associated sprite.
Web Button	Sets its associated sprite's layer and loads `http://www.epicsoftware.com` when the user clicks its associated sprite.
Exit Button	Sets its associated sprite's layer and plays the Exit marker when the user clicks its associated sprite.
Back Button	Sets its associated sprite's layer and plays the Main marker when the user clicks its associated sprite.
Yes Button	Stops any sound playing in channel 1 and plays the marker just after the playback head when the user clicks its associated sprite.
About Orb	Sets its associated sprite's cast member based on the second item of the `section` list when the sprite begins.
Clients Overlay	Sets its associated sprite's layer to 999 and sets the sprite's opacity based on the `section` list when the sprite begins.
Clients Text	Repeatedly moves down the screen with random opacity, velocity, and horizontal location for as long as the clients overlay is visible.

2. In the Cast window, double-click the Global member. Director will display the Global script within the Script window.

3. Use the Previous Cast Member and Next Cast Member buttons to view each of the Lingo scripts in the Scripts cast.

After browsing through the epic Portfolio interface's scripts and taking a look at its organization in the Score, you should have a good understanding of the logic behind this interface. If some of its aspects are still not clear, you may want to refer to Appendix B, "Guide to Lingo Programming." Although understanding the innerworkings of the epic Portfolio interface at this time is not completely necessary, it should make things easier for you as you re-create the interface throughout the rest of this chapter.

COMPLETING THE SPOTLIGHT BEHAVIOR

The moving spotlight is a popular effect used on the web and in various other multimedia interfaces. The method used in the Spotlight behavior is probably the simplest way to create this effect. The key to making the spotlight believable is the Add Pin ink. When the Add Pin ink is applied to a sprite, Director adds the RGB values of the sprite's pixels to the portion of the Stage it covers. This generally creates the effect of lightening a portion of the Stage. The `quad` property enables the programmer to distort a sprite by setting the locations of its four corners. All the programmer must do to produce a simple spotlight effect is create a generic image and then distort it so that it appears to shine on another sprite. To complete the Spotlight behavior, follow the steps outlined in Procedure 12.1.

Procedure 12.1 Completing the Spotlight Behavior

1. Open the `eptemp.dir` file from the 12 - epic Portfolio folder as specified in Appendix A.

2. In the Cast window, click the Spotlight member. Director will highlight the Spotlight member (see Figure 12.5).

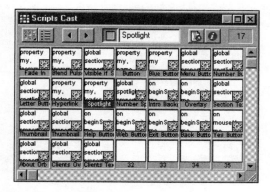

Figure 12.5 *The Spotlight member.*

3. Click the Cast Member Script button. Director will display the Spotlight script within the Script window.

4. Next, in the `prepareFrame` handler, type the following code:

```
topLeft = point(hSource, -100)
topRight = topLeft
bottomRight = point(leader.right+25, leader.bottom+10)
bottomLeft = point(leader.left-25, leader.bottom+10)
my.quad = [topLeft, topRight, bottomRight, bottomLeft]
```

Note that the preceding five lines calculate point values for each of the associated sprite's four corners and then set the sprite's `quad` property to a list containing those points. This distorts the associated sprite into a triangle with its top point at `hSource` and its base surrounding the leader sprite.

5. From the toolbar, click the Script Window button. Director will close the Script window.

The Spotlight behavior has the effect of creating a spotlight whose bottom corners appear 10 pixels below and 25 pixels on either side of the sprite it is following. You can adjust these numbers as you see fit. They are just an approximation based on trial and error. To aim the spotlight at smaller sprites, such as the interface's number buttons, you will probably need smaller values. The Number Spotlight behavior positions the bottom corners 7 pixels below and 20 pixels on either side of the leader sprite. If you want to create a truly generic Spotlight behavior that will work on images of any size, you should set the location of the spotlight's bottom corners based on the width of its leader sprite.

ACTIVATING THE MENU BUTTONS

The menu options that materialize in the epic Portfolio's main menu work much like any button. They all take advantage of the Button behavior, which sets their cast members based on mouse interaction. What makes the epic Portfolio interface's menu buttons unique is the way that they animate onto the screen in the main menu. The Menu Button behavior creates a link to a specified section but also causes its associated button to fall down the Stage until it reaches its desired vertical location. Actually, a menu button will fall slightly past its target vertical location and then snap into place. This adds to the effect by making it appear as if an invisible elastic string is holding each menu button in place. To complete the Menu Button behavior, follow the steps outlined in Procedure 12.2.

Procedure 12.2   Activating the Menu Button Behavior

1. In the Cast window, click the Menu Button member. Director will highlight the Menu Button member (see Figure 12.6).

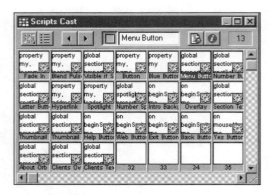

Figure 12.6   *The Menu Button member within the Cast window.*

2. Click the Cast Member Script button. Director will display the Menu Button script within the Script window.

3. Next, in the `prepareFrame` handler, type the following code:

```
if y < ty + 10 and not fallen then
  y = y + vy
  if y > ty + 20 then
    y = ty + 20
  end if
  vy = vy + 1.5
else
  fallen = true
  y = (y+ty)/2
end if
```

Note that the preceding conditional adds the value of `vy` to the `y` property, checks to make sure that `y` is no bigger than `ty` plus 20, and then adds 1.5 to the `vy` property if the sprite's `y` is less than 10 pixels past its target `ty` and the sprite has not yet reached its final destination. Otherwise, the conditional sets the fallen property to `true` and `y` to the average of `y` and `ty`. This creates the effect of allowing the associated sprite to fall until it is 10 pixels past a target `y` value and then sliding it into place. The fallen property keeps track of whether the sprite is falling down or sliding up.

```
my.locV = y
```

Note that the preceding line sets the associated sprite's vertical location to the value of the `y` property.

4. Within the Script window, in the `mouseUp` handler, type the following code:

```
section[1] = sectionlink.word[1]
section[2] = sectionlink.word[2]
play section[1]
```

Note that the preceding three lines set the first and second items in the `section` list to the first and second words in the `sectionLink` string, and then play the marker whose name matches the first item in the `section` list.

5. From the toolbar, click the Script Window button. Director will close the Script window.

If the menu buttons' opening animations ended with the Menu Button behavior, you would be finished with them by now. You may have noticed, however, that each menu button also contains the Fade In behavior. To use the Fade In behavior properly, a sprite must have either a white transparent background or no transparency at all. If the background is any color other than white, the sprite's image will shift colors when its `blend` property is below 100. The problem with having a white background is that Director will crop the image to remove any purely white borders. Therefore, your image's size may be changed. You should always keep the different states of a particular button the same size to avoid any quirky behavior. Aside from this, the Over and Down menu button states use white text, which could be made transparent. You can avoid these potential problems by using green backgrounds on the Over and Down images and white backgrounds on the normal button state images. By creating a simple behavior, you can set a menu button sprite's background color to green when it uses an Over or Down image and white otherwise. This means that the sprite's background will always be transparent, regardless of its color. Remember that, unlike the other button states, the blue menu buttons need white backgrounds so that they can fade in properly. To complete the Blue Button behavior, follow the steps outlined in Procedure 12.3.

Procedure 12.3   Completing the Blue Button Behavior

1. In the Cast window, click the Blue Button member. Director will highlight the Blue Button member (see Figure 12.7).

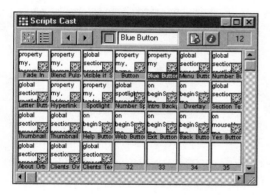

Figure 12.7   *The Blue Button member.*

2. Click the Cast Member Script button. Director will display the Blue Button script within the Script window.

3. In the `prepareFrame` handler, type the following code:

```
if my.member.name.word.count > 2 then
    my.bgColor = rgb(0, 255, 0)
else
    my.bgColor = rgb(255, 255, 255)
end if
```

Note that the preceding conditional sets the background color of the associated sprite to green if its cast member's name is more than two words long. Otherwise, it sets the background color to white. The sprite's cast member's name will contain two words normally and three in its Over and Down states. Because the sprite uses the Background Transparent ink, the value of `bgColor` will appear transparent.

4. From the toolbar, click the Script Window button. Director will close the Script window.

Hopefully, you understand the reasoning behind the Blue Button behavior by now. In short, the Blue Button behavior is a fix that is necessary because of Director's inability to distinguish white borders on an image or fade images with background colors other than white. Sometimes, when working with an authoring tool, you must accept its quirks and work around them. Preview your epic Portfolio interface now to make sure that the menu buttons work properly. You may notice that a menu button will not display its Over or Down state until its opacity reaches 100 percent. This is necessary because the menu buttons' green backgrounds are accomplished through the Button behavior. The Button behavior just ignores any mouse interaction until its sprite reaches full opacity.

ADDING THE OVERLAY SPRITE

The sole purpose of the Overlay sprite is to display the epic tag line and logo and the name of the interface throughout the interface's sections. The Overlay bitmap was actually created by taking a screen capture of the interface just after the appropriate foreground elements had moved into place. If you want to create the Overlay bitmap through Director, you can set layer 1 to be invisible, click frame 269 of the Score window, and take a screen capture of the Stage window. In an external paint program, you can then paste your screen capture and crop it to the 640 × 480 pixel Stage area. Next, paint over the blue interface buttons with black and then copy and paste the new image into Director. When the image is in the Score, you can set its background color to black and its ink to Background Transparent. If this all seems too complicated, don't worry. The Overlay bitmap has already been created for you. To position the Overlay sprite in the Stage and the Score and apply its appropriate behavior, follow the steps outlined in Procedure 12.4.

Procedure 12.4   Positioning the Overlay Sprite

1. Using the Cast window, click the Choose Cast button and select the Media option. Director will display the Media cast within the Cast window.

2. Drag the Overlay member from the Cast window into cell 270 of channel 2 of the Score window. Director will display the Overlay sprite within the Stage window.

3. In the Score window, drag cell 284 of channel 2 to frame 374. Director will extend the Overlay sprite to frame 374 (see Figure 12.8).

4. Click cell 271 of channel 2. Director will highlight the Overlay sprite.

5. In the Property Inspector window, in the Background Color field, type **#000000** and press the Enter key (Return on Macintosh). Director will set the background color of the Overlay sprite to black.

6. Click the Ink drop-down list and select the Background Transparent option. Director will remove the black background from the Overlay sprite (see Figure 12.9).

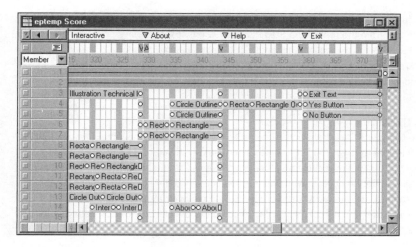

Figure 12.8   *Extending the Overlay sprite.*

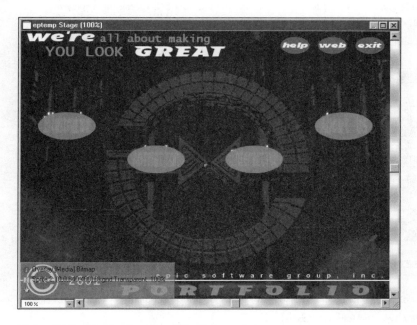

Figure 12.9   *The Overlay sprite within the Stage window.*

If you were to preview your movie right now, you would find that the elements of the Overlay sprite become invisible each time you enter a section. This is because the Overlay sprite is in a lower sprite channel than the background images of the sections and is therefore behind them. To make the Overlay sprite appear in front of the background images, you must set its layer to a high number with the Overlay behavior.

7. Apply the Overlay behavior to the Overlay sprite that begins in cell 270 of channel 2 as specified in Appendix A.

The Overlay sprite is not very useful without its Overlay behavior. The whole point of separating the epic tag line and logo and the name of the interface from the rest of the Stage is to ensure that they always appear in front of other Stage elements. If you wanted, you could accomplish this effect by just selecting the desired elements from frame 269 (all 17 sprites), dragging them down to around channel 1000, and extending to the end of the movie. Although it may not seem like it now, the screen capture method is less of a hassle.

ACTIVATING THE NUMBER BUTTONS

The most important feature of the Number Button behavior is its `checkVisible` function. The `checkVisible` function is just a series of conditions that test the `section` list to determine whether the current sprite should be visible. Each number or letter button calls its `checkVisible` function at the start of every frame to make sure it belongs in the current section. This function would not be necessary if each section contained the same number of items, but that is not the case. Besides setting its sprite's visibility, the Number Button behavior also sets its sprite to its Active member when necessary and guides the number spotlight. To complete the Number Button behavior, follow the steps outlined in Procedure 12.5.

Procedure 12.5   Completing the Numbered Button Behavior

1. In the Cast window, click the Choose Cast button and select the Scripts option. Director will display the Scripts cast within the Cast window.

2. Click the Number Button member. Director will highlight the Number Button member (see Figure 12.10).

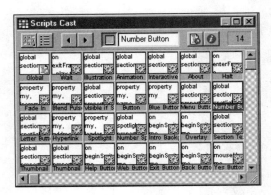

Figure 12.10   *The Number Button member within the Cast window.*

3. Click the Cast Member Script button. Director will display the Number Button script within the Script window.

4. In the `prepareFrame` handler, type the following code:

```
checkVisible

if number = 1 then
```

Note that the preceding calls the associated sprite's `checkVisible` function, which sets the sprite's opacity based on the current section.

```
if section[3].char[1] = string(number) and section[3].char[2] <> "0" then
    my.member = string(number) && "Button Active"
  else if my.member = member(string(number) && "Button Active") then
    my.member = string(number) && "Button"
  end if
else
```

Note that the preceding conditional sets the associated sprite's cast member to its Active state if the value of the third item in the section list begins with 1 but not a 10. (The script must check to see whether the third item begins with a 1, because the third value may be 1A. Checking to see whether the third item is equal to a 1 would not work in this situation.) Otherwise, the conditional sets the sprite's cast member to its normal state if it is currently set to its Active state.

Note that the following conditional sets the associated sprite's cast member to its Active state if the value of the third item in the `section` list begins with its `number` value. Otherwise, the conditional sets the sprite's cast member to its normal state if it is currently set to its Active state:

```
if section[3] starts string(number) then
  my.member = string(number) && "Button Active"
else if my.member = member(string(number) && "Button Active") then
  my.member = string(number) && "Button"
end if
end if
```

5. In the `mouseEnter` handler, type the following code:

```
if my.blend = 0 then exit
```

Note that the following two lines set the spotlight sprite's opacity to 100 percent and its `leader` property to the associated sprite. This creates the effect of pointing the spotlight at the associated sprite and turning it on:

```
spotlight.blend = 100
spotlight.leader = my
```

6. In the `mouseLeave` handler, type the following code:

```
if my.blend = 0 then exit
```

Note that the following line sets the spotlight sprite's opacity to zero percent. This creates the effect of turning the spotlight off:

```
spotlight.blend = 0
```

7. Next, in the `mouseUp` handler, type the following code:

```
if my.blend = 0 then exit
```

Note that the following two lines set the third item in the `section` list to the current button's number and then call the thumbnail image sprite's `reset` function. The `reset` function makes the thumbnail image sprite replay its opening animation:

```
section[3] = string(number)
sendSprite(5, #reset)
```

8. From the toolbar, click the Script Window button. Director will close the Script window.

The letter buttons work almost exactly like the number buttons. The only real difference between the Number Button and Letter Button behaviors, besides being numbers and letters, is their `checkVisible` functions. To determine whether its sprite should be visible, the Number Button behavior needs to check only the first and second items of the `section` list. Based on the section, the behavior then decides whether the current sprite's number is small enough to be visible. As for the Letter Button behavior, it must check all three items of the `section` list. If the *section* variable is equal to one of four combinations, all letter buttons should be visible, regardless of their letter.

MAKING ADJUSTMENTS

There's no getting around it: Taking the "epic" out of the epic Portfolio interface is going to take some work. Besides replacing most, if not all, of the interface graphics, you will, of course, want to replace the members of the Portfolio cast. And you might not end up with the same numbers as epic did. Nevertheless, if you follow a few simple rules, you will be sure to fit all your company's content into this portfolio format. First, you will have a much easier job converting the interface if you leave the section's named Illustration, Animation, Interactive, and About. For most multimedia companies, this shouldn't be a problem. Second, whatever you rename the subsections, make sure they have only one-word titles (no spaces). If you must, you can put a special condition into the Section Text behavior to display two words as the subsection's title (as epic did for Contact Us). When sorting your portfolio items, remember that no more than 10 items can fit into a section as number buttons, and only 3 more per number button fit as letter buttons. Good luck.

>> **part 4**
immersive interfaces

"Do not follow where the path may lead. Go instead where there is no path and leave a trail."
—Muriel Strode

▼▼▼ chapter 13
woodlands waterway

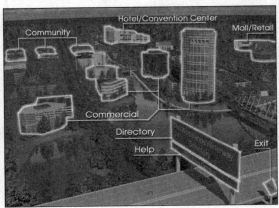

Figures 13.1-13.4 *The Woodlands Waterway interface in action.*

APPROACHING THE "WOODLANDS WATERWAY" INTERFACE

An immersive interface is one that makes the user feel as if he is actually surrounded by the images of the computer screen. Generally, the controls of an immersive environment will, in some way, try to mimic the real world. The Woodlands Waterway interface begins by positioning the user in the sky staring down at the city of The Woodlands. This alone would not be enough to classify the Woodlands Waterway as an immersive interface. When the mouse moves over specific portions of the screen, the interface presents the user with two-dimensional text labels and glow effects. Not until the user actually clicks one of the glowing buildings will he begin to feel immersed in the Woodlands Waterway interface. All it takes is a short QuickTime animation to transport the user into The Woodlands.

UNDERSTANDING THE WOODLANDS WATERWAY INTERFACE

Not all immersive interfaces are complex. When you look at the Lingo scripts of the Woodlands Waterway interface, you will see that the logic behind the interface is fairly simple. Most of the interface's effects, such as the Directory section's blurring and the Help section's transition, are achieved through the Score. In fact, the only effects in the Woodlands Waterway interface that actually require Lingo code are the building link captions and the glow effects that occur when the user moves her mouse over a particular sprite. To view the various Lingo scripts of the Scripts cast, follow these steps:

1. Open the `ww.dir` file from the 13 - Woodlands Waterway folder as specified in Appendix A, "Guide to Common Tasks." The Scripts cast contains the nine Lingo scripts shown in Table 13.1.

Table 13.1   The Scripts Cast Lingo Scripts

Script Name	Description
Global	Sets the global *section* variable to an initial value of Main.
Wait	Makes the movie repeat the current frame over and over until otherwise specified.
Play Section	Plays the marker whose name matches the value of the global *section* variable when the playback head exits its associated frame.
Section Link	Sets the global *section* variable to a specified value and plays the frame directly to the right of the playback head when the user clicks its associated sprite.
Halt Link	Stops the movie entirely when the user clicks the associated sprite.
Use Cursor	Sets its associated sprite's cursor to a cursor made up of the Point Cursor and Point Cursor Mask members of the Bitmaps cast.
Fade In	Gradually increases its associated sprite's opacity until it reaches a value of 100 percent unless the sprite's opacity is 0 percent.
Mouse Over	Signals its associated sprite to fade in when the user's mouse enters the sprite's bounds and sets the sprite's opacity to 0 percent when the mouse leaves the sprite's bounds.
Caption	Sets the location and cast member of the caption sprite based on the mouse location and building sprite opacities.

2. In the Cast window, double-click the Global member. Director will display the Global script within the Script window.

3. Next use the Previous Cast Member and Next Cast Member buttons to view each of the Lingo scripts in the Scripts cast.

After browsing through the Woodlands Waterway interface's scripts and taking a look at its organization in the Score, you should have a good understanding of the logic behind this interface. If some of its aspects are still not clear, you may want to refer to Appendix B, "Guide to Lingo Programming." Although understanding the innerworkings of the Woodlands Waterway interface at this time is not completely necessary, it should make things easier for you as you re-create the interface throughout the rest of this chapter.

ACTIVATING THE BUILDING LINKS

Nearly all the link sprites in the Woodlands Waterway interface (including the building links) make use of the Fade In behavior. When the user moves her mouse over a transparent link sprite, it should gradually increase its opacity until it is fully visible. However, the Fade In behavior does not handle mouse interaction on its own. Its only job is to increase its associated sprite's opacity when the opacity is already greater than zero percent. To put the Fade In behavior into action, you must also apply the Mouse Over behavior to the link sprites. The Mouse Over behavior works as a trigger that tells Fade In to display its associated sprite by setting its opacity to one percent each time the user's mouse enters its bounds. Of course, when the user's mouse leaves the sprite's bounds, Mouse Over must set its opacity back to zero percent. To complete the Mouse Over behavior, follow the steps outlined in Procedure 13.1.

Procedure 13.1   Completing the Mouse Over Behavior

1. Open the `wwtemp.dir` file from the 13 - Woodlands Waterway folder as specified in Appendix A.

2. In the Cast window, click the Mouse Over member. Director will highlight the Mouse Over member (see Figure 13.5).

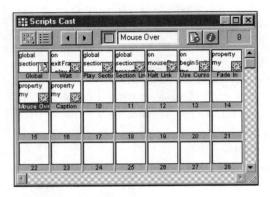

Figure 13.5   *The Mouse Over member.*

3. Click the Cast Member Script button. Director will display the Mouse Over script within the Script window.

4. In the `mouseEnter` handler, type the following code:

```
my.blend = 1
```

Note that the preceding line sets the associated sprite's opacity to one percent. If the associated sprite also contains the Fade In behavior, this will signal it to begin increasing the sprite's opacity.

5. In the `mouseLeave` handler, type the following code:

```
my.blend = 0
```

Note that the preceding line sets the associated sprite's opacity to zero percent.

6. From the toolbar, click the Script Window button. Director will close the Script window.

The building link sprites work just like the other link sprites in the interface. A link sprite should remain transparent throughout the movie unless the user's mouse is within its bounds. One aspect of the building links is unique, however. Each building link may contain several images of buildings, each of which should behave as its own link. Although the rectangular bounds of a building link sprite may stretch across most of the Stage, it may contain only a few small buildings with large gaps in between them. The areas in between buildings should not be considered part of a particular building sprite. To achieve such irregular clickable areas without creating a large number of sprites, you must take advantage of the Matte ink effect. As you may remember from earlier chapters, the Matte ink removes white borders from sprites by making them not only invisible but also no longer part of the sprite's bounds. Therefore, when you apply the Matte ink to the building link sprites, all white borders will be, in effect, removed from the sprites. To activate the building link sprites, follow the steps outlined in Procedure 13.2.

Procedure 13.2   Activating the Building Link Sprites

1. In the Score window, click cell 13 of channel 2, press and hold the Shift key, and then click cell 13 of channel 5. Director will highlight cell 13 of channels 2 through 5.

2. Using the Property Inspector window, click the Ink drop-down list and select the Matte option. Director will remove the white borders from the selected sprites (see Figure 13.6).

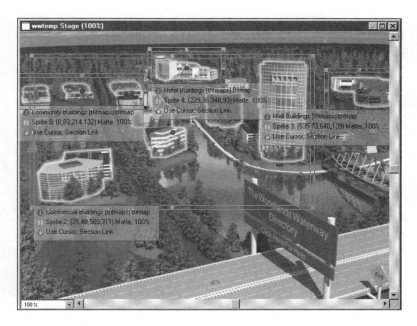

Figure 13.6   *The selected sprites within the Stage window.*

3. In the Blend drop-down list, type **0** and press the Enter key (Return on Macintosh). Director will set the opacity of the selected sprites to zero percent.

4. Apply the Mouse Over behavior to the selected sprites as specified in Appendix A.

5. Apply the Fade In behavior to the selected sprites as specified in Appendix A.

Now that the building links are fully functional, the Woodlands Waterway interface's main menu is looking about how it should. When the user's mouse moves over an active building link, the building gives off a glow effect to indicate that it is clickable. Of course, without some clue as to the building's function, the user may be hesitant to go ahead and click. In the Woodlands Waterway interface, text labels of some sort are a necessity. The most common type of rollover text label found in interfaces today consists of a small colored rectangle that appears near the mouse cursor, when the user's mouse moves over an item.

COMPLETING THE CAPTION BEHAVIOR

The Caption behavior has two functions. First, it must always keep its sprite near the mouse cursor so that the user never has to search the screen for a text label. In addition to controlling its sprite's location, the Caption behavior must also control its cast member. When the user's mouse is over a particular building link, the Caption behavior sets its associated sprite's cast member to one of the four building link bitmaps. Each building link sprite could handle its own rollover caption, but an easier method is to allow a single behavior on the caption sprite itself to check the opacities of the four building links and decide which of the caption bitmaps, if any, should display. To complete the Caption behavior, follow the steps outlined in Procedure 13.3.

Procedure 13.3   Completing the Caption Behavior

1. In the Cast window, click the Caption member. Director will highlight the Caption member (see Figure 13.7).

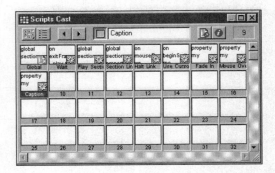

Figure 13.7   *The Caption member within the Cast window.*

2. Click the Cast Member Script button. Director will display the Caption script within the Script window.

3. In the `prepareFrame` handler, type the following code:

```
my.locH = the mouseH
```

Note that the preceding line sets the associated sprite's horizontal location equal to that of the mouse.

Note that the following conditional sets the associated sprite's horizontal location to half its width if its left border is less than 0 or to 640 minus half its width if its right border is greater than 640. This has the effect of keeping the associated sprite within the horizontal bounds of the Stage at all times:

```
if my.left < 0 then
  my.locH = my.width/2
else if my.right > 640 then
  my.locH = 640 - my.width/2
end if
```

Note that the following line sets the associated sprite's vertical location equal to 30 pixels below that of the mouse:

```
my.locV = the mouseV + 30
```

Note that the following conditional sets the associated sprite's vertical location to half its height if its top border is less than 0 or to 480 minus half its height if its bottom border is greater than 480. This has the effect of keeping the associated sprite within the vertical bounds of the Stage at all times:

```
if my.top < 0 then
  my.locV = my.height/2
else if my.bottom > 480 then
  my.locV = 480 - my.height/2
end if
```

Note that the following conditional sets its associated sprite's cast member to an appropriate caption bitmap and its opacity to 100 percent if one of the building links' opacities is greater than 0 percent. Otherwise, it sets the opacity of its associated sprite to 0 percent:

```
if sprite(2).blend > 0 then
   my.member = "Commercial Caption"
   my.blend = 100
else if sprite(3).blend > 0 then
   my.member = "Mall Caption"
   my.blend = 100
else if sprite(4).blend > 0 then
   my.member = "Hotel Caption"
   my.blend = 100
else if sprite(5).blend > 0 then
   my.member = "Community Caption"
   my.blend = 100
else
   my.blend = 0
end if
```

4. From the toolbar, click the Script Window button. Director will close the Script window.

Now that the main menu is complete, you really don't have much left to build. The original Woodlands Waterway interface played long video sequences when the user clicked one of the four building links. To simplify the interface and cut down its file size, those video sequences have been replaced with simple text fields. Only the short fly-through animations remain to take the user between the main menu and other sections of the interface. After working with video in Chapter 6, "Classic Jukebox," you should have no problem setting up such animations in your interfaces. Therefore, this discussion moves on to the Directory section's animation effects.

SETTING UP THE DIRECTORY SECTION'S BACKGROUND

The Directory section consists mainly of a wooden billboard filled with links to other sections. The directory billboard is an alternative to the main menu for those users who want to see clear, obvious links as opposed to the more entertaining building links. The billboard should slide into position when the user clicks the `The Woodlands Waterway Directory` link from the main menu. One complication is that the billboard does not cover the entire screen. The main menu's links should be replaced with those of the directory billboard, but many of them still appear active when the billboard is directly in front of the main menu. A good solution to this problem is to blur the background image that contains the main menu's controls. This forces the user's eye to focus on the billboard rather than the disabled building links. To position the Directory Billboard and Blur Background sprites within the Score and the Stage, follow the steps outlined in Procedure 13.4.

Procedure 13.4   **Positioning the Directory Billboard and Blur Background Sprites Within the Score and the Stage**

1. In the Cast window, click the Choose Cast button and select the Bitmaps option. Director will display the Bitmaps cast within the Cast window.

2. Drag the Directory Billboard member from the Cast window into cell 15 of channel 3 of the Score window. Director will display the Directory Billboard sprite within the Stage window.

3. In the Score window, click cell 16 of channel 3. Director will highlight the Directory Billboard sprite.

4. Using the Property Inspector window, type **200** into the X field, **280** into the Y field, and then press the Enter key (Return on Macintosh). Director will update the Directory Billboard sprite within the Stage window (see Figure 13.8).

>>>

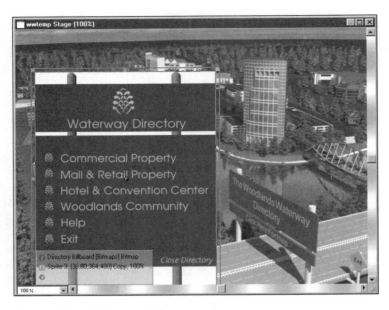

Figure 13.8 *The Directory Billboard sprite.*

5. Next click the Ink drop-down list and select the Background Transparent option. Director will remove the white background from the Directory Billboard sprite.

6. Drag the Blur Background member from the Cast window into cell 15 of channel 2 of the Score window. Director will display the Blur Background sprite within the Stage window (see Figure 13.9).

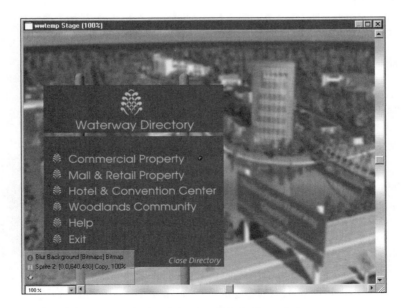

Figure 13.9 *The Blur Background sprite within the Stage window.*

7. In the Score window, click cell 16 of channel 2. Director will highlight the Blur Background sprite.

8. Click cell 29 of channel 2. Director will highlight cell 29 of the Blur Background sprite.

9. Click the Insert menu and select the Keyframe option. Director will mark cell 29 of channel 2 as a keyframe.

10. Click cell 29 of channel 3. Director will highlight cell 29 of the Directory Billboard sprite.

11. Click the Insert menu and select the Keyframe option. Director will mark cell 29 of channel 3 as a keyframe.

12. Next click cell 22 of channel 2. Director will highlight the Blur Background sprite (see Figure 13.10).

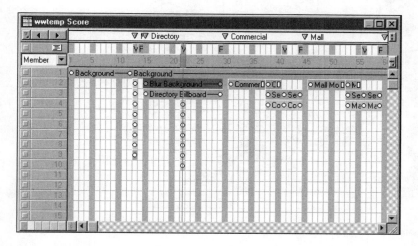

Figure 13.10   *The Blur Background sprite within the Score window.*

13. In the Property Inspector window, in the Blend drop-down list, type **0** and press the Enter key (Return on Macintosh). Director will set the opacity of the Blur Background sprite to zero percent.

14. Click the Insert menu and select the Keyframe option. Director will mark cell 22 of channel 2 as a keyframe.

15. Click the Blend drop-down list and select the 100 option. Director will set the opacity of cell 22 of the Blur Background sprite to 100 percent.

16. In the Score window, click cell 22 of channel 3. Director will highlight the Directory Billboard sprite.

17. Using the Property Inspector window, type **690** into the Y field and then press the Enter key (Return on Macintosh). Director will update the Directory Billboard sprite within the Stage window (see Figure 13.11).

18. Click the Insert menu and select the Keyframe option. Director will mark cell 22 of channel 3 as a keyframe.

19. In the Property Inspector window, type **280** into the Y field and then press the Enter key (Return on Macintosh). Director will update the Directory Billboard sprite within the Stage window.

20. Within the Score window, click cell 16 of channel 3. Director will highlight the Directory Billboard sprite.

21. Click the Modify menu, select the Sprite submenu, and then select the Tweening option. Director will display the Sprite Tweening dialog box.

22. In the Sprite Tweening dialog box, drag the Ease Out slider as far to the right as it will move. Director will update the Ease Out label to read 100%, (see Figure 13.12).

>>>

Figure 13.11 *The Directory Billboard sprite within the Score window.*

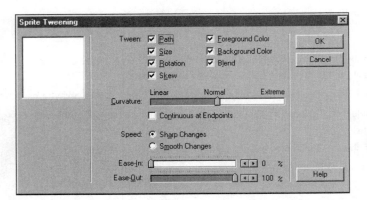

Figure 13.12 *The Ease Out slider within the Sprite Tweening dialog box.*

23. In the Sprite Tweening dialog box, click the OK button. Director will close the Sprite Tweening dialog box.

Preview your movie and test out the Directory section for yourself. When you click the main menu's `The Woodlands Waterway Directory` link, the directory billboard should slide up from the bottom of the screen. Because you adjusted the Ease Out slider from within the Sprite Tweening dialog box, the billboard's movement should seem more natural than if you had not. Notice that the billboard starts out moving fast and then seems to slow down a bit before stopping. Because the billboard movement is such a short animation, the differences are subtle; if you want to see what the animation would look like without the Ease Out slider set to 100 percent, however, you can set it back to 0 percent and preview your movie again.

SETTING UP THE HELP SECTION

The Help section is an important part of any interface that takes advantage of unique controls. In the case of the Woodlands Waterway interface, the user might not feel comfortable clicking the building links, but might still want to use the main menu rather than the directory billboard. In such a case, this cautious user should be able to click the main menu's `Click Here For Help` link and see exactly where the clickable areas of the screen are located. The easiest way to label the main menu's links is to create new images that appear directly in front of the main menu's background image. To return to the main menu, the user should be able to click anywhere on the Help section's image, which fills the entire Stage. To position the Help Background sprite within the Score and the Stage and apply its appropriate behaviors, follow the steps outlined in Procedure 13.5.

Procedure 13.5   Positioning the Help Background Sprite

1. Drag the Help Background member from the Cast window into cell 90 of channel 2 of the Score window (see Figure 13.13). Director will display the Help Background sprite within the Stage window.

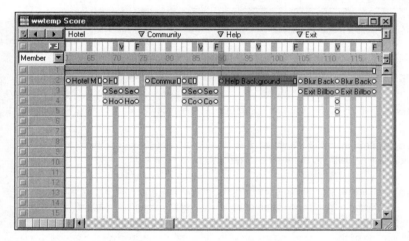

Figure 13.13   *The Help Background sprite within the Score window.*

2. In the Score window, click cell 104 of channel 2. Director will highlight cell 104 of the Help Background sprite.

3. Click the Insert menu and select the Keyframe option. Director will mark cell 104 of channel 2 as a keyframe.

4. Next click cell 97 of channel 2. Director will highlight the Help Background sprite.

5. In the Blend drop-down list, type **0** and press the Enter key (Return on Macintosh). Director will set the opacity of the Help Background sprite to zero percent.

6. Click the Insert menu and select the Keyframe option. Director will mark cell 97 of channel 2 as a keyframe.

7. Click the Blend drop-down list and select the 100 option. Director will set the opacity of cell 97 of the Help Background sprite to 100 percent.

8. In the Score window, click cell 91 of channel 2. Director will highlight the Help Background sprite (see Figure 13.14).

>>>

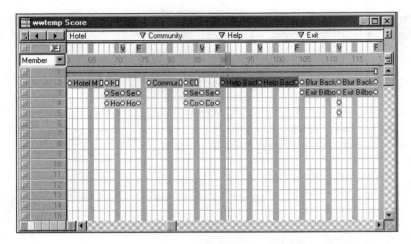

Figure 13.14 *The Help Background sprite within the Score window.*

9. Apply the Use Cursor behavior to the Help Background sprite that begins in cell 90 of channel 2 as specified in Appendix A.

10. Apply the Section Link behavior to the Help Background sprite that begins in cell 90 of channel 2 as specified in Appendix A.

11. When the Parameters dialog box prompts you for a value, press the Enter key (Return on Macintosh). Director will apply the Section Link behavior to the Help Background sprite.

The background transition effects of the Directory and Help sections look much more impressive from the user's perspective than the programmer's. By fading a modified version of an image over the original image, the programmer can fool the user into thinking that she is actually seeing the original image being modified. For example, in the Directory section, placing a blurred version of the background image with 50 percent opacity over the original background image gives the user the impression that she is seeing a partially blurred background image. This sort of effect can prove useful in an incredible variety of situations.

MAKING ADJUSTMENTS

Because of the graphics and video sequences of the Woodlands Waterway interface, you might find modifying the interface to suit your own purposes a nearly impossible task. However, you can use the Lingo and tweening techniques discussed in this chapter to enhance your own original interfaces. If you put forth the effort, you could replace all the media elements of the Woodlands Waterway interface with your own graphics, video, and text. In some situations, however, building an interface from scratch may be easier than modifying an existing interface.

"Imagination is more important than knowledge. Knowledge is limited. Imagination encircles the world."
—Albert Einstein

▼▼▼ **chapter 14**
chopper-bot

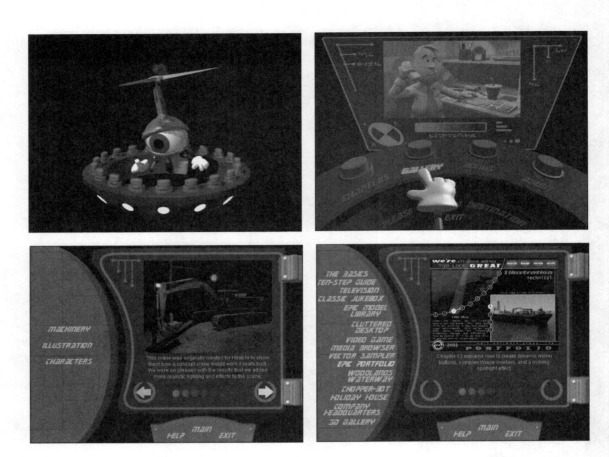

Figures 14.1-14.4 *The Chopper–Bot interface in action.*

APPROACHING THE "CHOPPER-BOT" INTERFACE

The most unique aspect of the Chopper-Bot interface is its first-person perspective. After the opening animation shows a robot flying up to the hovering console, the scene changes to make the user feel as if he becomes the robot. The only part of the robot used after the opening animation is a bitmap image of its hand. By just making the hand follow the user's mouse location and rotating the image appropriately, the Chopper-Bot interface succeeds in creating a believable first-person perspective. As soon as the user makes the robot hand push one of the console's buttons, the user seems to fly past the floating console and directly into three flat panels that provide access to the various elements of the selected section. Although the entire Chopper-Bot interface is not immersive, its main menu certainly is.

UNDERSTANDING THE CHOPPER-BOT INTERFACE

Much like the Woodlands Waterway interface, the animation effects of the Chopper Bot interface are created with a combination of tweening in the Score and Lingo behavior scripts. For example, the main menu's console moves only when told to do so by the Score, but the robot hand moves exclusively through Lingo code. As a rule, any animation effect that must be affected in any way by the user should be created through Lingo. Animations that are more static can usually be created in the Score. Just remember that you must choose either one method or the other. After you add a tweening effect to a sprite, you should never apply a behavior that could alter any property being set by the Score. To view the various Lingo scripts of the Scripts cast, follow these steps:

1. Open the cb.dir file from the 14 - Chopper-Bot folder as specified in Appendix A, "Guide to Common Tasks." The Scripts cast contains the 22 Lingo scripts shown in Table 14.1.

Table 14.1   The Lingo Scripts of the *Scripts* Cast and Their Descriptions

Script Name	Description
Wait	Makes the movie repeat the current frame repeatedly until otherwise specified.
Play Main	Plays the Main marker when the playback head exits its associated frame.
Set Sound Velocity	Sets the *vSound* variable to a specified value when the playback head enters its associated frame.
Volume Control	Adds the value of *vSound* to the current volume of the first sound channel each time the playback head enters a frame. Works with the Set Sound Velocity behavior.
Inactive When Invisible	Sets its associated sprite's horizontal location to negative 1000 when its opacity is 0 percent and back to normal otherwise.
Fade In	Gradually increases its associated sprite's opacity until it reaches a value of 100 percent unless the sprite's opacity is 0 percent.
Slide In	Sets its associated sprite's horizontal location to negative 100, and then gradually increases it until it reaches its original value if the *section* variable equals a specified value.
HUD	Sets its associated sprite's dimensions to fill the Stage while the zooming property is equal to one and back to normal while zooming equals two.
HUD Message	Sets the HUD sprite's cast member and zooming property based on mouse interaction. Works with the HUD behavior.
Console Button	Sets its associated sprite's cast member and plays sounds based on mouse interaction and its name property.
Console Prompt	Gradually transitions its associated sprite's opacity between 25 and 50 percent.
Console Exit Button	Gradually transitions its associated sprite's opacity from 50 to 100 percent when the user's mouse enters its bounds, and back again when it leaves.
Hand	Hides the cursor and follows the mouse when the user's mouse is within range of the main menu's console. Otherwise, shows the cursor and keeps its associated sprite near the console.
Item Image	Sets its associated sprite's dimensions to fill the Stage while the zooming property is equal to one and back to normal while zooming equals two. Sets its zooming property based on mouse interaction. Also handles scrollbar problems with the section text.
Help Overlay	Gradually increases its associated sprite's opacity until it reaches a value of 60 percent if the value of the *helpMode* variable is true.
Link	Sets its associated sprite's cast member and plays sounds based on mouse interaction and its cast member's order.
Show Item	Displays a specified section image and text when the user clicks its associated sprite.

>>>

Table 14.1 Continued

Script Name	Description
Back Arrow	Sets the section image and text to one less than the current image and text. Cycles through five images and descriptions.
Next Arrow	Sets the section image and text to one more than the current image and text. Cycles through five images and descriptions.
Main Link	Plays the frame directly to the right of the playback head when the user clicks its associated sprite.
Help Link	Plays the Help marker when the user clicks its associated sprite.
Exit Link	Stops the movie entirely when the user clicks its associated sprite.

2. In the Cast window, double-click the Global member. Director will display the Global script within the Script window.

3. Use the Previous Cast Member and Next Cast Member buttons to view each of the Lingo scripts in the Scripts cast.

After browsing through the Chopper-Bot interface's scripts and looking at its organization in the Score, you should have a good understanding of the logic behind this interface. If some of its aspects are still not clear, you may want to refer to Appendix B, "Guide to Lingo Programming." Although understanding the innerworkings of the Chopper-Bot interface at this time is not completely necessary, it should make things easier for you as you re-create the interface throughout the rest of this chapter.

COMPLETING THE SLIDE IN BEHAVIOR

The purpose of the Slide In behavior is to slide the current section's menu items into position and hide the rest. When the playback head enters the sprites' frame, each of the menu items sets its horizontal location to negative 100. Then, only the menu items of the current section slide into position. The remaining menu items hold their positions off the left side of the Stage. Remember that menu items use their original position on the Stage as a target destination for their sliding effect. Therefore, you must position the menu item sprites on the Stage exactly as you want them to appear in their respective sections. To complete the Slide In behavior, follow the steps outlined in Procedure 14.1.

Procedure 14.1   Completing the Slide In Behavior

1. Open the `cbtemp.dir` file from the 14 - Chopper-Bot folder as specified in Appendix A.

2. In the Cast window, click the Slide In member. Director will highlight the Slide In member (see Figure 14.5).

3. Click the Cast Member Script button. Director will display the Slide In script within the Script window.

4. Next, in the `beginSprite` handler, type the following code:

```
my = sprite(me.spriteNum)
x = my.locH + 1
my.locH = -100
```

Note that the preceding three lines set the `my` property equal to the associated sprite, the `x` property equal to 1 pixel more than the sprite's horizontal location, and the sprite's horizontal location equal to negative 100. The `x` property must be set to 1 past the original horizontal location because of the method used to move the associated sprite. The sprite's horizontal location will never equal the exact value of `x`.

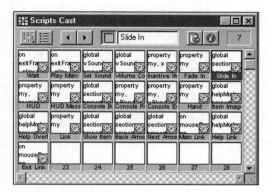

Figure 14.5 *The Slide In member.*

5. In the Script window, in the `prepareFrame` handler, type the following code:

```
if section <> sectionName then exit
```

Note that the following line adds one-third the distance between the associated sprite's horizontal location and the x property to the sprite's current horizontal location. This has the effect of moving the associated sprite into place quickly at first and then slowly. As mentioned earlier, the sprite's horizontal location will never reach the exact value of x:

```
my.locH = my.locH + (x - my.locH)/3
```

6. From the toolbar, click the Script Window button. Director will close the Script window.

Now that you have each section displaying its appropriate menu items, you will probably want to activate them. If you were to preview your movie right now and click one of the sections' menu items, you would find that nothing would happen. All the right behaviors have already been applied to the menu item sprites, but the Show Item behavior is not yet completed. To finish activating the menu items, you must enter code into the Show Item behavior that will handle mouse clicks.

COMPLETING THE SHOW ITEM BEHAVIOR

The Show Item behavior accepts a single parameter named `itemNum`. The `itemNum` property keeps track of the current menu item's order within its section. When the user clicks a menu item, the `itemNum` property tells the behavior which of the current section's images and text fields should display. The opacity of the image and text field sprites is set to one percent because the sprites also contain the Fade In behavior. When the Fade In behavior sees that the sprites are partially visible, it will gradually fade them both to full opacity. To complete the Show Item behavior, follow the steps outlined in Procedure 14.2.

Procedure 14.2 Completing the Show Item Behavior

1. In the Cast window, click the Show Item member. Director will highlight the Show Item member (see Figure 14.6).

>>>

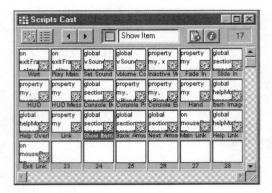

Figure 14.6 *The Show Item member.*

2. Click the Cast Member Script button. Director will display the Show Item script within the Script window.

3. In the `mouseDown` handler, type the following code:

```
sprite(7).member = section && "Image" && itemNum
sprite(7).blend = 1
sprite(8).member = section && "Text" && itemNum
sprite(8).blend = 1
```

Note that the preceding four lines set the cast member of the sprite in channel 7 to an image based on the `itemNum` property and the sprite's opacity to one percent. Then they set the cast member of the sprite in channel 8 to a text field based on `itemNum` and the opacity to one percent.

4. From the toolbar, click the Script Window button. Director will close the Script window.

At this point, the different sections of your Chopper-Bot interface should be functioning properly. The main menu, however, is still in a state of disrepair. The disembodied robot hand just sits in the interface's foreground serving absolutely no purpose. To make the main menu truly immersive and transform your interface into a nearly finished product, you must activate the robot hand.

ACTIVATING THE MAIN MENU'S ROBOT HAND

If you want to allow the user to control the robot's hand, the first step you must take is setting the registration point of the hand's bitmap to an appropriate location. By default, an image's registration point is located at its very center. When you set a sprite to a specific location on the Stage, the sprite will move so that its registration point matches up with the specified location. Therefore, because the robot hand should be following the location of the user's mouse, its registration point should occur right around the tip of its index finger. That way, when the user points to a button with her mouse, the robot hand will point at the same button with its index finger. To adjust the Hand Point member's bitmap's registration point, follow the steps outlined in Procedure 14.3.

Procedure 14.3 Activating the Main Menu's Robot Hand

1. In the Cast window, click the Choose Cast button and select the Media option. Director will display the Media cast within the Cast window.

2. Double-click the Hand Point member (see Figure 14.7). Director will display the Hand Point bitmap within the Paint window.

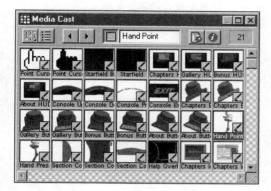

Figure 14.7 *The Hand Point member.*

3. In the Paint window, click the Registration Point button (see Figure 14.8). Director will indicate the Hand Point bitmap's current registration point.

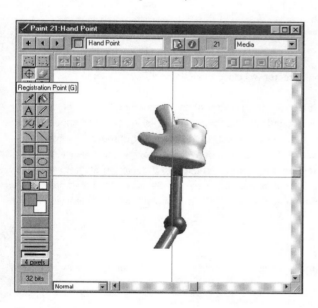

Figure 14.8 *The Registration Point button.*

4. Click to adjust the location of the Hand Point bitmap's registration point. Move the registration point to right around the middle of the robot hand's index finger (see Figure 14.9).

>>>

Figure 14.9 *The Hand Point bitmap.*

5. From the toolbar, click the Paint Window button. Director will close the Paint window.

Although the Hand behavior may seem complicated, it is really just a matter of finding, through trial and error, what looks right. Making the robot hand follow the mouse is not difficult. The tough part is making the hand appear as if its arm always points back to the same area. To do this, you must not only rotate the arm, but move it slightly as well. The arm should be rotated 0 degrees in the middle of the Stage and between approximately negative and positive 32 degrees at the edges. The more the sprite is rotated, the more you must shift it down the Stage to keep the user from seeing the bottom edge of the robot's arm. Of course, the robot hand can be allowed to move up the Stage only a certain distance. This also keeps the arm from appearing cut off. To complete the Hand behavior, follow the steps outlined in Procedure 14.4.

Procedure 14.4   Completing the Hand Behavior

1. In the Cast window, click the Choose Cast button and select the Scripts option. Director will display the Scripts cast within the Cast window.

2. Click the Hand member. Director will highlight the Hand member (see Figure 14.10).

3. Click the Cast Member Script button. Director will display the Hand script within the Script window.

4. Next, in the `prepareFrame` handler, type the following code:

```
my.loc = the mouseLoc
my.rotation = (my.locH-320)/10

if sprite(4).locV = 240 then
```

Note that the first two lines set the associated sprite's location to the location of the mouse and the sprite's rotation to one-tenth of its horizontal distance from the center of the Stage.

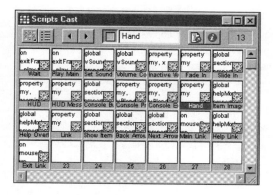

Figure 14.10 *The Hand member.*

Note that the following conditional sets the vertical location of the associated sprite to one-fifth its horizontal distance from the center of the Stage past the vertical center of the Stage, the sprite's cast member to the Hand Point member, and the cursor to normal if the sprite's vertical location is less than one-fifth of its horizontal distance from the center of the Stage past the vertical center of the Stage. Otherwise, it sets the sprite's cast member based on whether or not the user is pressing her mouse button and hides the cursor. This has the effect of keeping the robot hand outstretched only to a certain distance:

```
if my.locV < 240 + abs(my.locH-320)/5 then
  my.locV = 240 + abs(my.locH-320)/5
  my.member = "Hand Point"
  cursor(-1)
else
  if the mouseDown then
    my.member = "Hand Press"
  else
    my.member = "Hand Point"
  end if
  cursor(200)
end if
else
```

Note that the following three lines set the vertical location of the sprite to 50 pixels below the vertical location of the sprite in channel 4 and the cursor to normal. These lines execute only if the console is below its normal vertical position and have the effect of making the robot hand follow the console as it moves up and down:

```
my.locV = sprite(4).locV + 50
cursor(-1)
end if
```

5. From the toolbar, click the Script Window button. Director will close the Script window.

Now that you have finished the robot hand's behavior, preview your movie to ensure everything works properly. The robot hand should follow your hidden mouse cursor in the main menu, and the menu items should behave normally in the interface's sections. The only problem you should notice is the constant helicopter noise you hear throughout every section of the interface. To quiet this annoyance, you must continue on to the next section of the chapter.

ADJUSTING THE SOUND VOLUME THROUGH LINGO

The Set Sound Velocity behavior will not change the volume of the helicopter sound on its own. Its only purpose is to set the global *vSound* variable to a specified value when the playback head enters its associated frame. The *vSound* variable will eventually be used by the Volume Control behavior to adjust the volume of sound channel 1, where the helicopter noise is playing. To complete the Set Sound Velocity behavior and apply it to its appropriate frames, follow the steps outlined in Procedure 14.5.

Procedure 14.5   Completing the Set Sound Velocity Behavior

1. Click the Set Sound Velocity member. Director will highlight the Set Sound Velocity member (see Figure 14.11).

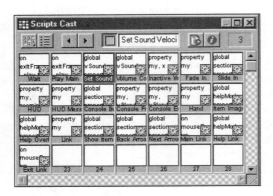

Figure 14.11   *The Set Sound Velocity member.*

2. Click the Cast Member Script button. Director will display the Set Sound Velocity script within the Script window.

3. In the enterFrame handler, type the following code:

```
vSound = vSoundNum
```

   Note that the preceding line sets the *vSound* variable to the vSoundNum property. The only purpose of vSoundNum is to be used as a parameter of the Set Sound Velocity behavior that modifies *vSound*.

4. In the toolbar, click the Script Window button. Director will close the Script window.

5. Apply the Set Sound Velocity behavior to frame 15 as specified in Appendix A.

6. When the Parameters dialog box prompts you for a value, type **-10** into the Sound Velocity field and then press the Enter key (Return on Macintosh). Director will apply the Set Sound Velocity behavior to frame 15.

7. Apply the Set Sound Velocity behavior to frame 31 as specified in Appendix A.

8. When the Parameters dialog box prompts you for a value, type **50** into the Sound Velocity field and then press the Enter key (Return on Macintosh). Director will apply the Set Sound Velocity behavior to frame 31.

9. Apply the Set Sound Velocity behavior to frame 45 as specified in Appendix A.

10. When the Parameters dialog box prompts you for a value, type **-10** into the Sound Velocity field and then press the Enter key (Return on Macintosh). Director will apply the Set Sound Velocity behavior to frame 45.

11. Apply the Set Sound Velocity behavior to frame 53 as specified in Appendix A.

12. When the Parameters dialog box prompts you for a value, type **50** into the Sound Velocity field and then press the Enter key (Return on Macintosh). Director will apply the Set Sound Velocity behavior to frame 53.

Sound channels are accessible through Lingo just as sprite channels are. To access a specific sound channel, you just type the word **sound** and then a number from one to eight, indicating which of the eight available sound channels you would like to use. Adjusting the volume of a sound channel is as simple as setting its `volume` property to a number from 0 to 255. The volume of each of the sound channels is set to 255, or 100 percent, by default. When incrementing a sound channel's volume, you must always check to make sure that you never attempt to set the volume to a number less than 0 or more than 255. A good example of how to do this is the Volume Control behavior's `enterFrame` handler. To complete the Volume Control behavior, follow the steps outlined in Procedure 14.6.

Procedure 14.6 Completing the Volume Control Behavior

1. In the Cast window, click the Volume Control member. Director will highlight the Volume Control member (see Figure 14.12).

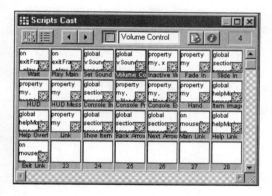

Figure 14.12   *The Volume Control member.*

2. Click the Cast Member Script button. Director will display the Volume Control script within the Script window.

3. In the `enterFrame` handler, type the following code:

```
if sound(1).volume + vSound > 255 then
   sound(1).volume = 255
else if sound(1).volume + vSound < 0 then
   sound(1).volume = 0
else
   sound(1).volume = sound(1).volume + vSound
end if
```

Note that the preceding conditional adds the value of the *vSound* variable to the current volume of the first sound channel. The volume may not be less than 0 or more than 255.

4. From the toolbar, click the Script Window button. Director will close the Script window.

Director's sound channels enable you to edit more than just their volume. By setting a sound channel's `pan` property to a value from negative to positive 100, you can adjust the sound's volume balance between your computer's left and right speakers. By accessing a sound channel's `member` property, you can even tell exactly which sound is playing. Each sound channel also makes several functions available that can do everything from test to see whether a sound is playing to play, pause, and stop sound. See Director's Lingo Dictionary for more information on manipulating sound channels.

MAKING ADJUSTMENTS

To begin customizing the Chopper-Bot interface, you must first decide exactly how many items you would like to have in each of your interface's sections. Then you should delete all the link sprites in channels 14 through 39 and create all your link images to replace the members of the Links cast. After you have all your links organized the way you want them, drag only the normal states of the links into the Cast window to replace the old link sprites. Apply the Link, Slide In, and Show Item behaviors to the new link sprites. Enter appropriate parameter values when necessary. Organize all the links on the Stage in their appropriate sections. When you are completely sure you have all the links where they should be with the appropriate behaviors and parameters, you can begin placing Image members in the Media cast and Description members in the Text cast. Each image should be 640 pixels wide and 480 pixels high, and each text field should be no more than four lines. The exception for the About section is that its Description text fields may use scrollbars and be as long as you want. Menu items in the Gallery section should point to groups of exactly five images. Image cast members other than the first of each section must end in capital letters to indicate their order. If you really must change the number of images in the items of the Gallery section, you will need to edit the Back Arrow and Next Arrow behavior scripts.

"Let no one come to you without leaving better and happier."
—Mother Teresa

>>> chapter 15

holiday house

Figures 15.1-15.4   *The Holiday House interface in action.*

APPROACHING THE "HOLIDAY HOUSE" INTERFACE

The Holiday House is an example of a fully immersive interface. The user must literally find her way around the house by clicking items that change the mouse cursor. Even the introduction letter is available only when the user clicks the envelope stuck on the front door. Unlike most interfaces, the Holiday House does not provide immediate access to its major sections from a main menu. The interface is more for entertainment than educational purposes and contains no vital information that the user might need to find quickly. When the user's goal is just to look around and explore an interface, a few of the rules of interface design can be bent.

UNDERSTANDING THE HOLIDAY HOUSE INTERFACE

The Holiday House interface is really not as complex as it seems. It consists mainly of simple animation effects created by Lingo code and triggered by mouse events. The hh.dir file is organized somewhat differently than the interfaces you studied earlier. Each section stores its own graphics, sounds, and scripts in a separate cast. The Scripts and Media casts are used only to store generic elements that may be used in any of the sections. Some of the scripts, such as Full Screen and Show Full Screen, may not make much sense to you now. If you browse through the interface and observe what happens when they are used, however, ambiguous scripts will eventually become clear to you. To view the various Lingo scripts of the Scripts cast, follow these steps:

1. Open the `hh.dir` file from the 15 - Holiday House folder as specified in Appendix A, "Guide to Common Tasks." The Scripts cast contains the six Lingo scripts shown in Table 15.1.

Table 15.1   The Scripts Cast Lingo Scripts

Script Name	Description
Wait	Makes the movie repeat the current frame over and over until otherwise specified.
Set Cursor	Sets its associated sprite's cursor to a specified value.
Set Sound	Plays a specified sound in an unoccupied sound channel when the user clicks its associated sprite.
Full Screen	Sets its associated sprite's horizontal location to negative 1000 when its opacity is 0 percent and back to normal otherwise. Also sets the sprite's layer to 0 when its opacity is 0 percent and to 1000 otherwise.
Show Full Screen	Sets the opacity of the sprite just above the associated sprite in the Score to 100 percent when the user clicks its associated sprite.
Enter Room	Sets its associated sprite's opacity based on mouse interaction and plays a specified marker when the user clicks its associated sprite.

2. In the Cast window, click the Wait member. Director will update the Cast window.

3. Click the Cast Member Script button. Director will display the Wait script within the Script window.

4. Use the Previous Cast Member and Next Cast Member buttons to view each of the Lingo scripts in the Scripts cast.

After browsing through the Holiday House interface's scripts and taking a look at its organization in the Score, you should have a good understanding of the logic behind this interface. If some of its aspects are still not clear, you may want to refer to Appendix B, "Guide to Lingo Programming." Although understanding the innerworkings of the Holiday House interface at this time is not completely necessary, it should make things easier for you as you re-create the interface throughout the rest of this chapter.

ACTIVATING THE KITCHEN WINDOW

The purpose of the Window behavior is to expose a film loop of falling snow and play an animation of Santa Claus when the user clicks its associated sprite. It uses a property variable named *animFrame* to keep track of its Santa animation by counting the frames as they pass. When the *animFrame* property is zero, it does not affect the associated sprite. When it is greater than zero, however, its value increments each frame to create the Santa animation. When the animation is complete, *animFrame* is set back to zero. To complete the Window behavior and apply it to its appropriate sprite, follow the steps outlined in Procedure 15.1.

Procedure 15.1   Completing the Window Behavior

1. Open the `hhtemp.dir` file from the 15 - Holiday House folder as specified in Appendix A.

2. Using the Cast window, click the Choose Cast button and select the Kitchen option. Director will display the Kitchen cast within the Cast window.

3. In the Score window, click cell 46 of channel 2. Director will highlight the Window sprite (see Figure 15.5).

>>>

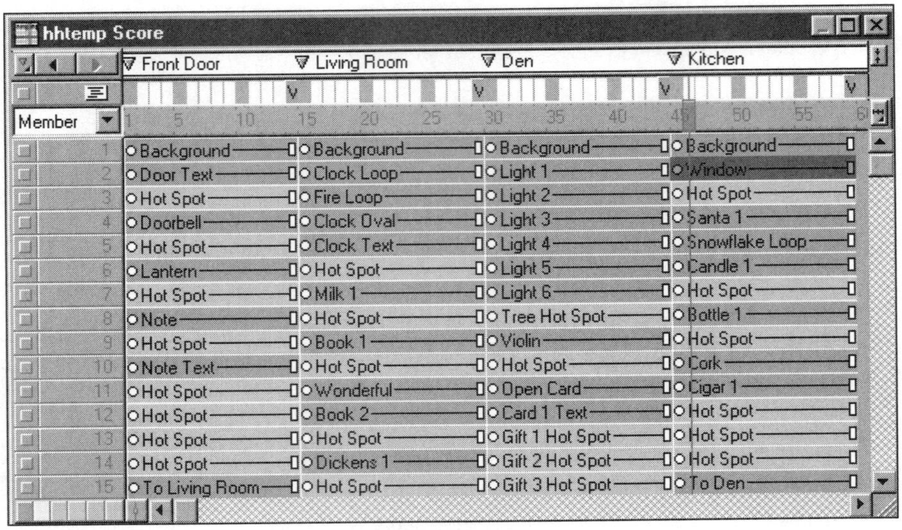

Figure 15.5   *The Window sprite.*

4. In the Property Inspector window, in the Blend drop-down list, type **0** and press the Enter key (Return on Macintosh). Director will set the opacity of the Window sprite to zero percent (see Figure 15.6).

Figure 15.6   *The Window sprite.*

5. Within the Cast window, click the Window member (the behavior script). Director will highlight the Window member (see Figure 15.7).

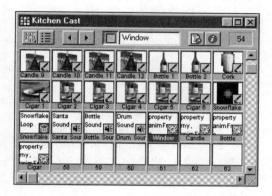

Figure 15.7 *The Window member.*

6. In the Cast window, click the Cast Member Script button. Director will display the Window script within the Script window.

7. Using the Script window, in the `enterFrame` handler, type the following code:

```
if animFrame = 0 then exit

if animFrame > 10 then
```

Note that the following conditional sets the opacity of Santa to 100 percent and plays the Santa Sound sound in channel 1 if the *animFrame* property is exactly 11. This triggers the Santa animation after the window has been visible for 10 frames:

```
if animFrame = 11 then
    sprite(me.spriteNum+1).blend = 100
    puppetSound(1, "Santa Sound")
end if
```

Note that the following lines set the cast member of the Santa sprite based on the *animFrame* property. Remember that this only happens when *animFrame* is greater than 10:

```
    sprite(me.spriteNum+1).member = member("Santa" && (animFrame-10), "Kitchen")
end if
```

Note that the following line increments the *animFrame* property. This causes the Santa animation to progress normally:

```
animFrame = animframe + 1
```

Note that the following conditional sets *animFrame* back to zero and Santa's opacity back to zero percent if the Santa animation has been completed or the window's opacity is zero percent. The window's opacity being zero percent indicates that the user has closed the curtains:

```
if animFrame > 35 or sprite(me.spriteNum-1).blend = 0 then
    animFrame = 0
    sprite(me.spriteNum+1).blend = 0
end if
```

>>>

8. In the Script window, in the `mouseDown` handler, type the following code:

```
if sprite(me.spriteNum-1).blend = 0 then
   sprite(me.spriteNum-1).blend = 100
   sprite(me.spriteNum+2).locH = 592
   animFrame = 1
else
   sprite(me.spriteNum-1).blend = 0
   sprite(me.spriteNum+1).blend = 0
   sprite(me.spriteNum+2).locH = -1000
end if
```

Note that the preceding conditional sets the window's opacity to 100 percent, the snowflake animation to a horizontal location of 592 pixels, and the *animFrame* property to 1 if the window's opacity is currently 0 percent. Otherwise, it sets the window and the Santa animation to opacities of 0 percent and moves the snowflake animation off the Stage to a horizontal location to negative 1000 pixels. Film loops like the snowflake animation cannot be affected by the `blend` property.

9. From the toolbar, click the Script Window button. Director will close the Script window.

10. Apply the Window behavior to the Hot Spot sprite that begins in cell 45 of channel 2 as specified in Appendix A.

11. Using the Score window, click cell 46 of channel 2. Director will highlight the Window sprite.

12. In the Property Inspector window, in the Blend drop-down list, type **0**, and press the Enter key (Return on Macintosh). Director will set the opacity of the Window sprite to zero percent.

You set the Window sprite's opacity to zero percent because the kitchen window begins in a closed state. When the Window sprite is visible, the window appears open. If you were to preview your movie with the Window sprite activated but still visible, the window would be open as you entered the kitchen. The problem with this is that neither the falling snow nor the Santa animation would be visible. The user triggers these animations by clicking the kitchen window. They cannot determine whether the window is open on their own.

LAYERING SOUNDS THROUGH LINGO

Lingo provides eight sound channels, which you can use to play up to eight sounds simultaneously. When working with multiple sound channels, the `soundBusy` function can come in quite handy. It accepts a sound channel number as an argument and returns either true or false depending on whether the specified channel is currently playing a sound. By accessing the sound channel's `member` property, you can even determine which sound the channel is playing. The Set Sound behavior chooses a channel to play a specific sound based on both the `soundBusy` function and the `member` property. To complete the Set Sound behavior and apply it to the champagne bottle's hot spot, follow the steps outlined in Procedure 15.2.

Procedure 15.2   Completing the Set Sound Behavior

1. In the Cast window, click the Choose Cast button and select the Scripts option. Director will display the Scripts cast within the Cast window.

2. Click the Set Sound member. Director will highlight the Set Sound member (see Figure 15.8).

3. Click the Cast Member Script button. Director will display the Set Sound script within the Script window.

4. In the `mouseDown` handler, type the following code:

```
channel = 8
```

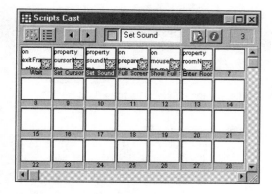

Figure 15.8 *The Set Sound member.*

Note that the preceding line sets a local variable named *channel* to a value of eight. Unless a better sound channel is found, the `soundName` sound will play in channel 8.

Note that the following loop checks sound channels 2 through 8 to find either one that is not currently playing a sound or one that is playing the `soundName` sound. If such a sound channel is found, the channel variable stores its number and the loop ends:

```
repeat with i = 2 to 8
  if not soundBusy(i) or sound(i).member = member(soundName && "Sound") then
    channel = i
    exit repeat
  end if
end repeat
```

Note that the following line plays the specified sound in a channel determined by the local *channel* variable:

```
puppetSound(channel, soundName && "Sound")
```

5. From the toolbar, click the Script Window button. Director will close the Script window.

6. Apply the Set Sound behavior to the Hot Spot sprite that begins in cell 45 of channel 9 as specified in Appendix A.

7. When the Parameters dialog box prompts you for a value, type **Bottle** into the Sound Name field and press the Enter key (Return on Macintosh). Director will apply the Set Sound behavior to the Hot Spot sprite.

Preview your movie and navigate the Kitchen section. Click the champagne bottle to make sure that your movie plays the bottle sound correctly. You should be able to interrupt the bottle sound by clicking the bottle again before its sound is finished playing. If you click another item such as the drum, however, the bottle sound will not be interrupted. Without the use of multiple sound channels, you could click the window and then click the champagne bottle and not even hear Santa's sleigh jingling by.

ACTIVATING THE CHAMPAGNE BOTTLE

When you previewed your movie, you found that you could click the champagne bottle over and over to have it replay its sound. Without any kind of accompanying animation, however, the sound doesn't make much sense. When you hear a cork popping out of a bottle and ricocheting across the room, you expect to see it happening as well. The purpose of the Bottle behavior is to animate a cork flying out of the champagne bottle when the user clicks it. Another important aspect of the Bottle behavior is that it must keep the user from popping the cork more than once. This can be achieved just by moving the bottle's Hot Spot spite off the Stage after it has been clicked. To complete the Bottle behavior and apply it to its appropriate sprite, follow the steps outlined in Procedure 15.3.

Procedure 15.3   Completing the Bottle Behavior

1. In the Cast window, click the Choose Cast button and select the Kitchen option. Director will display the Kitchen cast within the Cast window.

2. Click the Bottle member. Director will highlight the Bottle member (see Figure 15.9).

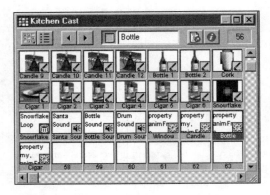

Figure 15.9   *The Bottle member.*

3. Click the Cast Member Script button. Director will display the Bottle script within the Script window.

4. Within the Script window, in the `enterFrame` handler, type the following code:

```
if animFrame = 0 then exit
```

Note that the following line sets the cork's vertical location to a value up to 90 pixels higher than its current vertical location:

```
sprite(me.spriteNum+1).locV = sprite(me.spriteNum+1).locV - 100 + animFrame*10
```

Note that the following two lines increment the *animFrame* property and then make sure it does not exceed a value of 10. If *animFrame* became greater than 10, the cork would actually begin moving down the screen because of the preceding line of programming code:

```
animFrame = animFrame + 1
if animFrame > 10 then animFrame = 10
```

5. Within the Script window, in the `mouseDown` handler, type the following code:

```
animFrame = 1
sprite(me.spriteNum-1).member = member("Bottle 2", "Kitchen")
sprite(me.spriteNum).locH = -1000
sprite(me.spriteNum+1).blend = 100
```

Note that the preceding lines set *animFrame* to one, the bottle sprite's cast member to a corkless version of the bottle, the bottle's clickable hot spot to a horizontal location of negative 1000 pixels, and the cork to an opacity of 100 percent. This triggers the cork animation and prevents the user from clicking the bottle again.

6. From the toolbar, click the Script Window button. Director will close the Script window.

7. Apply the Bottle behavior to the Hot Spot sprite that begins in cell 45 of channel 9 as specified in Appendix A.

When you preview your movie now, the champagne bottle should function just as it does in the original Holiday House interface. Notice that if you leave the kitchen and then return to it, everything will return to its original state. The curtain will be closed, the cork will be in, and the candle will be tall. Modified properties such as `locH` and `blend` immediately return to their default values upon the creation of a sprite. This may seem unrealistic, but it allows the user the freedom to look around as much as he wants. Just pretend that a housekeeper is following you around tidying anything you mess up.

MAKING ADJUSTMENTS

If you want to create your own version of the Holiday House interface, the first thing you will want to do is change the text on the front door from "epic software" to your company's name. The cast member is named Door Text and is located in the Front Door cast. Also you should change the Note Text member. Just remember to make sure that the text fits onto the paper image correctly. You also will want to fill the books' text fields with your own content and replace the Screen images and movie with your own portfolio items. Because the Holiday House interface is so centered on its graphics, just editing them is not an option. If you choose to build your own interface from scratch, however, you may find that many of the techniques used in the Holiday House interface can translate to other multimedia interfaces without much trouble.

"As long as you're going to think anyway, think big."
—Donald Trump

▼▼▼ chapter 16
company headquarters

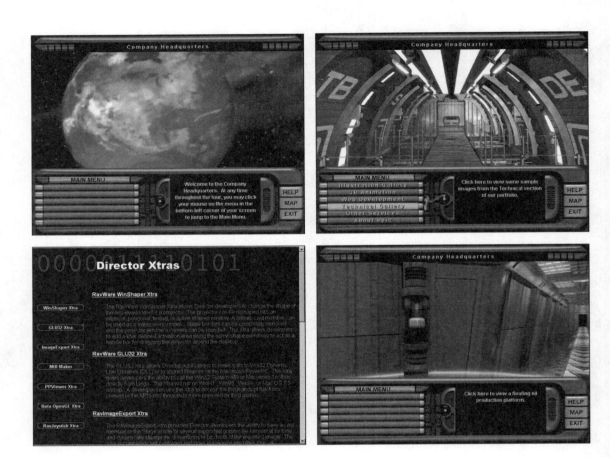

Figures 16.1-16.4 *The Company Headquarters interface in action.*

APPROACHING THE "COMPANY HEADQUARTERS" INTERFACE

The Company Headquarters interface combines video sequences and QuickTime VR with standard bitmaps to give the illusion that the user is actually immersed in a 3D environment. Unlike the Holiday House interface, Company Headquarters also provides the user with standard 2D controls. In the interface's main menu, the user can click directly on a door or go down to the console and choose one of the menu items instead. At any point in the interface when the user is not already at the main menu, he can click the blank menu in the lower-left corner of the Stage to go there. The Help, Map, and Exit buttons also are available throughout the interface. They provide the user with basic control over navigation in case he does not want to sit through animation sequences to get to a particular section.

UNDERSTANDING THE COMPANY HEADQUARTERS INTERFACE

By now, you've studied a wide variety of interfaces, and you should have a good idea of what goes into creating a good multimedia interface. The only major element of the Company Headquarters interface that you may be unfamiliar with is QuickTime VR. This chapter will not cover the creation of QuickTime VR movies. It will simply explain how to incorporate them into your Director interfaces. If you are interested in creating your own QuickTime VR movies, you should read about the QuickTime VR Authoring Studio at `www.apple.com/quicktime/qtvr/authoringstudio/`. To view the various Lingo scripts of the Scripts cast, follow these steps:

1. Open the `ch.dir` file from the 16 - Company Headquarters folder as specified in Appendix A, "Guide to Common Tasks." The Scripts cast contains the 15 Lingo scripts shown in Table 16.1.

Table 16.1   The Scripts Cast Lingo Scripts

Script Name	Description
Wait	Makes the movie repeat the current frame over and over until otherwise specified.
Play Marker	Plays a specified marker either when the playback head enters its associated frame or when the user clicks its associated sprite.
Mimic Sprite	Calls the event handlers of a specified sprite based on the event handlers of its associated sprite.
Set Message	Sets the $statusMessage$ variable to a specified string when the user's mouse enters the bounds of its associated sprite and back to $statusDefault$ when the mouse leaves.
Menu Button	Gradually transitions its associated sprite's opacity based on its `vBlend` property and mouse interaction. Also sets the visibility of the sprite just below the associated sprite in the Score and plays sounds based on mouse interaction.
Push Button	Sets its associated sprite's opacity and plays sounds based on mouse interaction.
Menu Link	Sets it associated sprite's cast member's background color based on its `vBright` property and plays sounds based on mouse interaction.
Help Button	Plays the `Help` marker when the user clicks its associated sprite.
Map Button	Plays the `Map` marker when the user clicks its associated sprite.
Exit Button	Stops the movie entirely when the user clicks its associated sprite.
Blank Menu	Sets the cursor and plays a sound based on mouse interaction.
Status Text	Sets the $statusText$ and $statusDefault$ variables based on the location of the playback head in the Score. Also sets its associated sprite's cast member's text to the value of the $statusText$ variable.
Room L1	Sets the value of the $statusText$ variable and displays the portfolio image sprite based on mouse interaction.
Room R1	Sets the value of the $statusText$ variable and displays the portfolio image sprite based on mouse interaction.
Portfolio Image	Sets its associated sprite's `visible` property to `false` and the QuickTime VR movie sprite's `visible` property to `true` when the user clicks its associated sprite.

2. In the Cast window, click the Global member. Director will display the Global script within the Script window.

3. Use the Previous Cast Member and Next Cast Member buttons to view each of the Lingo scripts in the Scripts cast.

After browsing through the Company Headquarters interface's scripts and taking a look at its organization in the Score, you should have a good understanding of the logic behind this interface. If some of its aspects are still not clear, you may want to refer to Appendix B, "Guide to Lingo Programming." Although understanding the innerworkings of the Company Headquarters interface at this time is not completely necessary, it should make things easier for you as you re-create the interface throughout the rest of this chapter.

COMPLETING THE ROOM L1 BEHAVIOR

The Room L1 behavior has two main functions. It must set the *statusText* variable based on the position of the mouse within the QuickTime VR movie, and it must display an appropriate portfolio image each time one of the movie's hot spots is clicked. The QuickTime VR movie itself takes care of the camera movement. The simplest way to test a single variable or function for a variety of values is to use a `case ... of` conditional. For more information on this sort of conditional, refer to Appendix A. To complete the Room L1 behavior script, follow the steps outlined in Procedure 16.1.

Procedure 16.1   Completing the Room L1 Behavior Script

1. Open the `chtemp.dir` file from the 16 - Company Headquarters folder as specified in Appendix A.

2. In the Cast window, click the Room L1 member. Director will highlight the Room L1 member (see Figure 16.5).

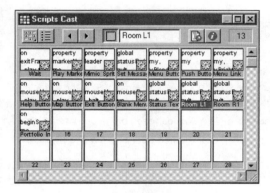

Figure 16.5   *The Room L1 member.*

3. Click the Cast Member Script button. Director will display the Room L1 script within the Script window.

4. In the `mouseWithin` handler, type the following code:

```
case my.ptToHotSpotID(the mouseLoc) of
    159: statusText = "Click here to jump back to the Main Menu."
    31: statusText = "Click here to view" && quote & "The Moment of Blue Spark." &
quote
    57: statusText = "Click here to view" && quote & "Hell Hath No Fury." & quote
    160: statusText = "Click here to view the cartoon character Augie sitting in
his desk."
    240: statusText = "Click here to view a fish jumping out of a lake."
    4: statusText = "Click here to view a cartoon space shuttle complete with pas-
sengers."
    17: statusText = "Click here to view a waterway and its surroundings from the
sky."
    otherwise: statusText = "Drag here to look around the room."
end case
```

Note that the preceding conditional sets the *statusText* variable based on the ID of the hot spot the mouse is currently over. If the mouse is not over a hot spot, *statusText* just instructs the user how to look around the room.

5. In the `mouseLeave` handler, type the following code:

```
statusText = statusDefault
```

Note that the preceding line sets the *statusText* variable to the value of *statusDefault*. The *statusDefault* variable stores the status text that should appear while the user's mouse is not over a sprite that uses the Set Message behavior.

6. In the `mouseDown` handler, type the following code:

```
if my.ptToHotSpotID(the clickLoc) = 0 then
   exit
else if my.ptToHotSpotID(the clickLoc) = 159 then
   play "Build Main"
else
   case my.ptToHotSpotID(the mouseLoc) of
      31: imageNum = 1
      57: imageNum = 2
      160: imageNum = 3
      240: imageNum = 4
      4: imageNum = 5
      17: imageNum = 6
   end case
   my.visible = false
   sprite(10).member = member("Illustration" && imageNum, "Portfolio")
   sprite(10).visible = true
end if
```

Note that the preceding conditional exits the current handler if the user has not clicked a hot spot. Otherwise, it plays the `Build Main` marker if the hot spot ID is 159. If neither condition is met, it sets `imageNum` based on the hot spot ID, hides the QuickTime VR movie, and shows the chosen portfolio image.

7. From the toolbar, click the Script Window button. Director will close the Script window.

The Room L1 behavior will make it so that when the user clicks one of the QuickTime VR movie's hot spots, one of the Illustration bitmaps will fill the Stage. The QuickTime VR movie must make itself invisible before displaying the portfolio image because it is in Direct to Stage mode. Direct to Stage means that no other sprites can appear in front of the movie. It is not completely necessary to keep your movies in Direct to Stage mode, but it generally makes things move much more smoothly.

ADDING THE ILLUSTRATION GALLERY ROOM

Now that you have completed the Room L1 behavior, you can really bring the Room L1 QuickTime VR movie to life. If you were to preview your movie right now, however, you wouldn't notice any change at all because the Room L1 behavior is not yet applied to a sprite. Before you can use the behavior, you must create a Room L1 sprite and position it appropriately. To position the Room L1 sprite within the Score and the Stage and then apply its appropriate behavior, follow the steps outlined in Procedure 16.2.

Procedure 16.2 Positioning the Room L1 Sprite Within the Score and the Stage

1. In the Cast window, click the Choose Cast button and select the Movies option. Director will display the Movies cast within the Cast window.

2. Drag the Room L1 member from the Cast window to cell 89 of channel 2 of the Score window (see Figure 16.6). Director will display the Room L1 sprite within the Stage window.

>>>

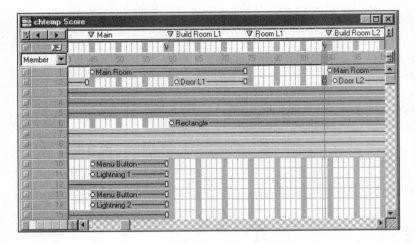

Figure 16.6 *The Room L1 sprite.*

3. Using the Property Inspector window, type **180** into the Y field and then press the Enter key (Return on Macintosh). Director will update the Room L1 sprite within the Stage window (see Figure 16.7).

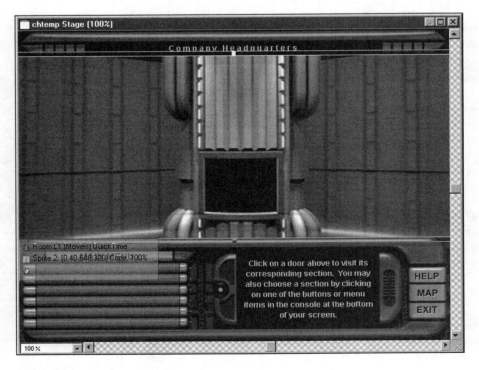

Figure 16.7 *The Room L1 sprite.*

4. Apply the Room L1 behavior to the Room L1 sprite that begins in cell 89 of channel 2 as specified in Appendix A.

If you preview your movie right now and navigate the Illustration Gallery section, the Room L1 QuickTime VR movie will appear to work properly. You will be able to drag your mouse to look around the room and even click the door at the end of the hallway to return to the main menu. Do not click any of the other hot spots, however. Because the Room L1 behavior refers to a portfolio image sprite, and you have not yet created one, clicking one of the image hot spots will have unpredictable results.

ADDING THE ILLUSTRATION PORTFOLIO IMAGE

After you create a portfolio image sprite, clicking an image hot spot will make it become visible. Because its dimensions match those of the Stage, it will fill the entire Stage window. To return to the Illustration Gallery room, the user will click the Stage. Because the portfolio image will be in front of all the other sprites, it will intercept the mouse click. Therefore, you must modify the Portfolio Image behavior to include a mouseDown handler that hides the portfolio image sprite and returns to the QuickTime VR movie. To position the Illustration 1 sprite within the Score and the Stage and complete and apply its appropriate behavior, follow the steps outlined in Procedure 16.3.

Procedure 16.3   Adding the Illustration Portfolio Image

1. In the Cast window, click the Choose Cast button and select the Scripts option. Director will display the Scripts cast within the Cast window.

2. Click the Portfolio Image member. Director will highlight the Portfolio Image member (see Figure 16.8).

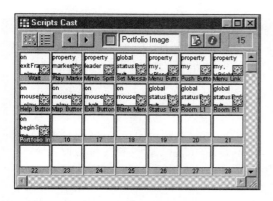

Figure 16.8   *The Portfolio Image member.*

3. Click the Cast Member Script button. Director will display the Portfolio Image script within the Script window.

4. In the mouseDown handler, type the following code:

```
sprite(me.spriteNum).visible = false
sprite(2).visible = true
```

Note that the preceding two lines hide the portfolio image and then show the QuickTime VR movie.

5. From the toolbar, click the Script Window button. Director will close the Script window.

6. Within the Cast window, click the Choose Cast button and select the Portfolio option. Director will display the Portfolio cast within the Cast window.

7. Drag the Illustration 1 member from the Cast window to cell 75 of channel 10 of the Score window (see Figure 16.9). Director will display the Illustration 1 sprite within the Stage window.

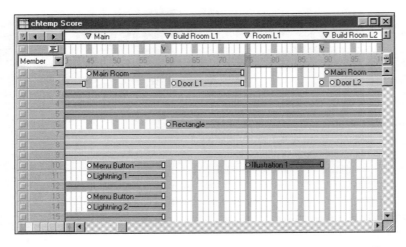

Figure 16.9 *The Illustration 1 member.*

8. Apply the Portfolio Image behavior to the Illustration 1 sprite that begins in cell 75 of channel 10 as specified in Appendix A.

Preview your movie again. The Room L1 QuickTime VR movie should work with the portfolio image to create a fully immersive Illustration Gallery section. Of course the section still has one very noticeable flaw. After the Door L1 movie has finished playing, the interface shows only black for a moment before displaying the Room L1 movie. The two movies cannot be placed directly beside each other in the Score because the Room L1 movie does not pick up where the Door L1 movie leaves off. The user would notice an uncomfortably large jump in camera position.

BRIDGING THE GAP BETWEEN DOOR L1 AND ROOM L1

To eliminate the pause between the end of the Door L1 movie and the beginning of the Room L1 QuickTime VR movie, you should create a smooth transition between them. The first is taking a screen capture of the Room L1 movie, as discussed in Chapter 12, "epic Portfolio." Once again, the screen capture has already been made into a cast member for you. The cast member is named Room L1 Screen and is located in the Graphics cast. To position the Room L1 Screen within the Score and the Stage, follow the steps outlined in Procedure 16.4.

Procedure 16.4 Positioning the Room L1 Screen Within the Score and the Stage

1. In the Cast window, click the Choose Cast button and select the Graphics option. Director will display the Graphics cast within the Cast window.

2. Drag the Room L1 Screen member from the Cast window to cell 75 of channel 1 of the Score window (see Figure 16.10). Director will display the Room L1 Screen sprite within the Stage window.

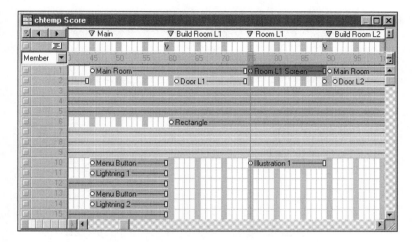

Figure 16.10 *The Room L1 Screen member within the Score window.*

Note that because the Illustration 1 sprite is located in a channel with a larger number than that of the Room L1 Screen sprite's channel, the Room L1 Screen sprite will not be visible in the Stage window unless you hide Illustration 1 or preview your movie.

3. Using the Property Inspector window, type **180** into the Y field and then press the Enter key (Return on Macintosh). Director will update the Room L1 Screen sprite within the Stage window.

4. Within the Score window, click cell 89 of channel 1. Director will highlight cell 89 of the Room L1 Screen sprite.

5. Click the Insert menu and select the Keyframe option. Director will mark cell 89 of channel 1 as a keyframe.

6. In the Score window, click cell 75 of channel 1. Director will highlight cell 75 of the Room L1 Screen sprite (see Figure 16.11).

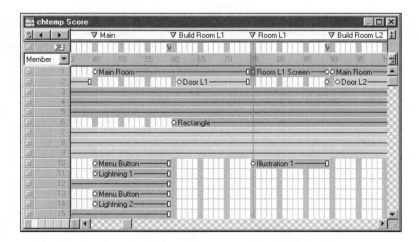

Figure 16.11 *The selected cell.*

7. Using the Property Inspector window, type **300** into the X field, **39** into the Y field, **1408** into the W field, **616** into the H field, and then press the Enter key (Return on Macintosh). Director will update the Room L1 Screen sprite within the Stage window.

Now that you have created a transition effect with the Room L1 Screen sprite, you should preview your movie to see how it looks. Normally, you wouldn't be able to create this transition so easily. First, you would have to open the Door L1 movie in QuickTime and scroll to its final frame. Then you would want to take a screen capture and place it on the Stage to give you an idea of where the Door L1 movie leaves off. When it was positioned correctly on the Stage, you would be able to adjust the Room L1 Screen sprite to create the transition effect. Of course the QuickTime screen capture would need to be deleted from your Director movie after you had finished the transition effect.

MAKING ADJUSTMENTS

To change the title that appears at the top of the Stage, you should edit the Title member of the Text cast. To change the names and content of the sections, you will have to edit nearly all the remaining members of the Text cast. Also remember to edit the parameters passed to the Button sprites through the Set Message behavior. Otherwise, your status messages may not match the buttons to which they correspond. If you choose to keep the QuickTime VR Gallery rooms, you should replace all the members of the Portfolio cast with items from your own portfolio. Just be sure to keep the cast members named exactly as they were prior to your changes.

"The world is not good enough. We must make it better."
—Alice Walker

>>> chapter 17
3d gallery

Figures 17.1-17.4   *The 3D Gallery interface in action.*

APPROACHING THE "3D GALLERY" INTERFACE

Director's new Shockwave 3D technology enables programmers to produce interactive 3D content for Windows, Macintosh, and the web. The Help section of Director 8.5 contains an incredibly vast library of new Lingo commands for dealing with Shockwave 3D content. Instead of attempting to browse through the 3D Lingo Dictionary right now, you should first understand the fundamentals of allowing the user to interact with models and overlays. As you become familiar with the basics of 3D Lingo, you will find that most commands are really quite self-explanatory. The most difficult part of programming in 3D Lingo is not learning the commands but learning how and when to use them.

UNDERSTANDING THE 3D GALLERY INTERFACE

If you glance at the Score window of the 3D Gallery, you might get the impression that the interface is much simpler than others you have built. This is true in that you will be working with only one sprite on only one keyframe. Within the sprite, however, are several models, each containing its own properties. In addition to working with 3D models, you will also learn to create 2D overlays and allow the user to interact with them as if they were individual sprites. Because Lingo's event handlers all refer to the single Shockwave 3D sprite and not any of its models or overlays, you will have to learn to work without them. Thankfully, Lingo is such a flexible language that this should be nothing more than a minor inconvenience. To view the various Lingo scripts of the Scripts cast, follow these steps:

1. Open the `3d.dir` file from the 17 - 3D Gallery folder as specified in Appendix A, "Guide to Common Tasks." The Scripts cast contains the seven Lingo scripts shown in Table 17.1.

Table 17.1 The Scripts Cast Lingo Scripts

Script Name	Description
Global	Initializes global variables, works with overlays and textures, and handles camera movement.
Wait	Makes the movie repeat the current frame over and over until otherwise specified.
Status Message	Sets the *useStatus* variable based on the user's interaction with a specified model.
Spinnable Model	Enables the user to rotate a specified model by clicking it and dragging.
Hovering Model	Moves a specified model back and forth along the Y axis to create a hovering effect.
Help Button	Displays the Help button's Over state and status message based on the user's mouse position.
Exit Button	Displays the Exit button's Over state and status message based on the user's mouse position. Stops the movie entirely when the user clicks the Exit button.

2. In the Cast window, click the Global member. Director will display the Global script within the Script window.

3. Use the Previous Cast Member and Next Cast Member buttons to view each of the Lingo scripts in the Scripts cast.

After browsing through the 3D Gallery interface's scripts and taking a look at its organization in the Score, you should have a good understanding of the logic behind this interface. If some of its aspects are still not clear, you may want to refer to Appendix B, "Guide to Lingo Programming." Although understanding the innerworkings of the 3D Gallery interface at this time is not completely necessary, it should make things easier for you as you re-create the interface throughout the remainder of this chapter.

SETTING UP THE SCORE

When you begin converting your interfaces into executable projectors, as specified in Appendix A, you will find that some movies may take a moment to load. While a projector movie is loading, it displays the movie's very first frame as it appears initially. Therefore, you should always make sure that the initial appearance of your movie's first frame will look right as a loader frame. For the purposes of the 3D Gallery interface, just placing the Shockwave 3D scene in the first frame of the movie will not work because the scene's initial camera position changes through Lingo code. If the scene were in the first frame of a projector movie, the user would see the default camera position while the movie was loading and then see the camera position set by Lingo. To avoid this inconsistency, just leave the Shockwave 3D scene out of the first frame of the 3D Gallery interface. To position the interface's sprites within the Score and the Stage, follow the steps outlined in Procedure 17.1.

Procedure 17.1   Positioning the Interface's Sprites Within the Score and the Stage

1. Open the `3dtemp.dir` file from the 17 - 3D Gallery folder as specified in Appendix A.

2. In the Cast window, click the Choose Cast button and select the Media option. Director will display the Media cast within the Cast window.

3. Drag the Scene member from the Cast window into cell 2 of channel 1 of the Score window. Director will display the Scene sprite within the Stage window.

   Remember that the first frame should remain blank if you want to convert your 3D Gallery interface into an executable projector.

4. Within the Score window, drag cell 29 of channel 1 to frame 14. Director will curtail the Scene sprite to frame 14.

5. Click cell 3 of channel 1. Director will highlight the Scene sprite (see Figure 17.5).

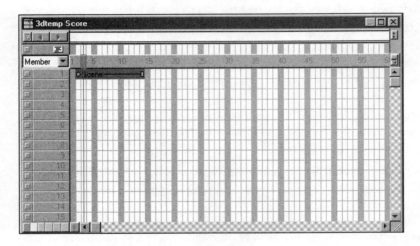

Figure 17.5   *The Scene sprite within the Score window.*

6. Using the Property Inspector window, type **640** into the W field, **480** into the H field, and then press the Enter key (Return on Macintosh). Director will update the Scene sprite within the Stage window.

7. Apply the Help Button behavior to the Scene sprite that begins in cell 2 of channel 1 as specified in Appendix A.

8. Apply the Wait behavior to frame 2 as specified in Appendix A.

Although the Help button is only a part of the interface's Shockwave 3D scene, you must apply its behavior to the Scene sprite. Director does not currently offer a method to apply behaviors directly to models and overlays. You might be wondering why the 3D Gallery interface uses behavior scripts at all instead of using one big movie script. The answer might not make sense to you until you progress a little further into the chapter. When you begin creating behaviors for models within the Shockwave 3D scene, you will need to apply multiple instances of a behavior to a single sprite. Each behavior instance will use a unique parameter value to affect only its specified model.

ACTIVATING THE EXIT BUTTON

The 3D Gallery interface uses the global variables *useCursor* and *useStatus* to keep track of the cursor and status message that the interface should display. At the beginning of each frame, the Global script sets the *useCursor* and *useStatus* variables to blank string values. Then the model and overlay behaviors each modify the variables if they find it necessary to do so. When the Global script checks the values of *useCursor* and *useStatus* again, it should receive either the names of a cursor and status message to display or blank string values. If the Global script receives a blank string from *useCursor* or *useStatus*, it just displays the default cursor or status message. The Exit Button behavior affects both *useCursor* and *useStatus*. To complete the Exit Button behavior and apply it to its appropriate sprite, follow the steps outlined in Procedure 17.2.

Procedure 17.2   Completing the Exit Button Behavior

1. In the Cast window, click the Choose Cast button and select the Scripts option. Director will display the Scripts cast within the Cast window.

2. Click the Exit Button member. Director will highlight the Exit Button member (see Figure 17.6).

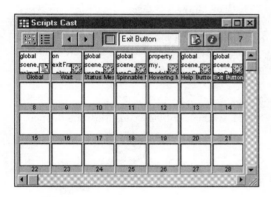

Figure 17.6   *The Exit Button member.*

3. Click the Cast Member Script button. Director will display the Exit Button script within the Script window.

4. In the `prepareFrame` handler, type the following code:

```
if (the mouseLoc).inside(rect(530, 440, 590, 470)) then
   useCursor = "Point"
   useStatus = "Exit"
   scene.camera(1).overlay[5].source = scene.texture("Exit Button Over")
else
   scene.camera(1).overlay[5].source = scene.texture("Exit Button")
end if
```

Note that the preceding conditional sets the *useCursor* variable to "Point", the *useStatus* variable to "Exit", and the `source` property of the camera's Exit button overlay to the button's Over state if the user's mouse is within the Exit button's bounds. Otherwise, it sets the camera's Exit button overlay to its normal state.

5. Next, in the `mouseDown` handler, type the following code:

```
if not (the mouseLoc).inside(rect(530, 440, 590, 470)) then
   exit
```

Note that the preceding conditional exits the current handler if the user's mouse is not within the bounds of the Exit button.

Note that the following line stops the movie entirely:

```
halt
```

6. From the toolbar, click the Script Window button. Director will close the Script window.

7. Apply the Exit Button behavior to the Scene sprite that begins in cell 2 of channel 1 as specified in Appendix A.

At this point, preview your movie and make sure that the Exit button functions properly. Each time you move your mouse over the Exit button, the interface's cursor and status message should change. When you move outside of the Exit button's bounds, the cursor and status message should return to normal. If you click the Exit button while previewing your interface, Director should immediately stop the movie and select the Scene sprite.

ADDING THE SCULPTURE STATUS MESSAGES

Because the Status Message behavior is meant to affect only a single model within a scene, it uses its `modelName` property to determine when the specified model should be affected. The behavior's `mouseWithin` handler first determines which model the mouse is currently over. Then, if that model matches the model specified by the `modelName` property, it allows the handler to proceed. If the mouse model does not match the `modelName` model, the handler exits before the remaining commands have a chance to execute. To complete the Status Message behavior and apply it to its appropriate sprite, follow the steps outlined in Procedure 17.3.

Procedure 17.3   Completing the Status Message Behavior

1. In the Cast window, click the Status Message member. Director will highlight the Status Message member (see Figure 17.7).

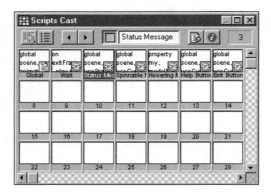

Figure 17.7   *The Status Message member.*

2. Click the Cast Member Script button. Director will display the Status Message script within the Script window.

3. In the `mouseWithin` handler, type the following code:

```
mouseModel = my.camera(1).modelUnderLoc(the mouseLoc)
```

Note that the preceding line sets a local variable named *mouseModel* to the model currently under the mouse cursor.

Note that the following conditional exits the current handler if the *mouseModel* variable's name property is not equal to the behavior's modelName property or the *mouseModel* variable is not a valid model. The conditional must make sure that the *mouseModel* variable is a valid model before attempting to access its name property:

```
if ilk(mouseModel) = #model then
  if mouseModel.name <> modelName then
    exit
  end if
else
  exit
end if
```

Note that the following line sets the *useStatus* variable to the value of the messageName property:

```
useStatus = messageName
```

4. From the toolbar, click the Script Window button. Director will close the Script window.

5. Apply the Status Message behavior to the Scene sprite that begins in cell 2 of channel 1 as specified in Appendix A.

6. When the Parameters dialog box prompts you for values, click the OK button (see Figure 17.8). Director will apply the Status Message behavior to the Scene sprite.

Figure 17.8 *The OK button.*

7. Apply the Status Message behavior to the Scene sprite that begins in cell 2 of channel 1 as specified in Appendix A.

8. When the Parameters dialog box prompts you for values, type **saucer:sculpt2** into the Model Name field, **2** into the Message Name field, and then press the Enter key (Return on Macintosh). Director will apply the Status Message behavior to the Scene sprite.

   Note that models such as saucer:sculpt2 must be named within your 3D editor prior to export as a Shockwave 3D scene.

9. Apply the Status Message behavior to the Scene sprite that begins in cell 2 of channel 1 as specified in Appendix A.

10. When the Parameters dialog box prompts you for values, type **saucer:sculpt3** into the Model Name field, **3** into the Message Name field, and then press the Enter key (Return on Macintosh). Director will apply the Status Message behavior to the Scene sprite.

11. Apply the Status Message behavior to the Scene sprite that begins in cell 2 of channel 1 as specified in Appendix A.

>>>

12. When the Parameters dialog box prompts you for values, type **saucer:sculpt4** into the Model Name field, **4** into the Message Name field, and then press the Enter key (Return on Macintosh). Director will apply the Status Message behavior to the Scene sprite.

After you have applied the four instances of the Status Message behavior to the Scene sprite, the interface's status bar should be fully functional. The Help button, the Exit button, and all four sculpture models should display their own unique status messages. Because the status bar is in the form of a camera overlay, the different messages must be in the form of textures created from bitmap cast members. This means that if you ever want to change the status messages that the interface currently displays, you will have to edit the Status bitmaps.

COMPLETING THE SPINNABLE MODEL BEHAVIOR

The Spinnable Model behavior enables the user to rotate a specified model on the X and Y axes. Thanks to Director's new 3D Lingo, this is not a complex task. The behavior starts to become a little complicated, however, when you use rotation velocity caps and friction. Don't worry. When you look at the Lingo code piece by piece, it will begin to make sense. The toughest part of enabling the user to rotate models is determining when a specified model should be affected. You should remember this technique from the Status Message behavior's `mouseWithin` handler. To complete the Spinnable Model behavior and apply it to its appropriate sprite, follow the steps outlined in Procedure 17.4.

Procedure 17.4   Completing the Spinnable Model Behavior

1. In the Cast window, click the Spinnable Model member. Director will highlight the Spinnable Model member (see Figure 17.9).

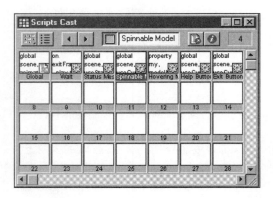

Figure 17.9   *The Spinnable Model member.*

2. Click the Cast Member Script button. Director will display the Spinnable Model script within the Script window.

3. In the `mouseDown` handler, type the following code:

```
mouseModel = my.camera(1).modelUnderLoc(the mouseLoc)
if ilk(mouseModel) = #model then
  if mouseModel.name <> modelName then
    exit
  end if
else
```

```
      exit
   end if
```

Note that the following line sets the `dragging` property to `true`. It will only execute if the preceding conditional does not cause the handler to exit:

```
dragging = true
```

4. In the `prepareFrame` handler, type the following code:

```
if the mouseUp then dragging = false
```

Note that the preceding line sets the `dragging` property to `false` if the user is not currently pressing the mouse button.

Note that the following conditional sets the *useCursor* variable to "Drag" if the value of the `dragging` property is `false`:

```
if dragging then useCursor = "Drag"
```

Note that the following conditional checks to make sure that either the `rotateH` or the `rotateV` property is equal to `true`. If the specified model is not meant to rotate on either axis, Lingo can ignore the rotation code.

```
if rotateH or rotateV then
```

Note that the following conditional sets the `vrx` property to half the distance between the vertical location of the mouse and the `oldV` property and then checks to make sure that `vrx` is no less than negative 45 and no more than positive 45 if `dragging` and `rotateV` are both `true`. Otherwise, it sets the `vrx` property to itself multiplied by the `friction` property. The `friction` property is generally a value between zero and one, so this has the effect of reducing the value of `vrx` and slowing down the specified model's rotation on the X axis:

```
if dragging and rotateV then
   vrx = (the mouseV-oldV)*0.5
   if vrx < -45 then
     vrx = -45
   else if vrx > 45 then
     vrx = 45
   end if
else
   vrx = vrx*friction
end if
```

Note that the following conditional sets the `vry` property to half the distance between the horizontal location of the mouse and the `oldH` property and then checks to make sure that `vry` is no less than negative 45 and no more than positive 45 if `dragging` and `rotateH` are both `true`. Otherwise, it sets the `vry` property to itself multiplied by the `friction` property:

```
if dragging and rotateH then
   vry = (the mouseH-oldH)*0.5
   if vry < -45 then
     vry = -45
   else if vry > 45 then
     vry = 45
   end if
else
   vry = vry*friction
end if
```

Note that the following rotates the specified model based on the `vrx` and `vry` properties:

```
scene.model(modelName).rotate(vrx, vry, 0)
    end if
```

Note that the following two lines store the position of the mouse cursor in memory through the `oldH` and `oldV` properties:

```
oldH = the mouseH
oldV = the mouseV
```

5. From the toolbar, click the Script Window button. Director will close the Script window.

6. Apply the Spinnable Model behavior to the Scene sprite that begins in cell 2 of channel 1 as specified in Appendix A.

7. When the Parameters dialog box prompts you for values, click the OK button (see Figure 17.10). Director will apply the Status Message behavior to the Scene sprite.

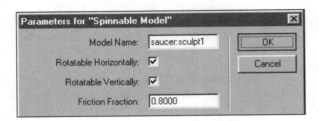

Figure 17.10   *The OK button within the Parameters dialog box.*

8. Apply the Spinnable Model behavior to the Scene sprite that begins in cell 2 of channel 1 as specified in Appendix A.

9. When the Parameters dialog box prompts you for values, type **saucer:sculpt2** into the Model Name field and then press the Enter key (Return on Macintosh). Director will apply the Spinnable Model behavior to the Scene sprite.

10. Apply the Spinnable Model behavior to the Scene sprite that begins in cell 2 of channel 1 as specified in Appendix A.

11. When the Parameters dialog box prompts you for values, type **saucer:sculpt3** into the Model Name field and then press the Enter key (Return on Macintosh). Director will apply the Spinnable Model behavior to the Scene sprite.

12. Apply the Spinnable Model behavior to the Scene sprite that begins in cell 2 of channel 1 as specified in Appendix A.

13. When the Parameters dialog box prompts you for values, type **saucer:sculpt4** into the Model Name field and then press the Enter key (Return on Macintosh). Director will apply the Spinnable Model behavior to the Scene sprite.

If you preview your movie right now, everything should function just about like the original 3D Gallery interface. The only difference you might notice is that the sculptures do not bob up and down slightly while hovering above their pedestals. This is only a minor effect, but it can add a great deal to the interface. Slightly moving the sculptures serves to separate them from the scene's background and let the user know that they are dynamic elements of the interface.

COMPLETING THE HOVERING MODEL BEHAVIOR

The Hovering Model behavior's only purpose is to cause its specified model to bob up and down rhythmically. There are four main components of a hovering model's vertical location: its current position, current velocity, current acceleration, and its normal position. The `normalPY` property stores the specified model's normal position, around which the model will move. A model's normal position should be a little higher than its initial position in the scene to make sure than no part of the model intersects with its pedestal. The `py` property stores the float value of the specified model's position on the Y axis. The model's velocity on the Y axis is stored in the `vpy` property, and the acceleration is always either 0.02 or negative 0.02. The initial value of `vpy` determines the amount that the specified model will deviate from its `normalPY` property. To complete the Hovering Model behavior and apply it to its appropriate sprite, follow the steps outlined in Procedure 17.5.

Procedure 17.5   Completing the Hovering Model Behavior

1. In the Cast window, click the Hovering Model member. Director will highlight the Hovering Model member (see Figure 17.11).

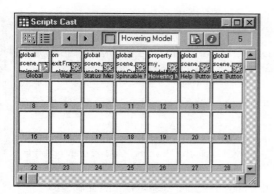

Figure 17.11   *The Hovering Model member.*

2. Click the Cast Member Script button. Director will display the Hovering Model script within the Script window.

3. Within the Script window, in the `prepareFrame` handler, type the following code:

```
if py < normalPY then
  vpy = vpy + 0.02
else
  vpy = vpy - 0.02
end if
```

Note that the preceding conditional adds 0.02 to the current value of the `vpy` property if the value of `py` is less than `normalPY`. Otherwise, it subtracts 0.02 from the `vpy` property.

Note that the following line adds the value of the `vpy` property to the *py* variable:

```
py = py + vpy
```

Note that the following line sets the specified model's position on the Y axis to the value of `py`:

```
my.member.model(modelName).transform.position.y = py
```

>>>

4. From the toolbar, click the Script Window button. Director will close the Script window.

5. Apply the Hovering Model behavior to the Scene sprite that begins in cell 2 of channel 1 as specified in Appendix A.

6. When the Parameters dialog box prompts you for a value, click the OK button (see Figure 17.12). Director will apply the Hovering Model behavior to the Scene sprite.

Figure 17.12 *The OK button within the Parameters dialog box.*

7. Apply the Hovering Model behavior to the Scene sprite that begins in cell 2 of channel 1 as specified in Appendix A.

8. When the Parameters dialog box prompts you for a value, type **saucer:sculpt2** into the Model Name field and then press the Enter key (Return on Macintosh). Director will apply the Hovering Model behavior to the Scene sprite.

9. Apply the Hovering Model behavior to the Scene sprite that begins in cell 2 of channel 1 as specified in Appendix A.

10. When the Parameters dialog box prompts you for a value, type **saucer:sculpt3** into the Model Name field and then press the Enter key (Return on Macintosh). Director will apply the Hovering Model behavior to the Scene sprite.

11. Apply the Hovering Model behavior to the Scene sprite that begins in cell 2 of channel 1 as specified in Appendix A.

12. When the Parameters dialog box prompts you for a value, type **saucer:sculpt4** into the Model Name field and then press the Enter key (Return on Macintosh). Director will apply the Hovering Model behavior to the Scene sprite.

Now that you have completed your 3D Gallery interface, preview your movie one more time and test all its major components. Move from side to side to test the Global script's camera rotation. After you have a sculpture in sight, make sure it is hovering properly and drag part of it to make it rotate. Try releasing click while you are dragging to make the sculpture model spin. When you are satisfied that everything works as it should, you might want to adjust the "friction fraction" parameter values of the Scene sprite's Spinnable Model behavior instances. The values can range anywhere from zero to one. A value of zero would cause a model to stop spinning as soon as the user releases a mouse click, and a value of one would allow the model to spin indefinitely.

MAKING ADJUSTMENTS

If you decide to create your own unique version of the 3D Gallery interface, you will almost definitely want to build your own Shockwave 3D scene. You could customize the existing interface to an extent by just changing the overlay graphics; if you want to fill the interface with your own 3D portfolio, however, you will need to create a scene within a popular 3D editor such as 3D Studio MAX or LightWave 3D, and then export it to the Shockwave 3D, or W3D, format. You should position your camera directly in the middle of the gallery room and surround it with 3D models from your own portfolio. Make sure that the camera is facing the wall that is opposite the gallery's door if you want the camera to move into the room as it does in the original 3D Gallery interface. When your W3D file is complete, import it into your director movie and then paste it over the original Shockwave 3D scene. You will need to rename the new cast member to **Scene** and adjust the behavior parameters to match your new scene's models before previewing your new interface.

▼▼▼ conclusion

CONGRATULATIONS

You have completed the entire book. By now, you should have the skills necessary for every major aspect of interface development. You should be able to create complex interfaces for CD-ROMs and the Internet without much trouble. Moreover, you will find that once you know how to create interfaces in Director, you also can build a variety of other applications. As Director's popularity grows, your skills will only increase in value.

As you build more applications in Director, you will develop your skills further. The best way to learn the details and quirks of a piece of software is to use it frequently. If you find yourself stuck, and you don't know what to do, just try something and see whether it works. If it doesn't, try something else. So long as you save backup copies of your movies, you can't go wrong with experimentation.

You may not have realized that your skills in Director can actually translate to other programming languages. Of course, you will need to learn the syntax of the new languages and become familiar with the interfaces of their editors, but the basic programming logic always remains the same. Learning to think like a computer is generally the most challenging part of learning to program, but after you have the logic down, you should be all right.

ONLINE DIRECTOR RESOURCES

You can find a wealth of information online to build your knowledge of Director. This section lists a number of helpful sites that will enable you to enhance your skills and expand on what you have learned in this book.

CLEVERMEDIA DEVELOPMENT RESOURCES (*WWW.CLEVERMEDIA.COM/RESOURCES/*)

The CleverMedia Development Resources site (see Figure C.1) consists of links to resources such as "Tips, Tricks, and Techniques," "Questions and Answers," and of course, "Behaviors, Xtras, and Scripts." If you need specific questions about Director answered, CleverMedia's Director Community Resource, or DCR, can be very useful. The rest of the CleverMedia site offers dozens of playable arcade games created in both Director and Flash.

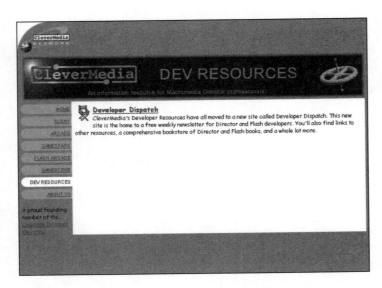

Figure C.1 *The front page of the CleverMedia Development Resources site.*

Director Intelligence Agency (www.director8.com/)

The Director Intelligence Agency, or DIA, offers one of the most extensive, well-organized Director libraries available (see Figure C.2). Of course there is one catch. The DIA requires a membership fee for total access to the site. Even if you don't want to register, however, you can still access the "Declassified" area, which contains a comprehensive library of Director information, resources, and categorized links to other web sites. The "Game Resources" section contains several categories of online tutorials about Lingo game programming. Even if you don't want to pay for membership, the DIA is well worth a visit.

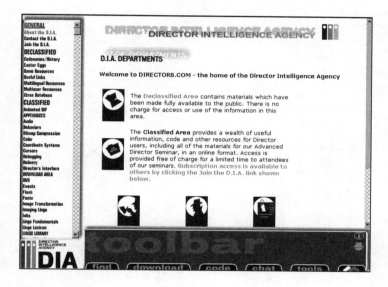

Figure C.2   *The front page of the Director Intelligence Agency site.*

Director Online User Group (www.director-online.com/)

The Director Online User Group, otherwise known as DOUG (see Figure C.3), is an online community of Lingo programmers complete with an extensive collection of articles written by DOUG members. An online forum enables you to post questions about Director or just browse through the questions that others have asked. DOUG also offers a wide variety of links and plug-ins to help you get more out of Director.

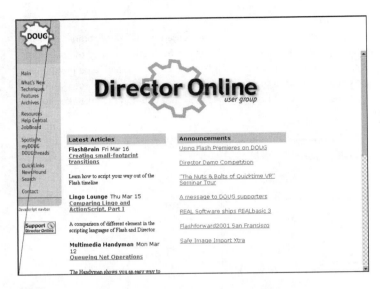

Figure C.3 *The front page of the Director Online User Group site.*

DIRECTOR WEB (*WWW.MCLI.DIST.MARICOPA.EDU/DIRECTOR/*)

Director Web (see Figure C.4) has been around since 1994, and in that time, it has compiled several searchable data-bases full of useful items like "Tips 'n' Scripts," "XStuff," and "Net Resources." If you want to catch up on the Direct-L newsletter, Director Web offers an archive of digests all the way back to 1995. Another helpful resource is their list of external applications that enable you to do things like create screen savers with Director or change the icon of your projector files. If you are looking for searchable libraries of Director content, you should visit Director Web immediately.

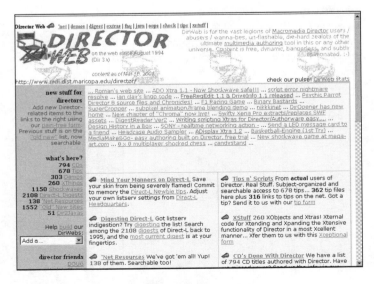

Figure C.4 *The front page of the Director Web site.*

MACROMEDIA DIRECTOR SUPPORT CENTER (*WWW.MACROMEDIA.COM/SUPPORT/DIRECTOR/*)

Macromedia's official Director support site offers a wide variety of information on Director, various tutorials, and free downloads of Director Xtras (see Figure C.5). The tutorials are organized into several different topics ranging from "The Basics" to "Top TechNotes." Registered users of Director also can obtain advice from certified Macromedia personnel. The Macromedia Director support Center is the site to visit if you are looking for official information from the people who know Director best.

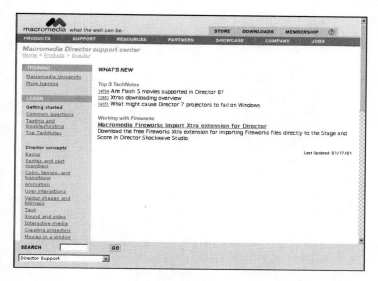

Figure C.5   *The front page of the Macromedia Director Support Center site.*

MEDIAMACROS (*WWW.MEDIAMACROS.COM/*)

The MediaMacros site contains searchable libraries of Lingo behaviors and even enables you to submit your own behaviors (see Figure C.6). Another unique feature is MediaMacros's Learning Arcade. You can play dozens of Shockwave games and then, if you like, download their source files to see how they were made. The Learning Arcade lets you learn Lingo while playing some very addictive arcade games. MediaMacros also offers a variety of other resources, but you will probably want to spend your time in the Learning Arcade.

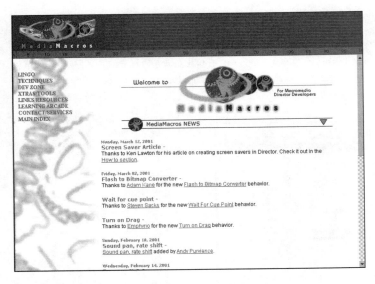

Figure C.6 *The front page of the MediaMacros site.*

UPDATE**STAGE** (*WWW.UPDATESTAGE.COM/*)

The updateStage site is an online newspaper centered on Director news and Lingo programming tips (see Figure C.7). You can browse through their archive of back issues, search their database of downloadable Xtras, or even see a complete list of the known bugs in Director. Being knowledgeable of Director's shortcomings can make debugging your Director interfaces a much easier task.

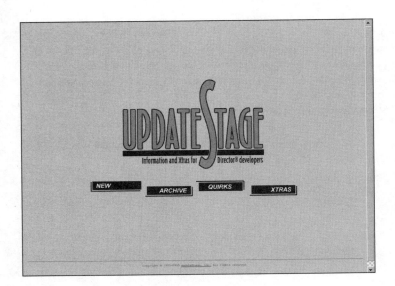

Figure C.7 *The front page of the updateStage site.*

ONLINE INTERFACE DESIGN RESOURCES

This section identifies a number of online resources related to interface design. Although these sites are not Director-specific, they can certainly help you realize the full design potential that Director promises.

EYEBALL DESIGN FXZONE (*WWW.EYEBALL-DESIGN.COM/FXZONE/*)

Eyeball Design puts their theories about graphic design into practice in this visually stunning site (see Figure C.8). The site contains a library of impressive PhotoShop effects, links to other design sites, and even a "Discussion Board" section that enables you to communicate with other designers and request new tutorials. The site is very well put together but probably won't be of much use to you unless you want to build your own interface graphics.

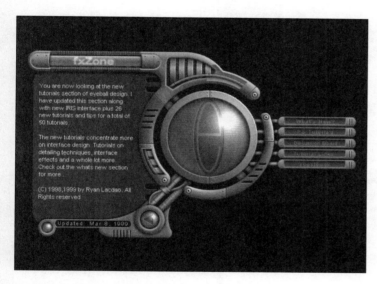

Figure C.8   *The front page of the Eyeball Design fxZone site.*

GLASSDOG WEB DESIGN (*HTTP://GLASSDOG.COM/DESIGN-O-RAMA/*)

The Glassdog Web Design site contains a host of information on web design and construction (see Figure C.9). Even though the Glassdog site offers some very nice design tips, its focus on web development means that, unless you plan to build web content, you may not find any useful information here. Still, the Glassdog Web Design site is a perfect example of how to apply (and sometimes even break) the rules of interface design.

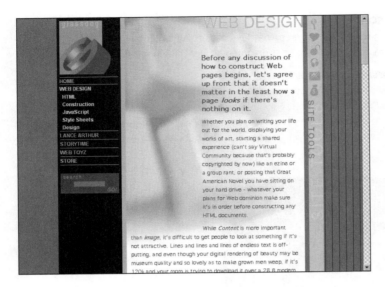

Figure C.9 *The front page of the Glassdog Web Design site.*

SOFTWARE DESIGN SMORGASBORD (*WWW.CHESCO.COM/~CMARION/*)

The Software Design Smorgasbord site (see Figure C.10) provides a wealth of knowledge on a number of different categories. With 10 sections to choose from, writer Craig Marion provides enough information to fill a textbook. The site is also well-organized and easy to navigate, so all this information is actually accessible.

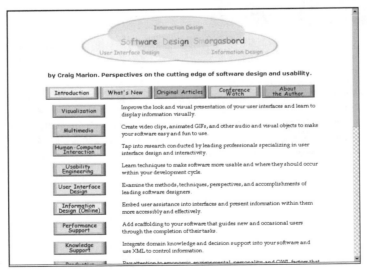

Figure C.10 *The front page of the Software Design Smorgasbord site.*

Web Developer Site Design (*www.webdeveloper.com/design/*)

As the name suggests, the Web Developer site covers only web aspects of interface design (see Figure C.11). If you don't intend to build web content anytime soon, you may as well forget about this site. Most of the Web Developer site deals with programming and graphics rather than design theory. Nevertheless, if you really want to find information on HTML, Flash, CGI, JavaScript, and other types of web development, this just might be the site for you.

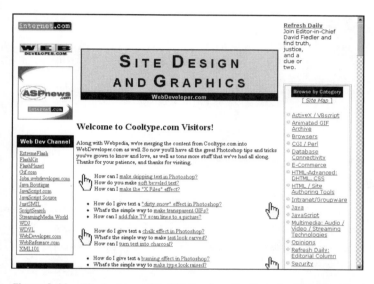

Figure C.11   *The front page of the Web Developer Site Design and Graphics site.*

XtraNet from Vertical Research (*www.vrix.com/*)

Vertical Research (see Figure C.12) covers the fundamentals of designing a modern user interface in the "Design" and "Style Guide" sections of the XtraNet site. The screen captures show a standard Windows environment, but the ideas discussed here can translate into any field of interface design. You should definitely visit the XtraNet from Vertical Research site if you want to understand more about the work that goes into designing a standard Windows user interface.

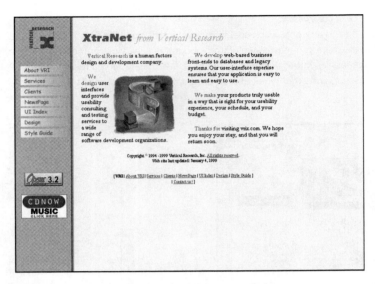

Figure C.12   *The front page of the XtraNet from Vertical Research site.*

PRODUCERS OF DIRECTOR XTRAS

The online resources listed in this section offer a wide variety of Xtras that you can access to enhance your Director project.

BEATNIK (WWW.BEATNIK.COM/SOFTWARE/XTRA_DIRECTOR.HTML)

Beatnik (see Figure C.13) is an Xtra for projectors or Shockwave that plays MP3 and MIDI format music using very little processing power. The Beatnik Audio Engine has become the standard both on and off the web. Beatnik enables the programmer to take advantage of up to 64 audio channels (as opposed to Director's 8). It even provides the ability to change the pitch of sounds through Lingo. For the professional developer concerned with quality audio, Beatnik is the only choice.

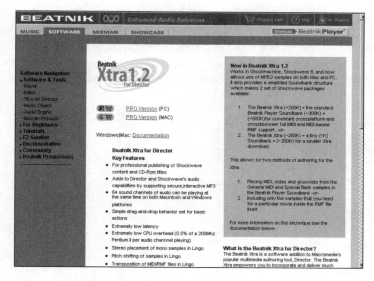

Figure C.13 *The Xtra page of the Beatnik site.*

DESIGNLYNX (*WWW.DESIGNLYNX.CO.UK/XTRAS/*)

DesignLynx produces a spell-checking Xtra named Speller that offers a variety of features (see Figure C.14). Three variations are available to fit your budget. The Behavior Xtra is designed to aid in the creation of complex behaviors. It makes adding behavior parameters as easy as filling out a form. DesignLynx also offers the BitChecker Xtra, which checks your Director movies for bitmap cast members that do not meet the bit depth and/or palette requirements you specify.

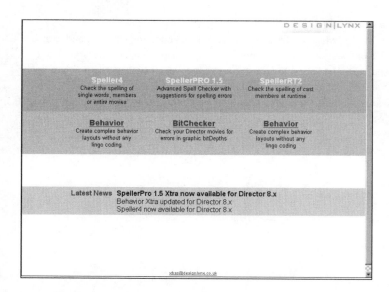

Figure C.14 *The Xtras page of the DesignLynx site.*

DIRECTXTRAS (*WWW.DIRECTXTRAS.COM/*)

The DirectXtras site contains a wide variety of Xtras (see Figure C.15). Some of the features offered by these Xtras include control over Internet connection, email, FTP, and the user's operating system. The DirectControl Xtra even offers programmers the ability to incorporate joystick control into their Director applications. The DirectXport Xtra enables you to apply a wide variety of effects to bitmap cast members and export them to 22 different file formats, including BMP, GIF, JPG, and PSD.

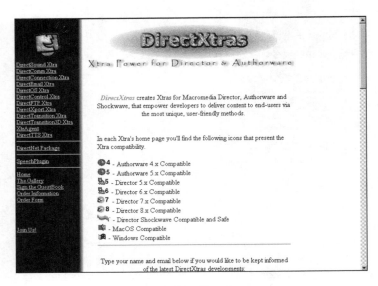

Figure C.15 *The front page of the DirectXtras site.*

ELECTRONIC INK (*WWW.PRINTOMATIC.COM/PRODUCTS.CFM*)

Electronic Ink's most famous Xtra is PrintOMatic, which enables the programmer to print images, text, and even a screen capture of the Stage (see Figure C.16). Electronic Ink also offers a "Lite" version that can give you most of PrintOMatic's functionality at absolutely no cost. They also produce the Table Xtra, which enables the programmer to create scrollable grids, and the Yak Xtra, which enables the programmer to convert text strings to speech. The Windows version of the Yak Xtra comes bundled with the Eloquent text-to-speech engine, so you may have to pay an additional fee.

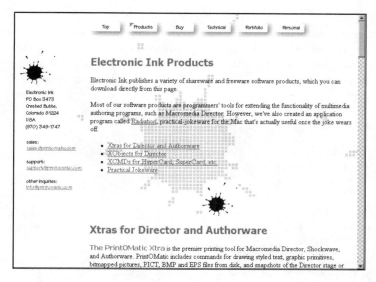

Figure C.16   *The products page of the Electronic Ink site.*

MACROMEDIA DIRECTOR XTRAS (*WWW.MACROMEDIA.COM/SOFTWARE/XTRAS/DIRECTOR/*)

Macromedia's official Director Xtras site (see Figure C.17) contains a comprehensive list of Xtra extensions ranging from transition packs to spell-checkers. All Xtras are organized alphabetically on the main page. If you click one of the links, it will lead to a page that contains the Xtra you requested and all others developed by its company. If you want to build your own Xtras in Visual C++, Macromedia even offers a link to its Xtra Extensions Developers Center.

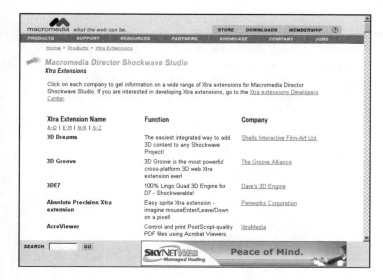

Figure C.17   *The Director Xtras page of the Macromedia site.*

MAGIC MODULES (WWW.MODS.COM.AU/)

Magic Modules is the company that makes Buddy API and Buddy Saver. The Buddy API Xtra gives the programmer incredible control over the Windows API or Macintosh Toolbox (see Figure C.18). Among other features, it enables the programmer to install fonts, control screen savers, and edit files through Lingo. Buddy Saver enables the programmer to create screen savers complete with Control Panel animations, configuration screens, and compressed installation programs.

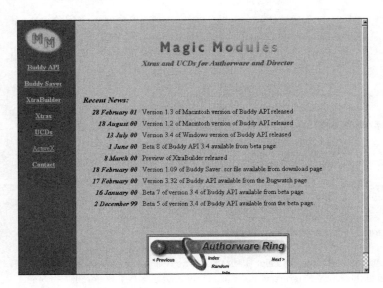

Figure C.18 *The front page of the Magic Modules site.*

MAGISTER LUDI (WWW.MAGISTERLUDI.COM/XTRAS/)

The Magister Ludi site offers Xtras to control Internet browsers, system sound volume, and monitor gamma (see Figure C.19). Magister Ludi also offers an absolutely free Xtra that enables the programmer to read keys in the Windows Registry. By accessing the Registry, the programmer can determine important information about Windows that would otherwise be hidden. Perhaps the most useful reason to read the Registry is to determine exactly which programs are installed on the user's system and to which directories.

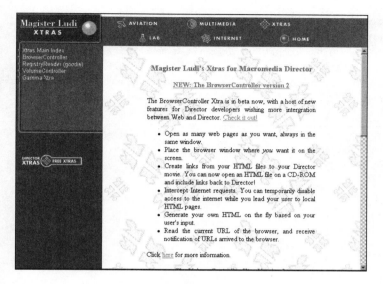

Figure C.19 *The Xtras page of the Magister Ludi site.*

PEGHOLE (*WWW.PEGHOLE.COM/XTRAS/*)

PegHole's OS Control Xtra enables the programmer to create actual system controls inside Director movies (see Figure C.20). Among other interface controls, the programmer can now add push buttons, scrollbars, sliders, radio buttons, and check boxes that match the appearance of the user's operating system. PegHole also offers the AutoComplete Xtra, which enhances Director's scripting environment by completing your Lingo commands for you as you type. The single user license is very affordable.

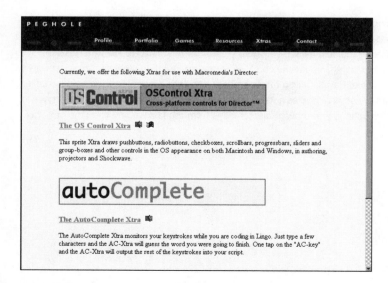

Figure C.20 *The Xtras page of the PegHole site.*

PENWORKS CORPORATION (*WWW.PENWORKS.COM/XTRAS/*)

Penworks has developed several Xtras to give the programmer control over such elements as CD audio, system dates, and projector icons (see Figure C.21). Using their Iconizer Xtra, you can make new icons, extract existing program icons, generate masks, and of course, set the icon of your Windows projector files. If you find yourself annoyed by the standard icon that Director inserts into your projectors, or you just want to give your applications a professional look, the Iconizer Xtra can help.

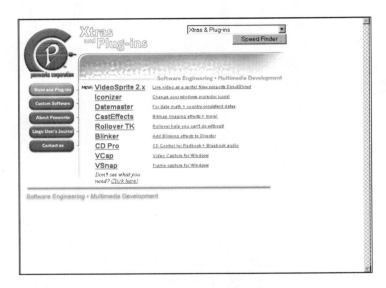

Figure C.21   *The Xtras page of the Penworks Corporation site.*

RAVWARE SOFTWARE (*WWW.RAVWARE.COM/XTRAS.HTM*)

RavWare is the producer of several powerful Xtras that give the programmer control over everything from PowerPoint to OpenGL to the Windows API (or Macintosh Toolbox) itself (see Figure C.22). The RavWare GLU32 Xtra gives the programmer access to dynamic linked libraries (or shared libraries on Macintosh) and the thousands of functions available in the Windows API (or Macintosh Toolbox). RavWare also offers probably the best window-shaping Xtra available. WinShaper will enable you to use a bitmap or vector image as a mask and set the shapes of your projector windows to whatever you desire. WinShaper also offers options to remove projector icons from the taskbar and keep the projector window on top of all others.

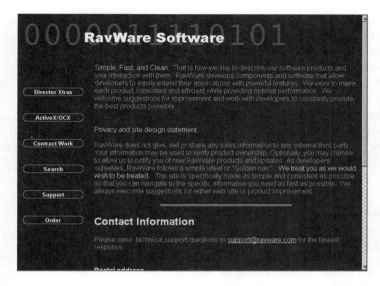

Figure C.22   *The Xtras page of the RavWare Software site.*

REACTION MEDIA (*WWW.REACTION-MEDIA.COM/DISKJOCKEY/*)

Reaction Media's DiskJockey is the ultimate tool for turning your Director movies into professional applications (see Figure C.23). DiskJockey can intelligently auto-run your CD-ROM applications, change the user's screen resolution to better suit your movies, read system information, and create complete installation programs. Based on your preferences, it will create program shortcuts and even an uninstaller for your Director applications. DiskJockey works on both Windows and Macintosh systems.

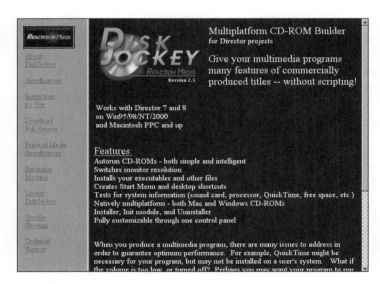

Figure C.23   *The DiskJockey page of the Reaction Media site.*

SCIRIUS DEVELOPMENT (*WWW.SCIRIUS.COM/*)

Scirius Development offers a few simple freeware Xtras that can prove quite convenient (see Figure C.24). DateTimeXtra offers several functions such as `getMonth` and `getWeekDay` that can make working with time values much simpler. `CapsLockXtra` just returns that state of the user's Caps Lock key, and `SetMouseXtra` sets the users mouse to a specified location. You may find better Xtras, but you'll never find them cheaper.

Figure C.24 *The front page of the Scirius Development site.*

TABULEIRO (*HTTP://XTRAS.TABULEIRO.COM/*)

Tabuleiro offers several Xtras, including MpegXtra, which enables you to import MPEG video, and WebXtra, which enables you to create a web browser inside a Director movie (see Figure C.25). Perhaps the most unique Xtra provided by Tabuleiro is ShapeShifter 3D, which works as a fully functional editor for Shockwave 3D content. It provides support for textures, bones, and even enables the user to import models of popular 3D formats directly into the editor. When a Shockwave 3D scene is complete, you can immediately incorporate it into your Director movies.

Figure C.25 *The Xtras page of the Tabuleiro site.*

UPDATESTAGE (*WWW.UPDATESTAGE.COM/XTRAS/*)

The updateStage site is simple and easy to navigate (see Figure C.26). It contains a large number of Xtras developed by a variety of authors. Their features range from changing the user's screen resolution to reading and writing binary files through Lingo. The updateStage site provides an Xtra search, but you may find it easier to just browse through the links in the frame located on the left side of your browser window.

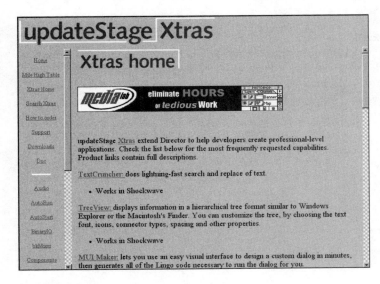

Figure C.26 *The Xtras page of the updateStage site.*

VISIBLE LIGHT (*WWW.VISIBLELIGHT.COM/PRODUCTS/*)

Visible Light (see Figure C.27) offers two categories of Xtras: OnStage and OnStage DVD. OnStage is the professional solution to distribution problems stemming from media playback. Through the OnStage CD Xtra, you can play MPEG, QuickTime, and AVI video without requiring the user to install anything. This is perfect for professional developers who need to be sure that the user can see multimedia CD content without any trouble. The downside of Visible Light is that their products tend to be a bit pricey.

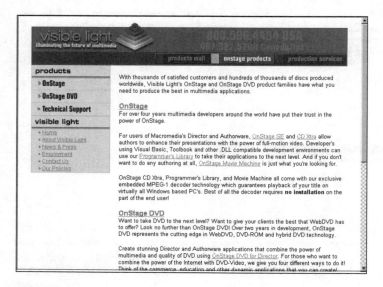

Figure C.27   *The products page of the Visible Light site.*

XTRAMEDIA SOLUTIONS (*WWW.XTRAMEDIA.COM/*)

XtraMedia Solutions (see Figure C.28) offers an Xtra named ChartsInMotion, which enables the programmer to plot visually appealing charts and graphs inside Director movies. It also enables the programmer to animate the charts with transition effects. The TableMaker Xtra enables the programmer to display scrolling tables and create spreadsheets through Lingo. XtraMedia's RearWindow Professional provides a variety of options for creating a background window behind the Stage.

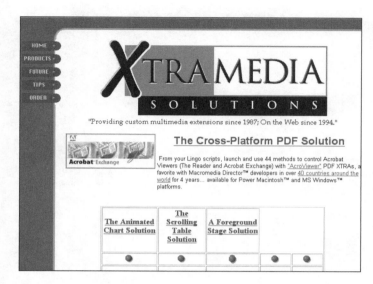

Figure C.28 *The front page of the XtraMedia Solutions site.*

The XtraZone site (see Figure C.29) offers a massive amount of transition effects ranging from fading to swirling. Each transition pack contains several transitions of a particular genre. Each transition is extremely customizable. The more complex transition packs provide screen captures for you to see them in action. Although transition effects may not be an absolute necessity to your Director projects, you might find that the aesthetic appeal they add to your interfaces is well worth the price.

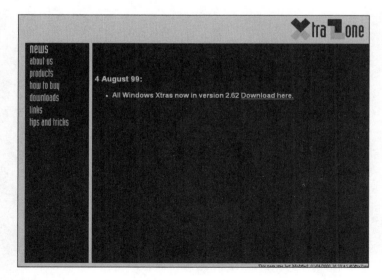

Figure C.29 *The front page of the XtraZone site.*

>>> **part 5**
appendixes

OPENING A MOVIE

At the beginning of almost every interface tutorial chapter, you will be instructed to open the interface's source movie and an incomplete version of the interface called a template. Director can have only one movie open at one time, so it closes any file you have open before it opens a new movie. To open a Director movie from the companion CD-ROM, follow these steps:

1. If the companion CD-ROM is not currently in your CD-ROM drive, insert it now.
2. Within Director, in the toolbar, click the Open button. Director will display the Open dialog box.
3. Click the Look In drop-down list and select your CD-ROM drive. Director will display the contents of your CD-ROM drive. (Macintosh users, select the Desktop option and then double-click your CD-ROM drive.)
4. Double-click the folder that pertains to the movie you want to open. Director will display the contents of that folder.
5. Next click the name of the movie you want to open. Director will update the Open dialog box.
6. Click the OK button. Director will open the movie that you selected.

As you become more familiar with Director, you will notice that recently opened files can be accessed through the File menu's Recent Movies submenu. This shortcut can prevent you from searching for a particular file in the Save Movie dialog box each time you want to open the file. You also can open a Director movie through your operating system directly by double-clicking its filename when browsing the contents of your hard drive.

SAVING A MOVIE

After opening a file from the companion CD-ROM, you must save a copy of it onto your hard drive before you will be allowed to modify the file. Because Director cannot write to the companion CD-ROM, all the interface source files are marked as read-only. Therefore, if you copy any of these files to your hard drive directly through your operating system, you must change the read-only file attribute before you will be allowed to modify the Director movie. Saving the source file to your hard drive through Director will bypass this step. To save a Director movie as a new file on your primary hard drive, follow these steps:

1. Click the File menu, and select the Save As option. Director will display the Save Movie dialog box.
2. Within the Save Movie dialog box, click the Save In drop-down list, and select your hard drive. Director will display the contents of your hard drive.

   If you have already created a folder in which to store your modified Director interfaces, you may skip to step 5.
3. Click the Create New Folder button. Director will create a new folder on your hard drive.
4. In the Save Movie dialog box, type **Director Interfaces** as the name of your new folder and press the Enter key (Return on Macintosh). Director will name your new folder Director Interfaces.
5. Double-click the Director Interfaces folder you created. Director will display the contents of the Director Interfaces folder.
6. In the File Name field, type a name for the file you want to create and press the Enter key (Return on Macintosh). Director will save a copy of the file you had open and name it what you typed into the File Name field.

After you have placed the Director movie on your hard drive, it is no longer marked as read-only. Director will activate the toolbar's Save button, which will enable you to update the movie's source file any time you modify it. Do this as often as possible to minimize the chances of losing changes made to a movie in case your computer crashes or shuts down unexpectedly.

PREVIEWING A MOVIE

After making any major change to a Director movie, you will generally want to make sure the movie still functions as expected. Previewing a Director movie is the quickest way to test it. Director will use the Stage window to display your movie just as if it were an executable projector or Shockwave content on a web site. To preview your movie within the Stage window, follow these steps:

1. From the toolbar, click the Rewind button. Director will move the playback head of your movie to frame 1 within the Score.

2. Click the Play button. Director will preview your movie within the Stage window. You may test virtually all aspects of your Director movie from within the Stage window at this time.

3. When finished, click the Rewind button. Director will stop previewing your movie within the Stage window and return it to frame 1.

Although previewing a movie within the Stage window will give you a good idea of how it will behave once it is compiled into an executable projector or Shockwave DCR file, some inconsistencies may occur. For example, certain Lingo commands are ignored in Shockwave DCR files to limit the ways in which a Shockwave file can access a computer's system. In addition, media files within projectors and Shockwave files may be compressed, which can affect their appearance.

Note:
If you want to stop your movie at a particular point, you must click the Stop button rather than the Rewind button. Your movie's sprites should remain in exactly the same positions that they were in before you stopped previewing.

WORKING WITH FRAME MARKERS

When developing any complex Director movie, be sure to keep it organized not only in the Cast window, but also in the Score window. The simplest and most effective way to keep track of major changes in the Score is by creating frame markers. A frame marker is just a text label for a particular frame. After you have created a marker, you can access its frame by name, as well as number, as specified in Appendix B, "Guide to Lingo Programming." To add a frame marker to the Score, follow these steps:

1. Within the Score window, click the Markers channel (the white strip near the top of the window). Director will create a marker named New Marker in the spot where you clicked.

2. In the Markers channel, type a name into the text field to the right of the marker you created and press the Enter key (Return on Macintosh). Director will rename the marker you created to whatever you typed.

3. If you want to move the marker that you created to another frame of the Score, drag the marker's icon (not its text label) horizontally to a new position.

4. If you want to delete the marker you created, drag the marker's icon vertically to a position outside of the Score window.

The most common mistake that Director users make when working with frame markers is trying to drag a marker's text label rather than its icon. Remember that if you click a marker's text label, Director will enable you to rename that marker. To create a new marker, you must click an empty spot of the Markers channel. If the label of another marker is covering up the spot where you need to create a new marker, just create the marker in an empty spot, and then drag it into position.

CREATING A SCRIPT

Before you begin writing a script, be sure to select an empty spot in the Cast window where you would like Director to create the script. Otherwise, Director will just use the next available spot after the selected cast member. To keep your Director movie organized, always be conscious of which cast member is selected within the Cast window. To create a new script cast member, follow these steps:

1. Within the toolbar, click the Script Window button. Director will display the Script window.

2. In the Cast Member Name text field, type a name for the script you want to create and press the Enter key (Return on Macintosh). Director will name the new script whatever you typed.

3. From the Properties window, click the Script tab. Director will display the Script sheet.

4. If you want to create a behavior script as opposed to a movie script, then click the Script Type drop-down list and select the Behavior option. Director will mark the script you created as a behavior script.

When working with any complex Director movie, you will find that the most convenient way to store your Lingo scripts is probably in a separate cast. By separating your movie's scripts from its media cast members, you will eliminate any confusion between cast members that will be used as sprites and those that will be applied to sprites. Such a distinction is not necessary in all cases. It is just a guideline.

Note:
As mentioned in Appendix B, movie script code affects the entire Director movie, but behavior script code affects only the sprites or frames to which the behavior is applied.

APPLYING BEHAVIORS

Behaviors are sections of Lingo programming code designed to affect the sprite or sprites to which they are applied. For more information on Lingo programming, please refer to Appendix B. Director offers two basic methods of applying behaviors to sprites. Generally the least confusing method involves the Property Inspector window. To apply a behavior to a sprite by using the Property Inspector window, follow these steps:

1. Within the Stage window or the Score window, click the sprite to which you want to apply a behavior. Director will update the Property Inspector window.

2. In the Property Inspector window, click the Behavior Popup (plus sign) button and select the name of the behavior you want to apply. Director will apply the behavior you selected to the sprite you selected.

When applying behaviors, Director also gives programmers the option to drag and drop behavior scripts from the Cast window into the Score window or even the Stage window. For users with large screen areas that are capable of viewing all Director's windows simultaneously, this can be a more convenient approach to behavior application. To apply a behavior to a sprite by using the Cast window, follow these steps:

1. Within the Cast window, click the Choose Cast button and select the name of the cast that contains the behavior you want to apply. Director will display the cast you selected within the Cast window.

2. Drag the behavior script you want to apply from the Cast window onto the sprite to which you want to apply the behavior within the Stage window or the Score window. Director will apply the behavior you selected to the sprite you selected.

You also can apply a behavior to a particular frame as opposed to a sprite. In such a case, the behavior would act much like a movie script but would not hold global handlers and would only be active while Director's playback head was in its frame. To apply a behavior to a particular frame, follow these steps:

1. Within the Cast window, click the Choose Cast button and select the name of the cast that contains the behavior you want to apply. Director will display the cast you selected within the Cast window.

2. Drag the behavior script you want to apply from the Cast window into the frame of the Behavior channel to which you want to apply the behavior within the Score window. Director will apply the behavior you selected to the frame you selected.

As you develop increasingly complex interfaces within Director, you will become familiar with the finer points of the Property Inspector window's Behavior sheet. It enables the programmer to add, remove, reorder, and even edit a sprite's associated behavior scripts. When dealing with a frame's behavior script, the Behavior sheet's functionality is somewhat abridged because only one behavior script can be applied to a single frame.

IMPORTING MEDIA

Although Director offers several ways to create media elements and enables you to paste media directly into the Cast window, importing is sometimes still the best method. If you want to turn a large number of image files into cast members, for example, pasting each image into Director's Cast window would be extraordinarily inconvenient. To import one or more media files into a Director movie, follow these steps:

1. From the toolbar, click the Import button. Director will display the Import Files dialog box.

2. Navigate to the folder that contains your media files and click a media file that you want to import. Director will update the Import Files dialog box.

3. Click the Add button. Director will add the media file's name to the File List field.

4. If you want to import more media files, repeat steps 2 and 3 until the File List field contains the names of all the media files you want to import.

5. After you have your files selected, click the Import button. Director will begin importing your media files.

6. If Director displays any dialog boxes prompting you to customize a media file's options, adjust any necessary settings and click the OK button. Director will import the files you selected.

7. If you want to rename any of the new cast members, within the Cast window click the cast member you want to rename. Director will update the Cast window.

8. Within the Cast window, in the Cast Member Name field, type a new name for the cast member and press the Enter key (Return on Macintosh). Director will rename the cast member you selected to whatever you typed.

After you import a media file into your movie, Director will name its cast member based on the media file's name. Generally, you should rename this cast member to fit in with the names of the other cast members in your movie. For example, perhaps your cast member names begin with capital letters or use spaces to separate words. You should always be sure that your cast members are named uniformly so that you can access them by name in Lingo code without running into any trouble.

CREATING A NEW CAST

Storing all your Director movie's cast members in a single cast is fine for simple movies, but as your interfaces become more complex, your need for multiple casts will become increasingly urgent. The most important thing to remember when developing any application is to keep things organized. At any point in the development process, you should be able to find a particular cast member without digging through too much garbage. To create a new cast within a Director movie, follow these steps:

1. In the Cast window, click the Choose Cast button and select the New Cast option. Director will display the New Cast dialog box.

2. In the Name field, type a name for the cast you want to create, and press the Enter key (Return on Macintosh). Director will create a new cast and display it in a new Cast window.

3. From the toolbar, click the Cast Window button. Director will close the new Cast window and return you to the original Cast window.

4. Click the Choose Cast button and select the name of the new cast you created. Director will display the cast you created within the Cast window.

You can move back and forth between casts by clicking the Cast window's Choose Cast button and selecting a menu option. If you ever need to move cast members from one cast to another, you can cut the cast members from their source cast, switch to the destination cast, and paste them into the destination cast. You can view two casts at once by clicking the Window menu, selecting the Cast submenu, and then selecting the name of the cast you want to view. Director will display the cast in a new Cast window. With two Cast windows open, you are free to drag and drop cast members as you want.

CREATING AN EXECUTABLE PROJECTOR

If you want people to use your Director interfaces, you will most likely want to create an executable projector file. After you build a projector, you will be able to distribute it as you want. Users will not need your original source file to run your interface. However, any external files that your interface requires to run will need to be distributed with the projector file. To create an executable projector file, follow these steps:

1. Click the File menu, and select the Create Projector option. Director will display the Create Projector dialog box.

2. Click the Look In drop-down list and select your primary hard drive. Director will display the contents of your primary drive.

3. Double-click the Director Interfaces folder. Director will display the contents of the Director Interfaces folder.

   If you have not yet created a folder in which to store your modified Director interfaces, do so now (as instructed in the "Saving a Movie" section).

4. Click the name of the movie from which you want to create an executable projector. Director will update the Create Projector dialog box.

5. Click the Options button. Director will display the Projector Options dialog box.

6. Next customize the available playback and compression options.

7. Click the OK button. Director will close the Projector Options dialog box.

8. Click the Create button. Director will display the Save Projector As dialog box.

9. Click the Save In drop-down list and select your primary hard drive. Director will display the contents of your primary hard drive.

10. Double-click the Director Interfaces folder. Director will display the contents of the Director Interfaces folder.

11. In the File Name field, type a name for the projector file you want to create and press the Enter key (Return on Macintosh). Director will create an executable projector file from the movie you selected.

Creating projector files does have one major drawback. After you build a projector file on your computer, anyone using a different operating system than yours may not be able to view the file. One simple solution to this problem is to build both a PC version of your interface and a Macintosh version. Of course, people who use other operating systems, such as Linux, may still not be able to run your interface. To create a truly cross-platform interface, you must publish in Shockwave format.

PUBLISHING SHOCKWAVE CONTENT

One of Director's most useful features is its capability to translate a fully functional application into a web applet that is accessible through an Internet browser. All Internet content created with Director is generally referred to as Shockwave content. Director offers a variety of compression options that will enable you to cut down the file size of your interface and let Internet users view it without waiting too long for it to download. To create a compressed Shockwave applet, follow these steps:

1. Click the File menu and select the Publish Settings option. Director will display the Publish Settings dialog box.

2. Click the Default button. Director will reset all publish settings to their default values.

3. Click the View in Browser check box unless it is already checked. Director will display your new HTML page in your computer's default Internet browser each time you publish a Director movie.

4. Click the Compression tab. Director will display the Compression sheet.

5. Next click the Standard Image Compression radio button. Director will update the Publish Settings dialog box.

   Any time your movie uses sprite with transparent colors, you should be sure to choose Standard compression over JPEG. JPEG compression tends to reduce image quality and works best with photos.

6. Click the Shockwave Audio drop-down list, and select the 16 option. Director will set your movie's audio compression to 16 kilobits per second.

   16 kilobits per second will generally be a high enough quality sound for your interfaces on the Internet. You should always choose audio quality as low as you can stand it because audio can greatly increase the file size of your movies.

7. Click the OK button. Director will remember your settings and close the Publish settings dialog box.

8. From the toolbar, click the Publish button. Director will create a Shockwave DCR file and an HTML file in your Director Interfaces folder. Because you checked the View in Browser check box earlier, Director will open your movie's HTML file in your computer's default Internet browser.

9. After you have finished viewing the Shockwave version of your Director movie, close your Internet browser and return to Director.

For someone to view your interface as a Shockwave applet, they can view either the Shockwave DCR file directly or an HTML file with a reference to the applet's filename. Each time you publish a Shockwave applet in Director, you will be presented with options about creating an HTML file. If you choose to create an HTML file, Director will place it in the same folder as your other interface files unless you specify a different directory. View the HTML file in a text editor. To place your Shockwave interface on another web site, you can copy the section of HTML code enclosed in an `<object>` or `<embed>` tag from the HTML file created by Director and paste it into the HTML code of another site. As long as your Shockwave DCR file is in the same directory, your interface should appear just as it did in the HTML file that was created by Director.

THE EVOLUTION OF LINGO

Several years ago, Director began as an animation program for making relatively simple presentations. It wasn't until two years later that its developers decided to add an interpreted scripting language to make movies built in Director more interactive. They named the language Lingo.

Lingo's original designers wanted the language to have a very plain-English, commonsense feel to it. They built the language to use real words rather than mathematical symbols as often as possible. The goal was to enable programmers to communicate with the computer the way they would communicate with other people. And for years, Lingo programmers typed phrases like

```
set the rotation of sprite 5 to 90
```

rather than shorter, more mathematical phrases like

```
sprite(5).rotation = 90
```

Eventually, Lingo's designers realized that trying to tell the computer what to do in plain English is just not practical. To address this problem, they developed an alternative syntax that more closely resembled other programming languages such as C++ and BASIC. A statement as confusing as

```
set stringVariable to word 2 to 5 of line 8 of the text of the member of sprite 2
```

could now be translated to

```
stringVariable = sprite(2).member.text.line[8].word[2..5]
```

Lingo still includes the option to type commands in the old verbose syntax, but most programmers feel more comfortable with the new dot syntax. The dot syntax makes code organization more obvious and, therefore, less prone to errors. Computers think in terms of mathematical operations, and so should programmers.

EVENT HANDLERS

Lingo is an event-driven language. This means that Lingo waits for an event such as a mouse click or the end of a movie to execute a set of programming commands, or code, instead of just executing the entire program's code in sequence. Of course programmers can create custom handlers (as discussed later). Think of event handlers as empty bags set aside by Lingo that you can fill with programming code. Remember that any commands not stored within an event handler will produce an error message and keep your program from running. An event handler should appear as follows:

```
on eventName
  statement(s)
end
```

Generally, you will place event handlers in behavior scripts that affect individual sprites or in movie scripts that affect the entire program. Most events can be placed in either type of Lingo script, although some are designed to specifically affect either a movie or a sprite. The following events are called automatically by Lingo throughout the run of a program and are listed in the order that they normally execute:

prepareMovie—**Handler that executes once just before a Director movie begins playing. Its common usage is to initialize global variables. This handler is available only in movie scripts.**

beginSprite—**Handler that executes once when the Score's playback head first encounters a sprite. Its common usage is to initialize property variables. This handler is available only in behavior scripts.**

prepareFrame—Handler that executes just before the beginning of each frame.

startMovie—Handler that executes once at the beginning of a Director movie's first frame. This handler is available only in movie scripts.

enterFrame—Handler that executes at the beginning of each frame.

exitFrame—Handler that executes at the end of each frame.

stopMovie—Handler that executes once at the end of a Director movie's last frame. This handler is available only in movie scripts.

endSprite—Handler that executes once when the Score's playback head leaves a sprite. This handler is available only in behavior scripts.

If several scripts refer to the same event handler, Lingo will execute behavior scripts applied to sprites one after another starting with sprite channel 1 and moving down the Score. If a sprite has more than one behavior, Lingo will execute them in the order that they were first applied to the sprite. If a behavior script is not applied to a sprite (or a frame), its code will never execute. After all the sprites' behavior scripts have executed, Lingo will look for the event handler in the program's movie scripts.

Some event handlers wait for user interaction to execute their code. This is the type of event handler that makes event-driven programming so convenient. The following event handlers are triggered in some way by either a mouse or a keyboard action:

mouseEnter—Handler that executes each time the mouse cursor moves within the bounds of an associated sprite. This handler is available only in behavior scripts.

mouseLeave—Handler that executes each time the mouse cursor moves outside the bounds of an associated sprite. This handler is available only in behavior scripts.

mouseWithin—Handler that executes constantly while the mouse cursor is within the bounds of an associated sprite. This handler is available only in behavior scripts.

mouseDown—Handler that executes each time the user presses the left mouse button. If this handler is used in a behavior script, the mouse cursor must be within the bounds of an associated sprite.

mouseUp—Handler that executes every time the user releases the left mouse button. If this handler is used in a behavior script, the mouse cursor must be within the bounds of an associated sprite.

rightMouseDown—Handler that executes each time the user presses the right mouse button. If this handler is used in a behavior script, the mouse cursor must be within the bounds of an associated sprite.

RightMouseUp—Handler that executes each time the user releases the right mouse button. If this handler is used in a behavior script, the mouse cursor must be within the bounds of an associated sprite.

keyDown—Handler that executes each time the user presses a key. This handler will not work in a behavior script unless it is that of an editable text field.

keyUp—Handler that executes each time the user releases a key. This handler will not work in a behavior script unless it is that of an editable text field.

Although these event handlers will function well in most situations, Lingo also provides other methods to check the user's mouse and keyboard for events. A wide variety of options are available to suit virtually any situation. However, you should gain a better understanding of Lingo programming before you concern yourself with these methods.

VARIABLES

A variable is a letter or a word that can represent a changing value. A variable can be accessible throughout the run of a movie or only in specific areas depending on how you define, or create, it. A local variable is accessible only within the block of code (such as an event handler) in which it was created. To create a local variable, you need only to set its value. To set, or assign, a variable's value, you must type the name of the variable, the equals sign, and then the value that you want the variable to represent. If Lingo does not recognize the name of the variable, it will assume that you want to create a new local variable as opposed to editing the value of an existing variable. A variable assignment should appear as follows:

```
variableName = value
```

The part of a movie in which a variable is accessible is called its *scope*. Global variables have a scope of their entire movie. This means that every Lingo script inside a movie has the capability to access a global variable. To define a global variable, you must type the `global` keyword and then the name of the variable at the beginning of each script that should have access to the variable. The following Lingo code defines a global variable named *playerScore* and then assigns it to five when the user presses a key:

```
global playerScore

on keyDown
   playerScore = 5
end
```

Property variables are usually accessed only within the script in which they were defined using the `property` keyword. However, you can access a property variable from a remote script by typing the name of the object (such as a sprite or cast member) to which the script containing the property has been assigned, a period, and then the name of the property you want to access. The following code defines a property variable named *score*, sets it to 100, and then sets a property variable named *timer* in a behavior script applied to the sprite in channel 2 to 30 when the user clicks the script's associated sprite:

```
property score

on mouseDown
   score = 100
   sprite(2).timer = 30
end
```

Almost every program requires the use of variables to keep track of different values. In fact, Director uses all sorts of variables behind the scenes to control everything from sprite locations to movie frame rates. To access a built-in property of an item such as a sprite or cast member, you must type the name of that item, a period, and then the name of the property variable you want to access. Setting a variable named *playerWidth* to the value of the `width` property of the sprite in channel 5 should appear as follows:

```
playerWidth = sprite(5).width
```

Each sprite within a Director movie automatically contains a number of predefined properties. The following sprite properties can replace `width` in the preceding code example:

spriteNum—Sprite property that indicates the channel number of a particular sprite.

member—Sprite property that indicates the cast member being used by a particular sprite

memberNum—Sprite property that indicates the number of the cast member being used by a particular sprite.

`loc`—Sprite property that indicates the location of a particular sprite within the Stage in the form of a point value.

`locH`—Sprite property that indicates the horizontal location of a particular sprite within the Stage in the form of an integer value.

`locV`—Sprite property that indicates the vertical location of a particular sprite within the Stage in the form of an integer value.

`locZ`—Sprite property that indicates the layer of a particular sprite within the Stage. Sprites with a higher `locZ` value appear in front of other sprites. If two sprites have the same `locZ` value, their channel numbers determine their order.

`width`—Sprite property that indicates the width of a particular sprite in pixels.

`height`—Sprite property that indicates the height of a particular sprite in pixels.

`rect`—Sprite property that indicates the locations of the borders of a particular sprite in the form of a rectangle value.

`left`—Sprite property that indicates the location of the left edge of a particular sprite.

`right`—Sprite property that indicates the location of the right edge of a particular sprite.

`top`—Sprite property that indicates the location of the top edge of a particular sprite.

`bottom`—Sprite property that indicates the location of the bottom edge of a particular sprite.

`quad`—Sprite property that indicates the coordinates of the upper-left, upper-right, lower-left, and lower-right corners of a particular sprite in the form of a list containing four point values.

`flipH`—Sprite property that indicates whether a particular sprite is mirrored.

`flipV`—Sprite property that indicates whether a particular sprite is flipped.

`rotation`—Sprite property that indicates the degree of rotation of a particular sprite in the form of a float value.

`skew`—Sprite property that indicates the degree of tilt of a particular sprite in the form of a float value.

`visible`—Sprite property that indicates whether a particular sprite is visible.

`blend`—Sprite property that indicates the translucency of a particular sprite. Its value can range from 0 (transparent) to 100 (opaque).

`color`—Sprite property that indicates foreground color of a particular sprite.

`bgColor`—Sprite property that indicates the background color of a particular sprite.

`puppet`—Sprite property that indicates whether a particular sprite is under Lingo control.

Lingo also allows access to a number of system properties. System properties have to do with attributes of the user's system or the movie itself. All system properties are preceded by the `the` keyword to distinguish them from ordinary variables and are accessible from within any of a movie's scripts. The following system properties are useful when dealing with user interaction:

`the mouseDown`—Property that indicates whether the user is holding down the left mouse button.

`the rightMouseDown`—Property that indicates whether the user is holding down the right mouse button.

`the mouseDownScript`—Property that indicates, in the form of a string value, the commands to execute each time the user presses the left mouse button within a Director movie.

`the mouseUpScript`—Property that indicates, in the form of a string value, the commands to execute each time the user releases the left mouse button within a Director movie.

the `mouseLoc`—Property that indicates the location of the mouse cursor within the Stage in the form of a point value.

the `mouseH`—Property that indicates the horizontal location of the mouse cursor within the Stage in the form of an integer value.

the `mouseV`—Property that indicates the vertical location of the mouse cursor within the Stage in the form of an integer value.

the `clickLoc`—Property that indicates the location in the Stage last clicked by the user in the form of a point value.

the `rollOver`—Property that indicates the channel number of the sprite the mouse cursor is currently over.

the `clickOn`—Property that indicates the channel number of the last sprite clicked by the user.

the `mouseChar`—Property that indicates the number of the character directly under the mouse cursor within a text field. If the mouse cursor is not over a character, the result is –1.

the `mouseWord`—Property that indicates the number of the word directly under the mouse cursor within a text field. If the mouse cursor is not over a word, the result is –1.

the `mouseItem`—Property that indicates the number of the item directly under the mouse cursor within a text field. If the mouse cursor is not over an item, the result is –1.

the `mouseLine`—Property that indicates the number of the line directly under the mouse cursor within a text field. If the mouse cursor is not over a line, the result is –1.

the `mouseMember`—Property that indicates the number of the cast member used by the sprite directly under the mouse cursor within the Stage. If the mouse cursor is not over a sprite, the result is void.

the `doubleClick`—Property that indicates whether the user has just double-clicked.

the `key`—Property that indicates the string value of the last key pressed by the user.

the `keyCode`—Property that indicates the integer value of the last key pressed by the user.

the `keyDownScript`—Property that indicates in the form of a string value the commands to execute each time the user presses a key within a Director movie.

the `keyUpScript`—Property that indicates in the form of a string value the commands to execute each time the user releases a key within a Director movie.

the `shiftDown`—Property that indicates whether the user is holding down the Shift key.

the `commandDown`—Property that indicates whether the user is holding down the Control key (Command key on Macintosh).

the `optionDown`—Property that indicates whether the user is holding down the Alt key (Option key on Macintosh).

A variable can represent a wide variety of types of data such as numbers or strings of text. To tell Lingo to convert the value of a variable into a different data type, you can type the name of the desired data type, an opening parenthesis, the value that you want to change, and then a closing parenthesis. This process is called *type casting*. A type cast should appear as follows:

```
variableName = typeName(variableName)
```

The following statements set the value of `number1` to the decimal number 3.5 and the value of `number2` to the integer value of `number1`, which is three:

```
number1 = 3.5
number2 = integer(number1)
```

A text value not in the form of a variable must always be enclosed in quotation marks. If it is not, Lingo will assume you are referring to the name of a variable. Number values do not require quotation marks because no variable name can begin with a number. Therefore, Lingo will never confuse a constant number value with a variable name. The following data types can replace `typeName` or `integer` in the preceding code examples:

> `integer`—Function that returns the integer, or nonfractional, value of a specified expression.

> `float`—Function that returns the decimal number value of a specified expression.

> `string`—Function that returns the string, or text, value of a specified expression.

Not only can you assign variables to values such as numbers and text strings, but you also can assign variables to other variables. Unless a variable is currently being assigned to a value, Lingo will see the variable as the value it represents. The following statement sets the *number1* variable to the value of the *number2* variable:

```
number1 = number2
```

Lists

Another way to store values is by creating a list. A list is a variable that can hold several different values simultaneously. To assign a set of values to a list, you must type the name of the list variable, an equals sign, an opening bracket, any number of values separated by commas, and then a closing bracket. The following statements are examples of list assignments:

```
numList = [4, 7.5, -8, 12, 0.2, 3]
name = ["Susie", "Johnny", "Billy Bob", "Herbert"]
randomStuff = [24, "hours a day", 5.4, 12, "AM"]
```

The simplest way to retrieve a value from a list is to access it by number. To access a single value contained within a list, you must type the name of the list, an opening bracket, the number of the value that you want to access, and then a closing bracket. The resulting value functions just as if it were a variable name. Setting a variable named *chosenName* to the value of the second item in the list variable *name* should appear as follows:

```
chosenName = name[2]
```

Property lists contain not only values, but also property names. For instance, a `car` variable might have a `year` property and a `model` property. To assign a set of properties to a list, you use basically the same syntax as with other lists. The only difference is that instead of just values, you must type the number sign, the name of the property you are creating, a colon, and then the value that you want to assign to that property. Assigning a set of properties to a list named `car` should appear as follows:

```
car = [#year: 1967, #model: "Beetle"]
```

You can treat property lists exactly the same as other lists, or you can access their properties by name rather than number by using dot notation. The following code accesses the properties of the `car` list:

```
carYear = car.year
modelName = car.model
```

Most predefined value types in Lingo such as color and point values consist of a property list with the properties already set up. For example, any color variable contains the properties red, green, and blue. Any point variable contains the properties locH and locV. Lingo defines several media types to make multimedia programming in Lingo quite a bit more convenient than it is in many other programming languages.

FUNCTIONS

Functions (also known as *custom handlers*) work almost exactly like event handlers. The main difference is that they execute only when they are told to do so by a special command generally referred to as a *call*. You can define your own functions by using the exact same syntax as you do when setting up event handlers. Defining a function named setUpGame might appear as follows:

```
on setUpGame
  score = 0
  lives = 5
  playerName = "Bob"
end
```

To call a function, or cause its code to execute, you must type the function's name, an opening parenthesis, and then a closing parenthesis in the section of your program that you would like the function's code to execute. After Lingo executes a function, it will return to the line directly after the function's call. A call for the setUpGame function should appear as follows:

```
setUpGame()
```

A function parameter is a value passed to a function to be used as a variable within that function. Parameters enable the programmer to create a single function that can perform a variety of different tasks. For example, a function to move the sprite in channel 5 a specified number of pixels horizontally and vertically on the Stage might appear as follows:

```
on moveSprite(changeH, changeV)
  sprite(5).locH = sprite(5).locH + changeH
  sprite(5).locV = sprite(5).locV + changeV
end
```

To call a function that uses parameters, you must type the name of the function, an opening parenthesis, a value for each parameter of the function, and then a closing parenthesis. A function call to the moveSprite function that moves the sprite 20 pixels to the left and 15 pixels down should appear as follows:

```
functionName(-20, 15)
```

If a function returns a value, you can treat its call as if it were a variable representing that value. You can call the function normally, or you can assign or compare a variable to the value of the function, which is its returned value. To cause a function to return a value, you must type the return keyword, and then the value that you want the function to return at the point in the function that you want its code to stop executing and return a value. If any programming code appears after the return line in a function, that code will not execute. A function named getSum that adds two numbers together and returns their sum should appear as follows:

```
on getSum(value1, value2)
  return value1 + value2
end
```

The preceding function's call acts just as if it were a constant value such as a number or a string. Assigning a variable named *total* to the resulting value of the getSum function's call should appear as follows:

```
total = getSum(2, 5)
```

A good example of a function that accepts a parameter and returns a value is built in to Lingo. The keyPressed function accepts a string or number value that represents a key on the keyboard and returns a Boolean value, either true or false, that specifies whether the specified key is currently being pressed. Setting a variable to the value of whether the user is pressing the Spacebar should appear as follows:

```
spaceDown = keyPressed(" ")
```

Every function has a scope just as variables do. The part of your movie in which a function is accessible depends on where you define that function. If you define a function inside a movie script, you will be able to call it from any script in the movie. If you define a function within a behavior script, however, you may directly call that function only from within its own script.

To call a function or an event handler of a behavior script from another script, you must use a function named sendSprite. The sendSprite function requires two parameters. The first parameter should be an integer value that represents the number of the sprite whose associated behavior scripts you want to access. The second value must be the name of the function or event handler you want to call immediately preceded by a number sign. Calling a function named resetGame from a script applied to the sprite in channel 5 should appear as follows:

```
sendSprite(5, #resetGame)
```

If extra parameters are supplied to sendSprite besides the two required parameters, they will be used as parameters to be passed to the specified sprite's function or event handler. Calling a function named moveSprite from a script applied to the sprite in channel 5 might appear as follows:

```
sendSprite(5, #moveSprite, -20, 15)
```

CONDITIONALS

A conditional is a structure that keeps one or several lines of Lingo code from executing unless a specified condition is met. The condition can be in the form of a Boolean value (true or false) or one or more mathematical equations or inequalities. If the final value of the condition is equal to the true keyword, the enclosed programming code will execute.

Lingo provides two forms of conditional structures. The most popular and generally most useful of the two is the if ... then conditional. An if ... then conditional should appear as follows:

```
if condition then
   statement(s)
end if
```

If only one command is enclosed within the if ... then conditional, the entire conditional can be placed on a single line and the end if statement can be omitted. An if ... then conditional on a single line should appear as follows:

```
if condition then statement
```

To make `if ... then` conditionals easier to use and understand, Lingo offers an optional `else` clause to be used when you want code to execute only if the preceding condition was not met. An `if ... then` conditional with an `else` clause should appear as follows:

```
if condition then
   statement(s)
else
   statement(s)
end if
```

To make the `if ... then` conditional even more convenient, Lingo enables you to expand the conditional to include as many `else` statements as you want. An `if ... then` conditional with two `else` clauses should appear as follows:

```
if condition then
   statement(s)
else if condition then
   statement(s)
else
   statement(s)
end if
```

The second type of conditional that Lingo has to offer is generally for situations in which you want to test a single variable for a large number of different values. The `case ... of` conditional is in no way necessary to any program. Any `case ... of` conditional could be replaced with an `if ... then` conditional with a series of else clauses. However, you will run into situations where a `case ... of` conditional is just more convenient. A `case ... of` conditional should appear as follows:

```
case variableName of
   value1: statement(s)
   value2: statement(s)
   value3: statement(s)
end case
```

The `case ... of` conditional has its own version of the `else` clause. If the `otherwise` keyword is typed in place of a value for the last condition of a `case ... of` conditional, its code will execute only if no other conditions have been met so far in the `case ... of` conditional. A `case ... of` conditional with the `otherwise` keyword should appear as follows:

```
case variableName of
   value1: statement(s)
   value2: statement(s)
   value3: statement(s)
   otherwise: statement(s)
end case
```

The reason that the `case ... of` conditional fits the definition of a conditional despite its unusual organization may be a bit difficult to grasp. Each time that Lingo reaches a value in a `case ... of` conditional, it checks to see whether the variable being tested is equal to that value. If the Boolean value that Lingo comes up with is `true`, Lingo executes the following code. Otherwise, Lingo moves on to test the next condition. As soon as a condition is met, no more are tested.

LOOPS

Loops are very similar to conditionals. A loop executes a section of programming code repeatedly as long as a speci-fied condition is met. Loops enable programmers to avoid typing similar statements over and over. A `repeat while` loop should appear as follows:

```
repeat while condition
   statement(s)
end repeat
```

To make a loop execute a set number of times, or iterations, you must use a loop control variable. By adding one to the loop control variable each time the section of code executes, you can count the iterations and end the loop when the variable is no longer below a certain value. However, Lingo will handle the entire process for you if you use a `repeat with` loop. A `repeat with` loop that uses a loop control variable named i and executes 50 times should appear as follows:

```
repeat with i = 1 to 50
   statement(s)
end repeat
```

The loop control variable of a `repeat with` loop does not have to increase in value after each iteration. A simple modification to the loop structure will cause the variable to decrease in value as the loop progresses. A `repeat with` loop that counts from 50 down to 1 should appear as follows:

```
repeat with i = 50 down to 1
   statement(s)
end repeat
```

One of the most common uses for `repeat with` loops is dealing with numbered elements, such as lists and sequential sprites. Using a loop control variable in place of sequential integer constants in the preceding code examples can shorten 50 lines of programming code down to only 3.

NAVIGATION

One of Lingo's most convenient features is its capability to work with Director's Score organization and playback head. Director's playback head is the translucent red block near the top of the Score window that indicates the cur-rent frame of the movie. Lingo offers several commands to move the playback head and thus display a new frame's contents within the Stage window. The following commands are used for navigation within and outside of Director movies:

`play`—Command that tells Director to move the playback head to a specified frame in the form of an integer, marker in the form of a string, or external Director movie and begin playing.

`go`—Command that tells Director to move the playback head to a specified frame in the form of an inte-ger, marker in the form of a string, or external Director movie.

`go next`—Command that tells Director to move the playback head to the next marker after the current frame of the movie.

`go previous`—Command that tells Director to move the playback head to the previous marker before the current frame of the movie.

`updateStage`—Command that updates the contents of the Stage immediately instead of waiting for the next frame.

`goToNetPage`—Command that opens the default Internet browser and loads a site from a specified URL in the form of a string.

`open`—Command that runs an external program from a specified path in the form of a string.

halt—Command that stops a Director movie and closes its window.

appMinimize—Command that minimizes a Director movie's window.

restart—Command that stops a Director movie and restarts the computer.

shutDown—Command that stops a Director movie and shuts down the computer.

Some Lingo commands, such as appMinimize, restart, and shutDown, are disabled in Shockwave applications made for the Internet. If you were to use these commands in a Shockwave movie, you would not receive an error message. Lingo would just ignore the disabled commands.

LINGO SYNTAX

When programming in Lingo, certain questions about code spacing may arise. The only time you are actually required to type a space into your Lingo code is when two words need to be separated. The following lines are perfectly equivalent:

```
variableName = (sprite(5).width + 10)*2
variableName=(sprite(5).width+10)*2
variableName = ( sprite ( 5 ) . width + 10 ) * 2
```

Although spacing does not matter to Lingo, using appropriate spacing can make your code easier to read and, therefore, more convenient for you, the programmer.

Unlike many programming languages, Lingo is not case-sensitive. This means that, as far as Lingo is concerned, the statements updateStage, updateSTAGE, and Updatestage are all equivalent. Because many commands and variables have names made up of more than one word and their names cannot contain spaces, many programmers choose to make use of camel notation to fix this problem. Camel notation is the method of using capital letters to separate words in the names of commands or variables. Often, long words are abbreviated to cut down on typing. A variable that represents the social security number of John Doe might appear as follows:

```
johnDoeSocSecNum
```

Although the basic syntax must always remain the same, Lingo offers each programmer the chance to develop his own style. The following operators are a vital part of Lingo's programming syntax:

+ (addition)—Operator that finds the sum of two numbers in an addition problem.

- (subtraction)—Operator that finds the difference of two numbers in a subtraction problem.

* (multiplication)—Operator that finds the product of two numbers in a multiplication problem.

/ (division)—Operator that finds the quotient of two numbers in a division problem.

= (equal to)—Operator that finds whether two expressions are of equal value.

<> (not equal to)—Operator that finds whether two expressions are of unequal value.

> (greater than)—Operator that finds whether the first expression is greater than the second.

>= (greater than or equal to)—Operator that finds whether the first expression is greater than or equal to the second.

< (less than)—Operator that finds whether the first expression is less than the second.

<= (less than or equal to)—Operator that finds whether the first expression is less than or equal to the second.

not—Operator that reverses the Boolean value of an expression.

and—Operator that finds whether two expressions are both true.

or—Operator that finds whether at least one of two expressions is true.

(. . .) (parentheses)—Operators that indicate a group of parameters or expressions.

" . . . " (string)—Operators that indicate a string. Any number of characters can be placed inside the operators.

[. . .] (list)—Operators that indicate a list. Any number of values can be placed inside of the operators separated by commas.

(symbol)—Operator that, when placed directly before a combination of characters not starting with a number, indicates a symbol.

\ (continuation)—Operator that, when placed at the end of a line, tells Director that the programming statement continues on to the next line.

– (comment)—Operator that tells Director to ignore any code following it in a line. Programmers use comments to explain ambiguous code or to temporarily hide lines of code to aid in debugging.

For more information about Lingo programming, click Director's Help menu and select the Lingo Dictionary option. Director has organized all the major Lingo commands into a system of hypertext pages complete with programming code examples. At any time, you can click the Contents button, the Index button, or the Search button for a different style of browsing.

>>> appendix c
guide to shockwave 3d

MULTIMEDIA AND THE INTERNET

The world today is full of more man-made excitement, astonishment, and even mystery than ever before. Each time a multimedia producer conjures up a new technique to astound an unsuspecting audience, it soon becomes just another trick. Merely keeping audiences entertained is not enough anymore. To make certain your audience keeps its focus on what you have to say, you must keep them in a state of amazement. They must feel totally immersed in the environment you are creating.

Even in seemingly mundane situations such as business meetings and college lectures, advances are constantly being made to bring information to audiences as efficiently as possible. Just speaking to a crowd or displaying passages of text results in audience members getting bored, thinking about unrelated topics, or losing interest entirely. Using overhead projectors, audio, video, and interactivity, presentations everywhere are holding people's interest longer and more completely than ever before. In a world where nanosecond attention spans rule, multi-media presentations must not only catch the audience's attention but also keep it long enough to deliver the desired message.

In the early days of the Internet, very little could be done about grabbing the attention of web surfers. Most comput-ers at the time could display only text in a single color, and their graphics capabilities left much to be desired. As technological advances enabled web developers to add entertainment value to information, however, the Internet exploded in popularity.

Today, most sites on the Internet are more than simple HTML documents with images thrown in here and there. As a web developer, it is no longer enough to be familiar with HTML, the most basic language for formatting informa-tion on the Internet. Developers must know how to integrate graphics, audio, animations, and even interactive appli-cations into their web sites. Applications designed to run within an Internet browser are generally referred to as *applets*.

One of the most popular tools for creating interactive applets for the web is Macromedia Director. Director enables programmers to create visually and aurally rich applications quickly and easily with nowhere near the number of hassles presented by other programming languages, such as Java and Perl. One of the main reasons Director is so easy to use is that it is more than a programming language. In fact, by using Director's Stage, Score, and prebuilt behavior scripts, a person can create a fully interactive, completely original application without a bit of programming knowledge. Of course to really unleash the power of Director, you should be totally familiar with both Director's authoring environment and its programming language, Lingo.

MOVIE FORMATTING OPTIONS

After creating an application, or "movie," in Director, you have quite a few options about how to present it to the world. Before trying to decide on a format, you should have a good understanding of the ways Director can play your movies. Generally, you will choose to turn your movie into either a standalone application, which can run completely independent of other programs, or a web applet, which requires a capable Internet browser and usually a host HTML document.

Standalone applications created in Director are called *projectors* because each executable projector contains code necessary to play all Director movies as well as a compressed version of the particular movie. *Shockwave* is the name given to Director's advanced method of compressing movies for very small file sizes. All web applets created through Director use Shockwave compression. A Shockwave applet is just a compressed version of a Director movie's data. Shockwave applet files (DCRs) do not include players. Therefore, a DCR file requires either a Shockwave player installed on the user's system or an Internet browser with an acceptable version of the Shockwave plug-in for its movie to play.

To minimize the amount of disk space required for projector movies, Director enables developers to create projector applications that use Shockwave compression. A Shockwave projector uses a player installed on the user's computer to play a movie. Ordinary projectors include the player within the same file as the movie's data. If a user tries to play a Shockwave projector and has no Shockwave player installed on her system, the projector will not work until the user downloads the latest player from the Internet. Shockwave projectors work much like Shockwave applets. The main difference is that applets look for the Shockwave player as a web browser plug-in.

Shockwave applets and standalone projectors offer several options for compressing Director movies just as much as is desired. Director can compress movie data, the player code, or both. The sacrifice is, when elements of a Director movie are compressed, they may take more time to access. In most situations, however, you would never notice the difference. In a Windows environment, the minimum disk space required for a standard projector is approximately 2.1MB. When the player code is compressed, however, this requirement can drop to 1.1MB for a compressed projector or even 60KB for a Shockwave projector. Macintosh requires 2.5MB standard and 1.2MB compressed but only 12KB for a Shockwave projector.

Another format you might choose when preparing to distribute your movies is the protected source, or DXR format. DXR files work almost exactly like normal source (DIR) files. Both formats can be played from a separate projector file, movie in a window, or Shockwave player. Their only difference is that DXR files do not make movie source data available to the user. Protected source files do not include information necessary to play or edit their movies. They rely completely on external players. To create a protected movie from Director, click the Xtras menu and select the Update Movie option. From the dialog box that appears, you can select the Protect radio button. Remember to create backup copies of your Director source files before converting them to protected movies.

To provide even more flexibility, Director offers the option to publish movies as Java applets. Java applets do not require the Shockwave plug-in and work in virtually all browsers. Because Director and Java are fundamentally differ-ent authoring environments, however, you must consider a number of issues before attempting to distribute your Director movie as a Java applet. Not all features of Director are available when saving a movie as a Java applet. For a more complete description of the considerations you must make when creating Java applets, see the "Save as Java" section of the Macromedia Director Support Center (located at www.macromedia.com/support/director/).

In most situations, you will have no need to create Java applets from Director. Virtually every distribution problem can be solved using some form of projector or Shockwave applet. For more information on creating executable projectors and publishing Shockwave content, refer to Appendix A, "Guide to Common Tasks."

WORKING WITH SHOCKWAVE MOVIES

The browser plug-in that enables Internet users to view Shockwave content is Shockwave Player. With more than 200 million users, it has become the web standard for powerful multimedia playback. Shockwave-enabled web browsers can view interactive presentations, games, advertising, and 3D content embedded in HTML documents or directly through the browser. Shockwave Player is so powerful that it now actually includes Flash Player, which plays content created by Macromedia Flash.

At this point, you might be wondering how Shockwave Player and Flash Player differ from one another. They are both free multimedia players developed by Macromedia. They are both capable of playing animations, audio, and video. They both add a great deal of interactivity to web sites across the Internet. The players are quite similar, but they have several very important differences. Flash Player is designed to work more with vector graphics, which are stored not as matrices of color values but as collections of points and curves that form shapes of varying complex-ity. Because of this difference, Flash Player is more suited to work with quick loading front-end web applications, online advertising, and cartoon animation. Conversely, Shockwave Player tends to work with more powerful web applications, multiuser games, and media files, such as Shockwave 3D, RealAudio, RealVideo, QuickTime, and even Flash applications.

Shockwave movies have the power to use the Internet in a number of ways. Through the Shockwave Multiuser Server, applets can host sessions such as chats and games that enable multiple users across the Internet to interact in real-time. Shockwave movies also can use data on the Internet to dynamically modify their content, open external web sites, interact with Internet scripting languages, and perform a variety of network activities.

To protect the end user, however, Macromedia has disabled the use of certain features of Director through Shockwave. These features could compromise the safety and privacy of web users by accessing, modifying, or even removing components of the user's computer that affect hardware. These restrictions do seriously limit the power of Shockwave developers. They might present occasional inconveniences, but most developers never find the need to execute tasks such as erasing files, printing pages, or shutting down the computers. Shockwave allows limited reading from and writing to a user's hard drives, but only within the Shockwave plug-in directory.

STREAMING SHOCKWAVE MOVIES

When authoring movies in Director, you must consider how they will display on the systems of the end users. If a movie will download from a source on the Internet, you may need to modify the movie for the best performance. You can use some of Director's prebuilt behaviors to cause your movie to wait while certain cast members load onto the user's hard drive. The process of allowing a movie to play at the same time that the user is downloading it from the Internet is known as *streaming*.

When distributing Shockwave movies on the Internet, streaming can provide nearly immediate access to the parts of your movies people want to access. If you do not set up a Shockwave movie for streaming, its users must wait for the entire movie to load before viewing even the first frame. A streaming movie begins to play as soon as a specified amount of data reaches the user's hard drive. As the movie plays, the remaining data continues to load in the background. Although the download time required is really the same, the user is happy because he can access the desired Shockwave movie immediately instead of waiting for a slow moving progress bar on a blank page.

When a Shockwave movie begins streaming over the Internet, it first downloads Score data, Lingo scripts, and other non-media information such as sprite properties. This type of information requires very little download time because it is quite small in file size, usually only a few kilobytes. Before the movie actually begins playing, Shockwave Player must download the cast members necessary to display its first frame. Shockwave Player may require data for additional frames to download depending on the movie playback options set by the movie's author. After the movie actually begins playing, Shockwave Player continues to download media cast members in the background in the order they appear in the Score.

If a movie's playback head jumps around in the Score or Lingo scripts reference its cast members prematurely, required cast members may not be available when they are needed. If a cast member is not available, the movie will either ignore it or display a placeholder depending on the specified movie playback properties. To avoid running into such a problem, you should begin by dividing your movie into sections. You should then make sure all cast members for a particular section have been loaded before playing that section, by using Director's prebuilt streaming behaviors or writing your own Lingo code.

However, the easiest way to create a streaming Shockwave movie is to arrange the Score with a small introductory scene at the beginning and no major jumps of the playback head. From the introductory scene, you can check to make sure the rest of the movie is loaded before allowing the user to proceed.

In general, it is a good idea to set up your Shockwave movies so that they keep the user entertained while data is loading in the background. You should never give the user a chance to get bored and move on to another web site. Because loading data from the Internet often requires quite a bit longer than loading it from a hard disk or CD-ROM, Lingo for the Internet must behave differently than ordinary Lingo behaves. Remember that loading data from the Internet for Shockwave movies is a more complex operation than loading it from a hard disk. Shockwave Player must first download the data onto the user's hard drive and then load it into memory.

Working in the 3D World

Each Shockwave 3D cast member in a Director movie contains a complete 3D world. This world generally contains objects, or models, illuminated by lights and viewed by cameras. At any given time, only one camera can be in use. If a sprite is created from a Shockwave 3D cast member, Director must know which camera view to display. Therefore, the first camera in the 3D world is active by default. Although the positions of objects within a world may appear to change when a camera is moved or a different camera becomes active, you must remember that this is not the case. Cameras are free to move just as lights and models are.

In a 3D cast member, a group can be a collection of models, cameras, lights, or other groups. Grouping elements together enables you to rotate or translate them simultaneously within the world. Each group has a name, a transform (for rotation and movement), a parent, and one or more children. The highest-level group in Shockwave 3D is called the *world group*. Each 3D cast member has its own world group, which means that all items in Shockwave 3D are contained within some kind of group.

When you think of 3D cast members, you must remember that only a 3D world can be a sprite. Individual models can be accessed only through a Shockwave 3D cast member. In Director, you can build a complex 3D application using only one 3D world and therefore only one sprite. Alternatively, if you prefer, you can use both 2D and 3D sprites within the same movie. Remember that the Score operates the same whether it contains 3D sprites or not, and you can set the cast members of 3D sprites through Lingo just as you can with other sprites.

Models and Model Resources

Unlike cameras and lights, models are a part of a 3D cast member that you can actually see. They make use of model resources and occupy a specific position and orientation within a 3D world. Models move according to Lingo or the motions assigned to them in their original 3D editing software. Model resources are elements of 3D geometry that are used to display models within a world.

To visualize the relationship between models and model resources, think of model resources as cast members and models as sprites. A single model resource can be used to create several models of the same geometry just as several sprites can use the same cast member. For example, a 3D world might contain a model resource for the geometry of a car's body and one for a car's wheel. To display a complete car within the world, you must create one model using the car body resource and four models using the wheel resource. Each wheel is identical but can be positioned differently within the 3D world.

Lights and Cameras

Lights illuminate models in the 3D world. Without at least one light in a 3D cast member, that world would appear completely black, and the models would serve no purpose. By default, each Shockwave 3D cast member contains one white light positioned in the center of the world above all the models. This keeps programmers from explicitly having to add lights to simple 3D scenes. Of course, Director enables you to modify this light and add new lights to the world. To disable the default light completely, set its `color` property to black, or `rgb(0, 0, 0)`. Because black is the absence of light, a black light will have absolutely no effect on the 3D world. Cameras do not control the appearance of models but the angle from which they are viewed. A 3D sprite will use a particular camera to display a 2D image of its cast member's world from that camera's position. However, a Shockwave 3D cast member is not limited to only one camera. If several sprites use the same 3D cast member, each one can display a different view of the world by making use of multiple cameras.

Shaders and Textures

Shaders are used to define the basic appearance of a model's surface within the 3D world. They define how models react to light. A simple shader will set a model's surface color, but shaders have the potential to alter completely the appearance of a model. The default shader style is called `#photorealistic` and makes surfaces appear normal with no added effects. Other available shaders include `#painter`, which looks like a painted surface, `#newsprint`, which looks like newspaper, and `#engraver`, which looks like an engraved surface. A texture is a 2D image that can be drawn onto the surface of a 3D model. A shader can make use of one or more textures when determining how a model's surface should appear. You can assign textures to your models within your 3D modeling software or through Lingo by creating a texture from a bitmap cast member.

CREATING 3D TEXT

In addition to working with 3D models and scenes, Director enables you to create 3D text and work with it as you would any other 3D cast member. You can apply behaviors to 3D text sprites, use the Shockwave 3D window to view or edit the 3D text cast members, and even manipulate the text through Lingo. To create a 3D text cast member, you must first create a normal text cast member. When a text cast member is highlighted, the Property Inspector window's Text sheet will contain a drop-down Display list. Choose the 3D Mode option from this drop-down list, and Director will convert your text cast member to 3D text. After your cast member has been converted, you can modify its properties through the Property Inspector window's 3D Extruder sheet.

USING SHOCKWAVE 3D BEHAVIORS

Because the Score cannot control 3D elements such as models, lights, and cameras, Shockwave 3D sprites are primarily controlled by Lingo. However, Director includes a library of behaviors that enable developers to control 3D sprites without any knowledge of Lingo. Although writing Lingo behaviors may still be required for complex projects, Director's prebuilt behavior library can come in handy for rapid 3D development.

The 3D behavior library contains two types of behaviors: triggers and actions. A trigger is a behavior that tells an action behavior when to execute its code. Action behaviors come in three forms: local, public, and independent. A local action can accept triggers only from the sprite to which it is attached; public actions can accept triggers from any sprite; and independent actions require no trigger at all.

You may notice that the distinction between triggers and actions occurs only within the 3D behavior library. In other libraries, the trigger code is included as an event handler, such as `mouseDown` or `prepareFrame`, inside the same behavior as the action code. Keeping triggers in separate behaviors makes it easy to reuse action code in any situation. Triggers can be used on any Shockwave 3D sprite in conjunction with an appropriate action.

You can access Director's 3D behavior library through the Library window. To open the Library window, click the Window menu and select the Library Palette option. Within the Library window, click the Library List button and select an option from the 3D submenu. To use any of the action of trigger behaviors, just drag the behavior from the Library window onto the Shockwave 3D sprite you want to affect. You also can drag behaviors into the Cast window to store them for later. Attach as many behaviors to your sprites as you need, but remember that each dependent action behavior must have a unique trigger behavior to activate it.

CHOOSING A 3D AUTHORING TOOL

So, you've decided to go to the next dimension in your web or multimedia project and add a Shockwave 3D component. Don't be surprised if you're more than just a little intimidated with the software programs available for creating 3D objects and scenes. Most 3D development tools have well-deserved reputations for complexity and require a significant investment of both time and money. No need to worry, however; the next few pages take a quick look at the 3D programs best suited for your needs.

If you are new to 3D development, you might be feeling just a bit overwhelmed right now. You may wonder why you should bother at all. Roger Chandler, Sr., Marketing Manager of Intel Architecture Labs, said it best. "Fundamentally, 3D makes content more engaging; it allows you to do things that you can't do in a normal 2D web environment; it really changes everything." It was reported that when 3D was added to their sites,

SharperImage.com saw a 500 percent increase in visits and a 100 percent increase in sales, and Land's End saw a 200 percent increase in sales. The bottom line is that 3D graphics and animation can help you communicate your ideas better, which often leads to higher profits.

The long list of powerful 3D features Macromedia has included in Director 8.5 is incredibly impressive. Shockwave applications on faster connections can download models at 10,000 polygons per second. The models are visible quickly and increase in clarity as the download is completed. Keyframe and bones deformations are built in to the Shockwave 3D (W3D) format and are fully controlled by Lingo. Simply put, an animator or 3D artist can create character animations in his 3D program of choice, and that animation will be fully controllable through Director's Lingo. The conversion is accomplished by using an *exporter*, which is designed to convert the native file format of the 3D program into the W3D format needed for Shockwave 3D. The following section contains a list of several 3D development tools that have exporters for their products.

Keep in mind that if you talk with most 3D artists, they will insist that their 3D program of choice is simply the best with no room for argument. However, you should test-drive several programs to see which one makes the most sense for the way you work. In some cases, you can even download a trial version of the software from the vendor's web site.

We contacted a number of software development companies to learn about products currently available and their feelings concerning the future of 3D in multimedia applications. In no way can we do justice to the specific features of the programs in this appendix. However, we will provide you with an overview and some helpful web sites where you can obtain additional information.

3D TOOLS WITH SHOCKWAVE 3D EXPORTERS

Now you are ready to take a look at some of the leading 3D programs from which you can choose. Remember, this is by no means a complete list. More than 40 companies have partnered with Macromedia for Director 8.5 Shockwave Studio.

3DS MAX BY DISCREET (*WWW.DISCREET.COM/*)

Discreet is a division of Autodesk and a leader in digital content creation, management, and distribution tools. Discreet develops systems and software for visual effects, 3D animation, editing, and production used in the creation of digital moving pictures for feature films, video, HDTV, broadcast graphics, interactive games, and the web. Discreet products are used extensively in film and video postproduction, games and multimedia, broadcast graphics, programming, and on-air event coverage. The company has received more than 300 awards in the past 10 years, including two Academy Awards for Technical Achievement from the Academy of Motion Picture Arts and Sciences. See Figure C.1.

The tagline for Discreet is, "We make tools that let you make magic," and their 3ds max program has been making magic for years. 3ds max 4 claims the bragging rights as the world's best-selling 3D animation tool. The program is the product of choice for web professionals and offers tight integration with Director 8.5. Discreet's initiative to bring 3D to the web includes the support for exporting 3ds max content to the new Shockwave 3D format. The company has Director 8.5 Shockwave Studio exporters for 3ds max 4 available for download.

The 3ds max Shockwave 3D exporter includes support for rich character animation from character studio, dynamic physics from reactor, and the same multiresolution mesh technology from Intel used in Shockwave 3D that gives web artists the ability to preview streaming and level-of-detail results directly within 3ds max.

Phillip Miller, Senior Director of Software Products at Discreet, said, "Interactive 3D animation provides developers and web viewers expanded opportunities to experience 3D on the web delivered in a scalable format at minimum bandwidth." With authoring and playback solutions jointly developed by Macromedia and Intel and a strong bridge to Discreet's leading 3D content-creation tools, artists can now deliver the rich web experiences that result in increased online sales, site stickiness, and customer satisfaction.

Figure C.1 *The Discreet 3ds max site.*

We asked Dan Prochazka, Product Manager for Discreet, why a Director developer might choose 3ds max for his 3D work. Dan said, "The Shockwave 3D exporter for 3ds max is the most advanced on the market. It is the only system that supports character animation with both bipedal animation and full skinning of characters. 3ds max, along with reactor, is the only 3D program that will allow for the preview and export of the Havok physics that are supported in Macromedia's Shockwave 3D. Using these programs, you can set up and preview sophisticated rigid body dynamics, export both the geometry and the physics, and bring them together in Director. Quite simply, a Director user would want to use 3ds max to generate his 3D content because no other program supports the exporting of so many 3D features and so much 3D content to Shockwave 3D."

AMAPI 3D BY EOVIA (*WWW.EOVIA.COM/*)

Eovia, founded in November 2000, is headquartered in San Diego, California. TGS acquired the company in March 2001. Although it is a young company, Eovia founders have more than 10 years of research and development and marketing experience with companies such as MetaCreations and Fractal Design. Formerly the home of AMAPI 3D, TGS has been in the graphics software business for more than 15 years. See Figure C.2.

AMAPI 3D 6.1 is the latest release and since July 2001 has included the Shockwave 3D exporter. The trial edition is available free with the exporter for a 30-day period. AMAPI 3D comes on hybrid CD and will work on Windows and Macintosh systems. The product is priced below $400, and the company offers numerous upgrade incentives.

AMAPI 3D is a very fast and powerful modeler with both low-polygon and NURBS editing capabilities. It offers five subdivision surface smoothing methods for organic modeling, but also allows for precise geometric modeling with measurements and numeric input. It is positioned as a companion modeler to more than 25 other formats and exports to LightWave, 3ds, OBJ, Strata, ElectricImage, Flash, Shockwave 3D, STL, VRML, Cinema 4D, DXF, and a number of other formats. It also includes a hybrid raytrace/cartoon rendering engine, which some animation professionals, furniture designers, architects, game content developers, sculptors, and creative artists primarily use as a modeler.

Figure C.2 *The Eovia AMAPI 3D site.*

ARGON BY ASHLAR-VELLUM (*WWW.ASHLAR-VELLUM.COM/*I)

Founded in 1988, Ashlar-Vellum is the leading developer and marketer of products that automate and simplify industrial, mechanical, and commercial design processes for drafting, design, and engineering professionals. Ashlar-Vellum's renowned user interfaces and powerful toolsets have earned the loyalty of conceptual thinkers around the world. Originally located in Santa Clara, California, Ashlar-Vellum now operates from headquarters in Austin, Texas. See Figure C.3.

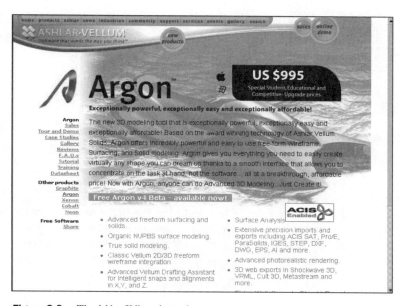

Figure C.3 *The Ashlar-Vellum Argon site.*

Argon 4 was created to bring high-end surface NURBS and solid modeling to a price point accessible by the new generation of 3D content creators. Argon is particularly suited to the precise modeling of manufactured objects and structures. Argon is an advanced 3D program that integrates precision, free-form NURBS surfaces and solids. It includes surface verification, advanced photorealistic rendering, and animation in an exceptionally powerful, easy-to-use package that sells for $995 with support for both Macintosh and Windows systems.

We asked Robert Bou, President of Ashlar-Vellum, about the kinds of 3D applications his products are now being used for. He said, "We feel that 3D on the web is best used for product presentations where the customer may wish to explore the look and feel of a real product prior to actually visiting a show room or placing and order. As bandwidth on the Internet increases, customers will demand 3D presentations for all products that they are evaluating."

CINEMA 4D BY MAXON COMPUTER (*WWW.MAXONCOMPUTER.COM/*)

MAXON Computer is the developer of professional 3D modeling, painting, animation, and rendering solutions. Their award-winning products have been used extensively in film, television, science, architecture, engineering, and other industries. MAXON products have been used for *The Mummy Returns*, *Gladiator*, *Tomb Raider*, *Logo*, *Inspector Gadget*, *Small Soldiers*, *Blast From the Past*, TiVO, NBC, DirecTV, *Mad TV*, *JAG*, Comedy Central, The WB, Fox Kids, and many more. MAXON has offices in Newbury Park, California, and Friedrichsdorf, Germany. See Figure C.4.

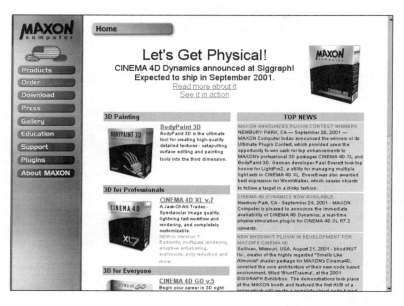

Figure C.4 *The MAXON Computer CINEMA 4D site.*

CINEMA 4D is a fully integrated 3D modeling, animation, and rendering package for Windows and Macintosh systems. It is well known for its surprisingly fast and photorealistic raytracer. You can download a free demo version of the program from their web site or purchase the full version for $1695. BodyPaint 3D, a companion product to CINEMA 4D, is an advanced 3D painting application for creating high-quality textures in a 3D environment. BodyPaint 3D seamlessly integrates into CINEMA 4D XL, offering artists the ability to add detail to surfaces at any point during the production process. It also can be used as a standalone application in combination with other popular 3D software packages.

We asked Paul Babb, the President of MAXON Computer, why a Director developer might choose his product for his 3D needs. Paul said, "We offer a great price/performance ratio, and our products are fast, both in the working environment and when rendering scenes."

He went on to say, "Our products are powerful. Both products handle very complex scenes in the millions of polygons, hundreds of shadow-casting lights, countless texture maps, particles, and complex animation with ease. Most programs cannot even open scenes of this size. Some have as many as one billion polygons per object. Our products allow you to have unlimited objects, unlimited materials and textures, unlimited lights, unlimited cameras, and unlimited animation tracks per object."

CINEMA 4D XL 7 works well with older hardware, requires less RAM than other 3D packages, and generates extremely efficient file size. The program will allow background rendering and enables you to open multiple projects at once. In a development shop where both Windows and Macintosh systems are running, CINEMA 4D XL is only 5 percent OS-dependent, so using it feels the same on all platforms. It is completely customizable, so you can define your own keyboard shortcuts and even change the dialog boxes and menu structure. The product is available in German, English, Italian, French, and Japanese.

D SCULPTOR BY D VISION WORKS (*WWW.D-VW.COM/*)

D Vision Works is an independently owned and operated UK company located at Milton Park near Oxford. The company specializes in image and video-processing solutions but offers a variety of products and services such as image processing, active lighting 3D capture, and stereoscopic filming. See Figure C.5.

Figure C.5   *The D Vision Works D Sculptor site.*

The D Vision Works D Sculptor product is an intuitive, image-based modeling program that enables the user to create 3D models of real-world objects using a digital camera. It differs from other 3D modeling software products covered in this section because the 3D objects are created from a series of photos of an object taken from a number of different views. The best way to understand D Vision is to look at how it is used to create a 3D object.

The first step in modeling with D Sculptor is to take a number of photographs of the object to be modeled. D Sculptor then helps you turn these into a fully textured 3D model, which can then be exported in a variety of file formats including DXF, WRL, 3ds, OBJ, and W3D (for use with Shockwave 3D). It also is possible for models to be exported for use with the supplied 3D viewer applet for license-free, platform-independent 3D display.

PRODUCER BY FAMOUS3D (WWW.FAMOUS3D.COM/)

Blaze International, the parent company of famous3D, is in the process of releasing commercial, Internet-based authoring tools that allow web production houses and businesses to create lifelike "talking heads" using text, audio, or video input. This content can then be streamed using their proprietary streaming format optimized for efficient display over the Internet. Applications for this type of technology include e-commerce, e-learning, entertainment, chat, call centers, and ultimately wireless devices. famous3D software has been used in the production of facial animation for broadcast applications since 1997. See Figure C.6.

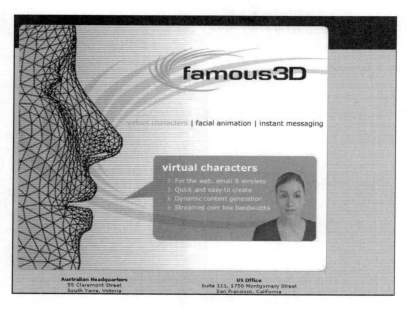

Figure C.6 *The famous3D Producer site.*

famous3D has been working with Intel for more than two years and has demonstrated its unique software at recent Pentium 4 launches. The combination of Macromedia Director 8.5 with the Intel Internet 3D Graphics software will provide developers with a flexible, extensive, and robust 3D development solution. The 3D technology will enable new types of web experiences to be delivered using the Macromedia Shockwave Player, which is already installed on a majority of web desktops.

famous3D's Producer software promises to empower developers around the world with an element clearly lacking from the web today—a human interface. Producer enables a user with little to no technical experience to create virtual characters for company mascots or human representatives. These virtual characters can be streamed from within a web site or HTML newsletter in three simple steps. A user of the software must first select a head from the library provided, or create a custom head from a photograph. The user then makes the head talk and emote audio or text, and seamlessly integrates the talking head into a web page using the publishing wizard.

Research in the e-learning market points to the fact that with dropout rates for online courses as high as 80 percent and onscreen reading retention 30 percent lower than printed material, the need for more compelling, interactive content is critical to the success of online learning initiatives. "The Internet is, on the whole, sterile and has failed to build strong and enduring relationships between businesses and their customers," pointed out famous3D's Vice President of Sales, Zac Jacobs. "As more businesses interact with their customers digitally, they are going to need tools to enhance that dialogue and make it more human." He goes on to say that this process naturally engenders loyalty and trust.

"With this joint development from Macromedia and Intel, the Internet community has a simple and compelling way to communicate more effectively to an immense user base," said David Skelton, CEO of Blaze International. "This richer, more immersive web experience will truly humanize the Internet."

IMAGEMODELER BY REALVIZ (*WWW.REALVIZ.COM/*)

Founded in March 1998, and based on technological research conducted by INRIA (The French National Institute for Research in Computer Science and Automation), REALVIZ develops and markets a portfolio of image-processing software that enables the production of 2D and 3D digital content for film, multimedia, CAD, architecture, video games, and digital imaging. The main focus of REALVIZ is democratizing access of such special effects and computer-generated images to a wide range of content creators in a variety of markets. REALVIZ has sales offices in Paris, London, Singapore, and San Francisco. The company generates more than 60 percent of its business in the United States. See Figure C.7.

Figure C.7   *The REALVIZ ImageModeler site.*

ImageModeler is a 3D modeling program that uses photographs. ImageModeler revolutionizes 3D model creation with a unique workflow for 3D and non-3D artists. It delivers impressive results that are automatically optimized for web player environments. With automated photographic texturing, the results are a perfect fit for today's visual requirements for e-merchandising and entertainment on the web. Low-polygon models with compressed textures deliver optimal file sizes for real-time web playback.

Developers can build 3D models using photographs that ease the transition into 3D authoring for non-3D multimedia developers and artists. Each model contains only a single texture for optimized web delivery with automatic placement and wrapping. Low-polygon models can be produced for optimal file size for delivery over low-bandwidth connections. The software allows for photorealistic texturing for impressive rendering on the web. REALVIZ ImageModeler 2.1 costs $2100.

LightWave 3D by NewTek (*www.lightwave3d.com/*)

NewTek is headquartered in San Antonio, Texas, and is a leading provider of full-featured video editing, animation, and special-effects tools including LightWave 3D, Video Toaster, and Aura. The company's products are used worldwide on projects ranging from home video to feature film. Recent film projects using NewTek software include *Driven*, *AI*, *Final Fantasy*, *The Time Machine*, *How the Grinch Stole Christmas*, *The 6th Day*, and *Jurassic Park III*. Recent game titles include Deus Ex, Serious Sam, Twisted Metal: Black, Quake 3 Arena, Moto Racer World Tour, Baldur's Gate II, EverQuest, and Escape from Monkey Island. The company's founder, Tim Jenison, commented, "The NewTek team is insanely committed to providing the highest quality tools and services to support our extended family of end users in their creative drive for success." See Figure C.8.

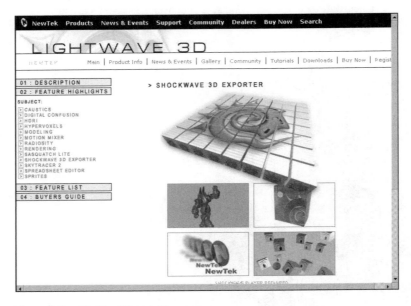

Figure C.8   *The NewTek LightWave site.*

LightWave 3D is well known for its use in television and film, as well as gaming, web design, and print media. It is a fully comprehensive modeling, animation, and rendering program with a very loyal user base. We asked Brad Peebler, Executive Vice President of NewTek, about the product. "While its feature set is considered 'high-end,' the price point is a fraction of the competition, and the learning curve is much shorter," said Peebler. LightWave is available for Windows NT, 2000, and XP, as well as Mac OS 9 and OS X. LightWave 3D sells at $2495.

LightWave is especially useful for Director developers because it is one of the only polygon native systems on the market. The 3D format inside of Director (and all real-time engines) uses polygons, which are the basic building blocks of the 3D objects. LightWave uses the same core technology, so translation from LightWave data into Director 8.5 is smooth and gives excellent results. The Director Exporter for LightWave is completely free for all LightWave owners (6.5 or higher).

We asked Peebler why he believes Macromedia will be successful with its 3D efforts where others have failed. Peebler replied, "The main difference in Macromedia's approach to 3D on the web is that they already have a deployment mechanism. With VRML and other splinter formats, the end user was forced to seek out an appropriate player for the 3D content. With SW3D, Macromedia already has hundreds of thousands of Shockwave users who auto-update into a 3D-ready version when they connect to a site with 3D content. That solves the biggest obstacle for the consumer. Secondarily, the time is right for 3D on the web. There are more 3D-enabled video cards on the market than ever before. Most of these cards have greater performance than workstation class computers of just a few years past." Peebler continued, "The key uses for 3D on the web will be gaming, product visualization, and of course, there will be innovative uses that only creative users will discover. As with any emerging technology, we have no idea where this technology may lead us. However, because of the incredible power and flexibility of 3D, there is no doubt that interesting new uses will emerge."

MAYA BY ALIAS|WAVEFRONT (*WWW.ALIASWAVEFRONT.COM/*)

Alias|Wavefront develops award-winning solutions for film and video, games, interactive media, industrial design, and visualization markets. These solutions give artists a distinct creative advantage no matter what their discipline. Alias|Wavefront Maya customers include CNN, Digital Domain, Disney's The Secret Lab, Electronic Arts, Industrial Light and Magic, Nintendo, Pixar, Sega, Sony Pictures Imageworks, Weta, and Square Co. See Figure C.9.

Figure C.9   *The Alias\Wavefront Maya site.*

Maya 4 is the sixth major release of this professional 3D software program from Alias|Wavefront. Maya is widely used in the film, game, and broadcast markets for the creation of high-quality 3D graphics and animation. Today, the 3D web market is the fastest growing sector in which Maya is used. The company took its first steps toward creating animation software for Internet and intranet graphics markets in 1999, when it released Maya Builder, a competitively priced version of the world-renowned Maya software tailored to the needs of web designers and game developers. Maya Builder has a full set of those features needed to create quality 3D artwork for real-time deployment through the leading web 3D technologies. These features include polygonal modeling, texture mapping, and lighting tools for the creation and animation of skinned characters and visually detailed environments that are optimized in the real-time interactive world. Maya has been used to create award-winning animations and includes a powerful set of modeling, rendering, and visual-effects tools. Maya can be used on Windows, IRIX, and Linux platforms.

Mike Wilson, Director of Maya Interactive at Alias|Wavefront, said, "We are committed to the Shockwave platform as a high-quality 3D web content-publishing path for Maya customers. The new 3D capabilities of Shockwave will introduce the broad base of Internet users to fully interactive 3D games, educational, and e-commerce material. We are very excited to be helping further this goal, through the development of an industrial-strength export path that is optimized specifically for Director and the Shockwave platform."

Wilson continued, "3D web content development is an iterative process, with repeated exports and modifications necessary to assure top compatibility, performance, and appearance in the target player. The Maya Shockwave 3D Exporter checks the Maya scene for compatibility with the Shockwave Player and then suggests scene optimizations that will improve performance. Moreover, it keeps track of changes and injects only these, as opposed to the whole scene, on subsequent exports. The result being that data conversion, which normally takes a number of minutes, is reduced to seconds. This function alone will quickly add up to hours of production time saved with the Maya Shockwave 3D Exporter solution." Alias|Wavefront has provided a tutorial to help developers convert objects from Maya into Shockwave 3D at www.aliaswavefront.com/sw3d/.

SHAPESHIFTER 3D BY TABULEIRO (HTTP://XTRAS.TABULEIRO.COM/)

Tabuleiro is a well-known name to those in the Director community and has been associated with Macromedia to extend the capabilities of Director since 1995. The company is located in Sao Paulo, Brazil, and shipped its first Director Xtra (MpegXtra) with the Director 5 CD, the first version of Director to support Xtras. When we asked Mauricio Piacentini, the Founder of Tabuleiro, about the company, he replied, "We are 100 percent focused on extending Director, and we have a good understanding of the problems faced by the Director developer and the workflow of a Director production." See Figure C.10.

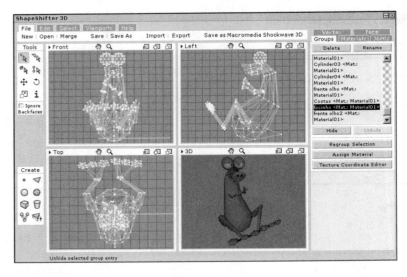

Figure C.10   *The Tabuleiro ShapeShifter 3D site.*

ShapeShifter 3D was created to address the needs of a Director-centric developer. All modeling and texturing is actually done inside of Director. The 3D modeler runs inside the Director development environment, not in a separate application. All ShapeShifter 3D operations and functions are optimized for low-polygon models, best suited for real-time applications. The Xtra runs on Windows and Macintosh systems and files can be transported seamlessly from one platform to another. ShapeShifter 3D users are always working inside Director with the limitations and strengths of a modeler developed specifically for Shockwave 3D. Unlike other full-featured 3D modelers, ShapeShifter 3D does not require a huge investment of time in training. The Xtra is focused on modeling and texturing of low-polygon models, and a couple of hours are typically all that is needed to become familiar with its commands. ShapeShifter 3D offers an attractive price of $199.

SOFTIMAGE|XSI BY SOFTIMAGE (*WWW.SOFTIMAGE.COM/*)

Softimage, a division of Avid Technology, is an industry leader in 3D animation, 2D cell animation, compositing, and special-effects software. SOFTIMAGE|XSI is the flagship product offering from Softimage and an integral player in Avid's "make, manage, and move" media strategy. It is the industry's first truly nonlinear animation (NLA) system that gives animators and digital artists the freedom to make anything from major motion pictures to cartoons and commercials, to animated content for video games and web sites. The Softimage product family is designed to help users throughout the production process. See Figure C.11.

Figure C.11   *The Softimage SOFTIMAGE|XSI site.*

The development of SOFTIMAGE|XSI has been driven by a single and consistent goal: "To build the best creative tools for digital artists." Version 2.0 sells for $9495 and boasts more than 2500 new features and feature enhancements aimed squarely at artists in the broadcast, interactive, and multimedia industries. The SOFTIMAGE|XSI package features an integrated compositor, real-time shaders, integrated hair and fur simulators, increased performance, expanded interoperability, and improved stability. It builds on the product's trademark features of nondestructive animation mixing, interactive rendering, and an Internet-enabled workflow.

"SOFTIMAGE|XSI continues our unprecedented pace of product development and innovation, with over 2500 new features and enhancements inspired by our customers from around the world," stated Michael Stojda, Managing Director of Softimage. "The latest version of XSI will enable digital artists to innovate, create, and collaborate in new ways providing our customers with a distinct creative advantage and accelerated return on investment."

"This release also pushes the envelope in terms of animation tools and workflow," said Michael David Smith, Technical Product Manager at Softimage. "In particular, SOFTIMAGE|XSI 2.0 includes an array of new features across all toolsets to facilitate character creation, rigging, and animation." These include new tools for symmetry drawing; manipulation and attribute painting; volume; pose-based and cage deformations; blending of IK, FK, and constraints; creating and editing complex flexible envelopes; and editing and manipulating textures. In addition, a series of new curve and keyframe editing tools to ease the manipulation of dense animation data have been added to the animation editor, which also supports the ability to manipulate clip-based motion data in context easily.

TRUESPACE BY CALIGARI (*WWW.CALIGARI.COM/*)

The Caligari Corporation was founded in 1986 with the mission to develop the easiest and most powerful tools for 3D authoring. Today, the Company focuses intently on developing affordable 3D solutions that enable designers to create visual communication quickly and easily within immersive 3D environments. Caligari has a proven track record in innovative 3D interface design and over the past 13 years has continued to develop and improve their core 3D technologies. With its roots in multimedia products, Caligari was a pioneer in transitioning its business practices and products to the web. See Figure C.12.

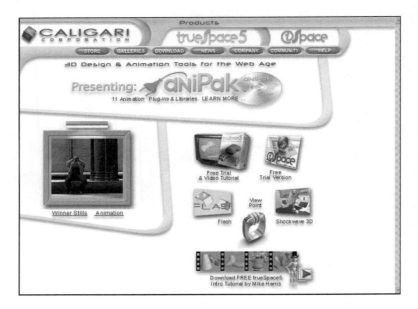

Figure C.12   *The Caligari trueSpace site.*

Caligari trueSpace combines high-end modeling, rendering, and animation power with an intuitive user interface that allows for real-time direct manipulation in a hardware-accelerated, integrated, 3D perspective workspace. Used extensively for product design, web design, graphic design, and multimedia, the software delivers advanced features such as hybrid radiosity rendering, a full complement of NURBS-based modeling tools, and advanced surfacing features. trueSpace also offers both linear keyframed animation and nonlinear physics-based animation with properties such as wind, gravity, and collision detection.

The latest version of trueSpace has an updated software development kit for third-party plug-in developers. Roman Organdy, the President of Caligari, said, "We offer a 'protean' program: a comprehensive array of online tools, training programs, libraries, and support services available so our users can now output their trueSpace models and animations to Macromedia's new Shockwave 3D and Director 8.5 formats, opening up vast new delivery options for distributing rich, interactive 3D content on the web."

Caligari's new Shockwave 3D Exporter plug-in streamlines conversion of trueSpace objects and scenes to the Macromedia Shockwave 3D format, including all trueSpace geometry, materials, lights, views, and animation. trueSpace can be used alone to create Shockwave 3D content or as a 3D authoring complement to Macromedia Director. trueSpace has the capability to generate HTML files directly for export to Viewpoint format, providing a one-step solution for creating Viewpoint-based web sites. A Flash plug-in for trueSpace is currently being developed. The trueSpace 5.1 package, including Shockwave 3D output, is $795 initially with annual renewal fees of $495.

TAKING THE LEAD

Moving into the realm of 3D software can be filled with both frustration and expense; if you consider the size of the market, however, there are great opportunities for 3D developers ahead. "With the Shockwave Player already in use by more than 200 million web users, we are in a unique position to improve online entertainment, e-merchandising, and learning experiences by adding 3D," said Peter Ryce, Senior Director of Product Marketing at Macromedia. "With the platform in place, we needed to integrate Macromedia Director 8.5 with 3D tools that deliver the highest quality experience for developers and artists. Yet the learning curve is well worth climbing because the results can be truly breathtaking."

The creative power that comes from exporting objects from your favorite 3D program into Director and breathing interactive life into them can make even the most stoic client's jaw drop. Years from now, people will regard the release of Director 8.5 Shockwave Studio as a milestone in the evolution of 3D on the web. As a multimedia developer, you can sit back and watch, or take the lead by creating innovative interface designs, incredible graphics, and amazing 3D animations.

THE FUTURE OF 3D ON THE INTERNET

There is an old saying that "the man who looks into a crystal ball to see into the future can end up with glass in his eye." Even so, no discussion about 3D on the Internet would be complete without at least an educated guess or two about what is in store for the future. Has 3D on the web finally arrived with the advent of Director 8.5's Shockwave 3D? To get a better understanding of this, we talked with visionaries from two research companies that have studied the question in some detail.

Wanda Meloni is the principal analyst of M2 Research and has tracked 3D and graphics technologies for more than five years. She is the author of the "Digital Media Market Study," which looks at the impact 3D and video are making on the digital media industry. Samantha Staples is principal software analyst and author of "3D on the Web" for Jon Peddie Associates (JPA), a leading market research firm that reports on digital media and presents the annual Web 3D Conference.

"For a number of years now, 3D on the web has been a presumed 'coming thing,' and many companies placed their bets early," said Ms. Meloni. Although there have been advances in 3D technology, the market has been slow to respond. Ms. Meloni cited three problems that have held back the proliferation of 3D on the web: bandwidth, 3D players, and content. 3D files are typically large and require significant bandwidth. Most consumers do not have access to high-speed Internet connections. Most 3D content requires specialized players, which are often proprietary and require a download before a user can view a file. Creating 3D content requires skilled developers who have mastered complex 3D authoring software. Professionals compared an estimated 200,000 3D graphics to the more than 10 million users who are currently deploying 2D web content.

The good news is that advances in technology and 3D development tools are reducing these barriers. Currently, the industry is measuring the success of 3D on the web primarily from a player-penetration angle, which is somewhat effective in the short term. M2 Research estimates that by the end of 2001, 3D players will have already reached 32 percent of all Internet users. There also will be a significant jump in the development of 3D content.

By the end of 2001, 15 percent of all content developed using 3D animation programs will be created specifically for web use, nearly double the percentage at the start of 2001. The bottleneck of content production may actually be the driving factor to the deployment of inexpensive, high-quality 3D applications. "These 3D tools must be as easy to use as others on which creative professionals and digital designers currently depend," continued Ms. Meloni.

In the long term, Ms. Meloni believes that the real measurement for determining the success of 3D on the web will have to reach far beyond simple player penetration. Because 3D player penetration will reach 100 percent within the next several years, it will soon be a moot point. What will drive real opportunity for the market will boil down to the extent 3D succeeds to increase the user's perception of 3D content and his interaction with that content. Early tests have shown that 3D content has increased traffic to web sites by 150 percent and in some cases increased web sales by 200 percent. Users are more likely to retain content and messaging if it is presented to them in 3D. Fortunately, or unfortunately depending on your view, commerce will be what ultimately drives the market to success.

One of the most comprehensive studies on the future of 3D, titled "3D on the Web" (available at www.jpa.com/), was conducted by Samantha Staples of JPA. This study includes research into topics such as the current and forecasted size of the web 3D universe as defined by access to the Internet, 3D-enabled browsers, and Internet connection speeds and bandwidth. The challenges that have to date hindered the deployment of 3D over the web include consumer resistance, bandwidth limitations, 3D file sizes, installation of plug-ins, and digital asset management. The report also includes an analysis of web 3D technologies and products and their business models and growth potential through the year 2007.

According to the "3D on the Web" market study, dial-up access to the Internet will continue to dominate over broadband for the remainder of this decade. One million active web sites will use some form of 3D by the year 2007, and B2B applications will continue to expand the horizons for 3D on the web, even though e-commerce is currently touted as the best application for web 3D.

In our interview with Ms. Staples, she took us behind the scenes to uncover the trends driving the market. She began by pointing out that the market for 3D on the Internet is still in its early days. "It's not enough to just put 3D on the web," said Ms. Staples. "Applications have to be developed to enhance user experiences, or web 3D will remain a novelty or niche technology."

"Much of the growth we forecast will be due to the success of companies that exhibit the foresight to work together to grow the market as a whole," added Ms. Staples. "Though the technologies are themselves important, their mere existence will not drive users to web 3D. The real jackpot is waiting for those who can pool their resources to concentrate on compelling applications in an effort to survive this tough embryonic phase."

The report forecasts strong growth in the number of sites using 3D technologies to deploy new types of content for e-commerce, entertainment and gaming, business collaboration, and other applications. 3D sites are expected to expand from just a handful in 2001 to more than one million by 2007. At the same time, browsers with installed 3D viewing technologies, such as Shockwave 3D, will grow from just more than 21 million in 2001 to more than 559 million by 2007.

"The first successful implementations of web 3D will likely be instances where repurposed 3D assets are used in applications such as 3D product catalogs, training, and customer service," said Ms. Staples. Other applications will require the creation of new 3D assets, and a content bottleneck is anticipated. Mrs. Staples then added, "Web developers with 3D skills will find themselves in demand, as compelling web 3D applications are developed and implemented."

A

alignment   The idea that all interface elements should be connected by their locations relative to screen edges and each other.

antialiasing   The process of smoothing an image to avoid the appearance of jagged edges due to sharp changes in the colors of pixels.

applet   An application that can be viewed only through an Internet browser with the proper plug-in.

application   See *program*.

argument   See *parameter*.

array   See *list*.

ASCII   The American Standard Code for Information Interchange used for defining alphanumeric characters.

B

behavior script   A Lingo script designed to affect only the sprite(s) to which it has been applied as opposed to affecting an entire Director movie.

bitmap   An array of color values that make up an image.

Boolean   Having to do with a value of either true or false.

C

cast   Stores scripts, images, sounds, and other media to be used within a Director movie.

cast member   A script, image, sound, or other medium stored within a cast to be used within a Director movie.

cell   A section of a channel that holds the contents of that channel for exactly one frame.

channel   A numbered row of cells that represents a single layer of a Director movie.

character   A single letter, numeric digit, or symbol that could be a component of a string.

color   The predefined Lingo type consisting of a red value, a green value, and a blue value that indicate a single color.

command   Any line of lingo programming code. Generally refers to built-in Lingo functions.

commenting   The process of hiding a line of source code from the rest of the Director movie for the purpose of clarifying unclear code or debugging a movie.

conditional   A structure that keeps one or several lines of code from being executed unless a specified condition is met.

constant   A value incapable of changing its worth.

contrast   The idea that interface elements that do not appear exactly alike should appear very different.

D

.DCR   The file extension used for Shockwave web applets.

.DIR   The file extension used for Director source files.

Director The multimedia development utility created by Macromedia designed to make multimedia programming easy.

dot syntax The new style of Lingo programming that resembles mathematical equations.

.DXR The file extension used for protected Director source files.

E

effects channels The six channels that can hold effects such as transitions, sounds, and behaviors as opposed to visual sprites.

event handler A function built in to Director that executes at set intervals or based on user interaction.

.EXE The file extension used for standalone applications.

F

feedback Informs the user about his interaction with an interface.

film loop A type of cast member that can contain multiple frames and/or sprites within itself.

float The predefined Lingo type indicating decimal, or floating-point, numbers.

font A style in which text graphically displays.

frame A numbered column of cells that represents a single point in a Director movie.

frame marker See *marker*.

frame rate The number of frames that a movie displays per second.

function A section of code that executes only when it is specifically told to do so.

future feedback Feedback given to the user before an interaction occurs.

G

global variable A variable that exists throughout a movie in any script that references it.

graphic A visual representation of an item either directly or indirectly made up of pixels.

H

handler See *event handler*.

hard return A break in a block of text caused by the writer pressing the Enter (Return on Macintosh) key to insert a carriage return.

I

icon An image or symbol used to represent an action or idea.

integer The predefined Lingo type indicating numbers that do not contain any decimal fractions.

interface An interactive means of bringing information to the user.

K

keyframe   A frame of a movie designated to signify a change in a sprite channel.

L

linear list   A list variable that contains only a list of ordered values.

Lingo   The programming language used to create scripts within Director.

list   A single variable that holds zero or more values within itself.

local variable   A variable that exists from the point it was first assigned a value to the end of the handler or function in which it began.

loop   A structure that makes a group of code execute repeatedly as long as a specified condition is met.

M

marker   A special kind of frame that can be accessed by its given name.

mask   An image that indicates (usually with only two colors) a certain portion of another image that is active, clickable, or visible.

member   See *cast member*.

metaphor   A representation of a physical object that is meant to give the user an idea of how an interface operates.

model   A representation of a model resource after it has been placed in a 3D world.

model resource   Elements of 3D geometry used to display models within a 3D world.

movie   Any application, presentation, or game created within Director.

movie script   A Lingo script designed to affect an entire Director movie.

N

nested   A conditional or loop enclosed within another conditional or loop.

O

opacity   The amount of visibility a visual item conveys.

opaque   The characteristic of a visual item to be completely visible.

operating system   The shell application required to run all other applications on a computer.

operator   A term or function indicating some operation to be performed.

P

parameter   A value passed to a function or behavior to be used as a local variable within the function.

past feedback   Feedback that is given to the user after an interaction has occurred.

pixel A single dot of color within a raster image or video buffer.

platform See *operating system*.

playback head Indicator that moves through the Score to show the frame currently displayed on the Stage.

point The predefined Lingo type consisting of a horizontal value and a vertical value that indicate a single 2D location.

present feedback Feedback given to the user as an interaction is taking place.

program A series of ordered instructions that tell the computer what to do.

programmer The person writing a particular application.

property list A list variable that contains not only values, but also property names.

property variable A variable that exists only within a single script or as an attribute of a specified sprite.

proximity The idea that the positioning of interface elements close together indicates a relationship.

puppet A sound or sprite that is under Lingo control as opposed to Score control.

R

raster graphics Graphics that work directly with pixels rather than shapes.

registration point The point on a graphic element that positioning and rotation is based on.

repetition The idea that similar styles should be reused throughout an interface to convey a sense of continuity.

rotating The process of distorting a graphic element by changing its angular orientation.

runtime The point in the development of a program when the program is actually executed.

S

Score The visual display of all frames, channels, and cells within a Director movie.

script A section of Lingo code that makes up exactly one member of a cast.

Shockwave The name given to all Internet content created with Director.

simplicity The idea that an interface should not contain so many elements as to confuse the user.

skewing The process of distorting a graphic element by slanting it horizontally.

soft return A break in a block of text caused by a line of text being too long and wrapping onto the next line.

sprite A representation of a visual cast member after it has been placed on the Stage or within the Score.

sprite channel See *channel*.

Stage The visual area of a Director movie where all action takes place.

string The predefined Lingo type indicating a group of zero or more characters organized in a specific order.

T

tick One sixtieth of a second.

translucent The characteristic of a visual item to be partially visible.

transparent The characteristic of a visual item to be completely invisible.

tweening The process of creating transitions between keyframes.

type A classification of a value such as integer, string, color, and so forth.

type casting The process of converting a value of one data type into a value of another.

U

user The person using a particular application.

V

value Any number, section of text, or other item of a set worth.

variable Constant letter or word that can represent a changing value.

vector graphics Graphics that work with shapes rather than directly with pixels.

verbose syntax The old style of Lingo programming that resembles English sentences.

vertex A point at which two line segments intersect.

visual channels All channels that can hold visual sprites as opposed to transitions, sounds, or behaviors.

void Without any set value.

W

.W3D The file extension used for Shockwave 3D scenes.

white space Screen area in an interface that does not contain any active elements.

word wrap Characteristic of a text field that allows entire words to move to the next line when the preset width of the field would otherwise be exceeded.

X

Xtra A plug-in application designed to expand the functionality of Director in some way.

Z

zooming The process of resizing an image to make it appear closer or farther away.

Note:
If you have any difficulties with this CD, you can access our web site at www.newriders.com.

The accompanying CD-ROM is packed with all sorts of exercise files and products to help you work with this book and with Director 8.5 Shockwave Studio. The following sections contain detailed descriptions of the CD's contents.

For more information about the use of this CD, review the readme.rtf file in the root directory. This file includes important disclaimer information as well as information about installation, system requirements, troubleshooting, and technical support.

SYSTEM REQUIREMENTS

This CD-ROM was configured for use on systems running at least Windows 95 or Mac OS 9. Your machine will need to meet the following system requirements for this CD to operate properly:

- ➤ Pentium II 400MHz or PowerPC CPU
- ➤ 700MB free disk space (depending on installation)
- ➤ 128MB RAM
- ➤ 36× CD-ROM drive
- ➤ 16-bit sound card with speakers or headphones
- ➤ 16-bit (High Color) display setting

LOADING THE CD FILES

Note:
This CD-ROM uses long and mixed-case filenames, requiring the use of a protected-mode CD-ROM driver.

To load the files from the CD, insert the disc into your CD-ROM drive. If AutoPlay is enabled on your machine, the CD-ROM setup program starts automatically the first time you insert the disc. You can copy the files to your hard drive or use them right off the CD.

EXERCISE FILES

This CD contains all the files you need to complete the exercises in *Director 8.5 Shockwave Studio Interface Design*. You can find these files in the root directory's numbered folders. Note, however, that you will not find any folders for Chapter 1, "Designing Interfaces," or Chapter 2, "Using Director"; these chapters contain exercises for which you do not need to access any project files. For information on accessing and modifying exercise files, refer to Appendix A, "Guide to Common Tasks."

DIRECTOR 8.5 DEMO FROM MACROMEDIA

Director enables programmers to create quality interactive multimedia quickly and easily for the Internet, Macintosh, and PC. Director's drag-and-drop interface and simplified programming language help to free programmers from wasting their time on common or repetitive tasks. The Shockwave player lets Internet users view online Director applications. Most computers with Internet access currently use the Shockwave player, and virtually all computer manufacturers preinstall the player on new computers.

This book's CD-ROM carries a demo of Director. Check it out to see firsthand what you can do.

READ THIS BEFORE OPENING THE SOFTWARE

By opening the CD package, you agree to be bound by the following agreement:

You may not copy or redistribute the entire CD-ROM as a whole. Copying and redistribution of individual software programs on the CD-ROM is governed by terms set by individual copyright holders.

The installer, code, images, actions, and brushes from the authors are copyrighted by the publisher and the authors.

This software is sold as-is, without warranty of any kind, either expressed or implied, including but not limited to the implied warranties of merchantability and fitness for a particular purpose. Neither the publisher nor its dealers or distributors assumes any liability for any alleged or actual damages arising from the use of this program. (Some states do not allow for the exclusion of implied warranties, so the exclusion may not apply to you.)

index

C

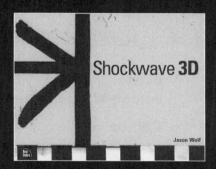

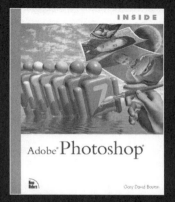

Solutions from experts you know and trust.

www.informit.com

- OPERATING SYSTEMS
- WEB DEVELOPMENT
- PROGRAMMING
- NETWORKING
- CERTIFICATION
- AND MORE...

Expert Access.
Free Content.

New Riders has partnered with **InformIT.com** to bring technical information to your desktop. Drawing on New Riders authors and reviewers to provide additional information on topics you're interested in, **InformIT.com** has free, in-depth information you won't find anywhere else.

- **Master the skills you need, when you need them**
- **Call on resources from some of the best minds in the industry**
- **Get answers when you need them, using InformIT's comprehensive library or live experts online**
- **Go above and beyond what you find in New Riders books, extending your knowledge**

As an **InformIT** partner, **New Riders** has shared the wisdom and knowledge of our authors with you online. Visit **InformIT.com** to see what you're missing.

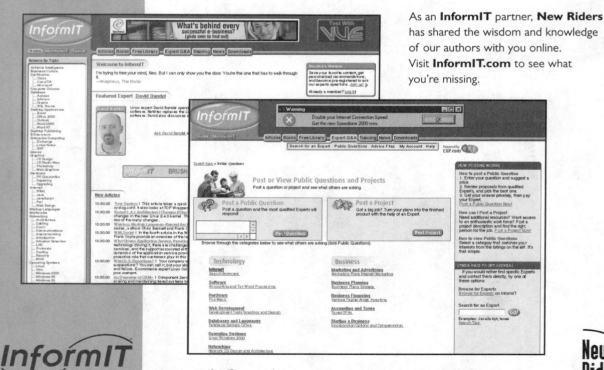

InformIT

www.informit.com ■ www.newriders.com